Antonio Negri

Key Contemporary Thinkers
Published:

Antonio Negri
Modernity and the Multitude

Timothy S. Murphy

polity

First published in 2012 by Polity Press

Polity Press
65 Bridge Street
Cambridge CB2 1UR, UK

Polity Press
350 Main Street
Malden, MA 02148, USA

ISBN-13: 978-0-7456-4319-9
ISBN-13: 978-0-7456-4320-5(pb)

A catalogue record for this book is available from the British Library.

Typeset in 10.5 on 12 pt Palatino
by Toppan Best-set Premedia Limited
Printed and bound in Great Britain by MPG Books Group Limited, Bodmin, Cornwall

For further information on Polity, visit our website: www.politybooks.com

For Juliana

Table of Contents

Acknowledgements

This is not an "authorized" study, so Toni Negri has not been involved in its composition beyond the verification of biographical details, but his example, support and encouragement have been crucial to all my intellectual work over the past twenty years. I would like to thank Dan Cottom, Michael Hardt, Vince Leitch and Steve Wright for their careful readings of the manuscript and their many extremely helpful suggestions for improvement. I am also grateful for the patience of Emma Hutchinson, my editor at Polity, who has waited a long time for this book. Iris and Daisy were my constant desktop companions while I wrote it, and Juliana never lost hope that it would get done, even when I wasn't so sure.

Publication of this book was supported in part by a grant from the Vice President for Research of the University of Oklahoma.

Parts of chapters 3 and 4 appeared previously, in a different form, in *Genre: Forms of Discourse and Culture*, volume 43, numbers 3–4 (fall/winter 2010), and volume 44, number 1 (spring 2011). They are reprinted here by permission of the University of Oklahoma and Duke University Press.

The publishers and the author wish to acknowledge permission to reprint the following copyright material:

From *Multitude: War and Democracy in the Age of Empire*, by Michael Hardt and Antonio Negri. Copyright © 2004. Used by permission of the Penguin Press, a division of Penguin Group (USA) Inc.

From *The Savage Anomaly: The Power of Spinoza's Metaphysics and Politics*, by Antonio Negri, trans. Michael Hardt. Copyright © 1991. Used by permission of the University of Minnesota Press.

From *In Praise of the Common: A Conversation on Philosophy and Politics*, by Cesare Casarino and Antonio Negri. Copyright © 2008. Used by permission of the University of Minnesota Press.

From *Insurgencies: Constituent Power and the Modern State*, by Antonio Negri, trans. Maurizia Boscagli. Copyright © 1999, 2009. Used by permission of the University of Minnesota Press.

From *Labor of Dionysus: A Critique of the State-Form*, by Michael Hardt and Antonio Negri. Copyright © 1994. Used by permission of the University of Minnesota Press.

From *Political Descartes*, by Antonio Negri. Copyright © 1970. Used by permission of Verso Books.

From *Books for Burning*, by Antonio Negri. Copyright © 2005. Used by permission of Verso Books.

From *Marx beyond Marx*, by Antonio Negri. Copyright © 1984. Used by permission of Autonomedia.

Reprinted by permission of the publisher from *Empire*, by Michael Hardt and Antonio Negri, Cambridge, MA: Harvard University Press. Copyright © 2000 by the President and Fellows of Harvard College.

Reprinted by permission of the publisher from *Commonwealth*, by Michael Hardt and Antonio Negri, Cambridge, MA: The Belknap Press of Harvard University Press. Copyright © 2009 by Michael Hardt and Antonio Negri.

1

Who Is Toni Negri, and Why Are They Saying such Terrible Things about Him?

The Italian philosopher and political theorist Antonio Negri has been alternately praised and reviled for his ideas and activities since the nineteen-sixties. Some view him primarily as a militant who revived the insurrectionary aspect of Marxist politics against the electoral accommodations of the established left parties in Italy – a provocateur who offered an apology for revolutionary violence and, according to his detractors, a coded rationale for terrorism. Others consider his most important work to be the philosophical analysis of power and subjectivity in modernity and postmodernity, which extends the poststructuralist problematic launched by Michel Foucault, Gilles Deleuze and Félix Guattari. Moreover, like his controversial predecessors, Negri is sometimes accused of depriving subjects of the agency necessary to accomplish the political transformations he promotes. Both perspectives contain some truth, although, when they degenerate into abstract ideological presuppositions, they ultimately become mutually exclusive. But the paradox that their juxtaposition presents is instructive. Perhaps a change of perspective can help us to sort the truths from the falsehoods and to see Negri more clearly, across the full range of his intellectual and practical achievements. To do so we must embrace contradiction, antagonism and paradox as Negri himself has, throughout his tumultuous life.[1]

Militant and Professor

Antonio Negri – known as "Toni" to his comrades – was born on August 1, 1933 in Padua, Italy, a traditional right-wing stronghold where he would later attend the university and teach for more than two decades. His father, who helped found the Communist Party of Bologna, was killed by Fascists in 1936, and his older brother was killed in action in 1943. He was raised by his mother, who was a primary-school teacher, and by his older sister's husband, a communist partisan from Trento. After the war Negri entered the University of Padua to study philosophy; something of an intellectual prodigy, he soon became editor of the university journal *Il Bo* and a student leader of the group Gioventù Italiana Azione Cattolica (GIAC: Italian Catholic Youth Action), where he met Umberto Eco, Gianni Vattimo and other young intellectuals of the Catholic left. During his second year at university he lived on a kibbutz (rural community) in Israel where he experienced collective organization and labor at first hand, and thereafter he left the GIAC. Fellowship study at the École normale supérieure in Paris and at the universities of Oxford, Tübingen and Munich gave him first-hand knowledge of contemporary French, English and German thought. When he completed his Libera docenza (a degree equivalent to the PhD) in 1958 with a dissertation on German historicism and a draft of the book *Stato e diritto nel giovane Hegel* (*State and Right in the Young Hegel*) (Negri 1958), he had already been a professor of political science at Padua for two years. His area of expertise was "state doctrine," an Italian discipline that effectively corresponds to Anglo-American philosophy of law and that, ironically enough considering Negri's Marxist commitments, was instituted under Fascism. Negri published a book on the historicism of Dilthey and Meinecke in 1959, and this was followed by a translation of Hegel's early writings on philosophy of law and by a book on Kantian jurisprudence in 1962. He was named to the university's Chair of State Doctrine in 1966 and became director of its Institute of Political Science in 1967, just in time for the student strikes, demonstrations and occupations that swept the country and the world for the next two years. Through the seventies Negri also held an appointment at the Italian National Research Center in Rome and was invited to conduct research or teach at the Free University of Berlin, at the University of Freiburg, at the University of Paris and, most famously, at the École normale supérieure at the invitation of Louis Althusser.

In parallel with this distinguished academic career, Negri carried on a constant engagement with dissident elements within Italian society. In 1958 he joined the Italian Socialist Party and became intellectually and organizationally active in party circles, serving as a local councilor and writing regularly for the socialist journal *Progresso Veneto*. During the sixties and seventies he helped to found and edit four key journals of the extra-parliamentary left – *Quaderni rossi* (*Red Notebooks*, 1960–1), *Classe operaia* (*Working Class*, 1963–6), *Contropiano* (*Counterplan*, 1967–8), and *Rosso* (*Red*, 1973–9) – which brought together many of the most important thinkers in Italy, including Massimo Cacciari, Raniero Panzieri, Mario Tronti and Manfredo Tafuri.[2] In 1963, together with his wife Paola Meo and with Cacciari (later on, the leftist mayor of Venice), he organized a *Capital* reading group among the workers of Porto Marghera – the largest petrochemical complex in Italy, which is adjacent to Venice. Negri and his family (including a daughter born in 1964 and a son born in 1967) lived in Venice, which allowed him to move freely between the vibrant cultural milieu of that city, the academic world of the University of Padua, just fifty kilometers away, and the industrial landscape of Porto Marghera. After Panzieri persuaded Negri to study Marx's writings during his time with *Quaderni rossi*, Negri's research began to shift from the scholarly studies of philosophy of law, on which his academic career had been based, to more directly political analyses and interventions. At first this shift manifested itself primarily in analyses carried out for small independent groups within the workers' movement and intended to identify innovative models of worker struggle. Meanwhile Negri produced a small number of scholarly books, including *Political Descartes* (Negri 1970b), in order to maintain his position within the university. Most of his energy, however, was directed toward immediately political activity.

Negri's early political experiences were centered on large factories like Porto Marghera and the FIAT plant at Mirafiori (which employed tens of thousands of workers at the time), and the first large-scale organization that he helped to found, Potere Operaio ("Potop": Workers' Power), in 1969, reflected this perspective. Like other similar groups to the left of the Italian Communist Party (PCI) – for example Lotta Continua or Avanguardia Operaia – Potere Operaio represented a break with the centralized, party-oriented union tradition of proletarian political organization, yet also a continuation of that tradition's privileging of the hetero-sexual male assembly-line worker as the subject of revolutionary activity. As a result of internal dissension – as well as on account of criticism directed at this bias by the rising Italian feminist and anti-war movements – Potere Operaio formally dissolved itself in 1973. As "Potop" collapsed, a much more diffuse, de-centered set of progressive movements that came to be called Autonomia (Autonomy) inherited its provocative role. Negri took this shift in his stride, working hard through the middle and late seventies to keep up theoretically with the constant phenomenological and organizational mutations of Autonomia. His writings in this period focused on defining new forms of militant organization and new methods of confrontation with corporations, parties and the state. This was the objective of the pamphlets later collected as *I libri del rogo* (*Books for Burning*, 1971–8) (Negri 2005) and of his 1977 book derived from his seminars on Lenin, *La fabbrica della strategia* (*The Strategy Factory*). New forms of resistance, beyond the comprehension of traditional party/trade union strategy – like the "self-reduction" of prices and the establishment of unofficial "free radio" stations and autonomous cultural centers – burgeoned across the country. The Italian Communist Party, eager to join a centrist coalition government for the first time since the Liberation, denounced Autonomia and its tactics almost as stridently as the Italian right did.[3]

Autonomist activity climaxed in the Movement of '77, rallies for which were held at the Institute of Political Science at the University of Padua. Like in Potere Operaio, some elements of Autonomia and of the Movement of '77 operated on the principle that the "legal" violence of the state had to be met with the mass resistance of the working class, which could also use violence legitimately, both defensively and offensively. Negri defended this principle in many of his writings during the seventies, and as a result he was sometimes accused of instigating specific acts of violence or property damage. For example, during some of the 1977 Padua events, unruly militants damaged university facilities, and Negri, as the movement's most visible participant on campus, was held responsible. He was also charged with inciting riots off campus, on the streets of Padua. As these charges were being investigated, Negri accepted Althusser's invitation to teach a series of seminars at the University of Paris VII and at the École normale supérieure (ENS). The course he gave at the ENS, on Marx's *Grundrisse*, resulted in his 1979 book *Marx oltre Marx* (*Marx beyond Marx*) (Negri 1984). During his absence the investigations cleared him of all charges and he returned to Padua in 1978, to pick up his work where he had left it. He continued to commute between Padua and Paris for the next year, until he was finally arrested upon his return to Italy on April 7, 1979 and charged with masterminding the Red Brigades' 1978 kidnapping and assassination of former Italian Prime Minister Aldo Moro – and, by extension, with organizational responsibility for all the terrorism that Italy had experienced since the early seventies. The most inflammatory charge, however, was that of "armed insurrection against the powers of the state." Across the country hundreds of other well-known militants, including many of Negri's colleagues at Padua's Institute of Political Science, were arrested at the same time on related charges, in a drastic attempt by the state (and its allies, including the PCI) to "behead" the burgeoning counter-culture.

Negri was imprisoned for nearly four years before coming to trial, on charges that were completely different from the ones originally brought against him by PCI-affiliated prosecutor Pietro Calogero. The original charges involving the Moro case were soon dropped for lack of evidence, but other, vaguer charges were immediately brought in order to keep Negri and his comrades in prison. Many of these subsequent charges relied heavily on the testimony of the *pentiti* – "repentant" terrorists, who were encouraged through special legislation to reduce their own sentences by implicating people in terrorist activity under the pretext of "confessing." Negri's political writings were also entered as evidence against him, despite their rejection of clandestine terrorist strategies in favor of open mass resistance, collective violence and illegality. All these extraordinary elements of the case were decried by the international left and regularly denounced in Amnesty International's annual reports on human rights violations from 1980 to 1988.[4] During this initial period of imprisonment Negri published six books, including his 1981 study of Spinoza, *L'anomalia selvaggia* (*The Savage Anomaly*) (Negri 1991). Negri's trial officially began on February 24, 1983, but it was interrupted by his surprise election to the Italian Chamber of Deputies on June 26 of the same year.

The unorthodox left libertarian Italian Radical Party, led by the theatrical Marco Panella, had proposed that Negri run as a way to draw attention to the flagrant violations of civil rights and constitutional protections that had become commonplace during the Italian state's "war on terror." To the consternation of many observers, Negri was elected as a representative for Rome, Milan and Naples; and, in conformity with Italian law, which grants immunity to elected representatives, he was released from prison and allowed to take his seat in the Chamber of Deputies during the summer of 1983. Immediately upon the opening of the legislature, motions were launched to strip Negri of his immunity and to return him to prison. During the debate over these motions Negri delivered his only speech to the Chamber, in which he argued, on constitutional grounds, for repeal of the special anti-terrorism legislation and for the release of prisoners held under its terms (Negri 2010a: 174–83). The vote was called for September 20, and the motion to strip Negri of his immunity was carried by a vote of 300 to 293. The ten Radical Party deputies elected along with Negri abstained from voting, allegedly as a result of intimidation. The police was ordered to return Negri to prison for the continuation of his trial; but he had already fled to France by boat, with the help of wealthy sympathizers. Many other members of Autonomia and related movements had sought refuge in Paris. The Italian prosecutors immediately made extradition claims to the French government, but these claims (and all subsequent ones) were rebuffed, both by the Mitterrand administration and by the Chirac administration, because the charges against Negri and his comrades were perceived as being essentially political. However, in order to avoid antagonizing their Italian counterparts, the French authorities refused to grant Negri and other Italian exiles formal refugee status, which would have made them eligible for French citizenship.[5] Negri's trial resumed without him, and a few months later he was convicted *in absentia*, on the abstract charges of "subversive association" and "membership in an armed band" (crimes originally defined under Fascism in order to outlaw the Communist Party), as well as of "moral co-responsibility" for a murder committed without his participation or knowledge. He was initially sentenced to 30 years in prison. With this, the Italian state's effort to criminalize the counter-culture reached its climax; the mass imprisonment of militants inaugurated the long-term process of enforced forgetting and erasure of the movements from official history.

Negri remained in precarious exile in France for 14 years, working as an instructor of political science at the University of Paris VIII (St. Denis) and as a researcher for the French ministry of labor. As the most prominent intellectual among the Italian refugees, he was welcomed by the French philosophical left. Félix Guattari found Negri an apartment and collaborated with him on the book *Les nouveaux espaces de liberté* (*New Lines of Alliance, New Spaces of Liberty*) (Guattari and Negri 1985). Jacques Derrida and Jean-François Lyotard invited him to join the Collège International de Philosophie (CIPH), and Jean-Pierre Faye invited him to participate in the Université Européenne de la Recherche (UER); these unconventional venues provided Negri with the chance to pursue and present his own original philosophical and political research, and also to establish the journal *Futur antérieur*. He published fourteen books during his years of exile, including *Il potere costituente* (*Insurgencies: Constituent Power and the Modern State*) (Negri 1999) and his first collaboration with Michael Hardt, *Labor of Dionysus* (Hardt and Negri 1994). His uncertain status as a political refugee without citizenship documents prevented him from participating in French public life and from traveling abroad, though he followed the vicissitudes of global militancy with passionate attention. All the while Negri's case was winding its way through the Italian judicial system in his absence. His original sentence of 30 years was reduced, on appeal, to 12 years.

In 1997, as Negri and Hardt finished the original draft of what would become their international bestseller *Empire*, Negri resolved to return to Italy to serve out his remaining prison sentence, in hopes that his gesture would catalyze a systematic resolution to the untenable situation of a whole generation of Italian militants exiled or imprisoned on purely political charges. Although his return did inspire a petition drive and the introduction of a bill of amnesty in the European Parliament, it did not succeed in focusing public sympathy on the legacy of the Italian counter-culture. The majority of the Italian public preferred to forget that legacy, as the state had hoped, and Negri's case soon vanished from the media. He remained in custody in Rome until he reached the midpoint of his overall sentence, taking into account the four years of his original preventive detention from 1979 to 1983. At that point he was granted limited parole: he was permitted to leave prison during the day, but had to return each night. Later he was permitted to move into an apartment in Rome to which he had to return every night. Finally, in 2003, he was granted full parole, given back his passport and granted the freedom to travel outside of Italy. Since the success of *Empire* (Hardt and Negri 2000) and of its sequels *Multitude* (Hardt and Negri 2004) and *Commonwealth* (Hardt and Negri 2009), Negri has been invited to speak in scores of countries around the world, from England and France to China and Iran. As of this writing, the only nations he is not permitted to visit are the

United States and Japan. In 2004 his first play, *Essaim* (*Swarm*), was produced in France; two further plays followed in 2005 and 2006 to complete the *Trilogy of Resistance* (Negri 2011). After several years spent traveling the world with his companion, French philosopher Judith Revel, Negri currently divides his time between Venice and Paris.

Two Modernities

Negri's life and work have been defined by a series of dilemmas that are simultaneously metaphysical and quotidian: the intellectual life of speculation against the practical life of militancy; an academic specialty in philosophical idealism against a materialist bias for direct political action; solitary research versus collaboration; objective pedagogy versus partisan inquiry; transcendent Power [*potere*] versus immanent power [*potenza*]. His critics see these dilemmas as contradictions that undermine or invalidate his work, while his supporters see them as productive paradoxes that have kept him relevant as a thinker and as a militant for many decades. Among supporters, Jason Read has perhaps best expressed the way that paradox has energized Negri's work:

> Negri's position is irreducible to either term of the opposition [between philosophy and politics]; it is best defined as *developing a new philosophy of praxis through a new practice of philosophy*. In other words, a philosophy of praxis, of the constitutive dimension of human activity, cannot simply be developed speculatively, as a pure movement of thought, but must be developed through a continual encounter with its constitutive conditions and limitations, with the materiality of the world. (Read 2007: 29)

As his biography demonstrates, Negri has constantly sought out material encounters with the world.

In the first, most academic and individualistic phase of his career, Negri immersed himself in the continental idealist tradition, in an effort to demythologize and historicize it. Tracing idealism backward from its highest point, Hegel, Negri sought to identify the ideological function of Kant's critical philosophy through its influence on juridical formalism and that of Descartes' rationalism through its accommodation of monarchical absolutism. His challenge in each case was to explicate the operation of a dualistic logic that claimed to resolve social contradictions absolutely, and at the same time to reveal the repressed third term that would return to destabilize the original polarity. Negri's general term for this disenchanted dialectic is antagonism, a conflict of historical forces that exceeds and resists dialectical resolution; the excluded third that underpins it is living labor, the socialized worker or the multitude. The danger facing this fundamentally Marxist analytical strategy is the seductive power of Hegelian dialectics itself, which crowns the idealist line of philosophical development and retroactively rewrites the earlier stages in its own image. Many of the most prominent Marxist philosophers of the twentieth century have been seduced back to Hegel, despite their efforts to resist. Georg Lukács' work on reification in *History and Class Consciousness* is a triumph of Marxist reconstruction, but it also re-inscribes the Hegelian assumption of a universal, abstract human essence, designed to act as an ahistorical standard against which historical modes of subjective alienation are assessed. Even more disheartening is the case of the Director of the Frankfurt Institute of Social Research, Theodor W. Adorno, whose Hegelian elaborations of the Marxist critique of administration ultimately led him to a position of purely speculative theoretical radicalism, allied with a conformist social and institutional practice: at the end of his life he effectively admitted to being a Young Hegelian as he denounced the German student movements to the state police. After a youthful flirtation, Negri managed to resist the seductions of Hegel and remained poised on the knife-edge that separates materialist antagonism from dialectical reduction – first by means of his engagement with Renaissance humanism and with Spinoza's metaphysics of radical immanence, and later by means of an alliance with the Nietzschean philosophies of non-dialectical difference articulated by Michel Foucault, Gilles Deleuze and Félix Guattari.

The defining paradox of the second, militant phase of Negri's career is captured in the phrase used by the Italian press to demonize him after his arrest in 1979: *cattivo maestro* ("wicked teacher"). All university professors in Italy are civil servants, and historically their political commitments have been predictably reactionary or quietist; paid by the state, they generally work to legitimate it. The individualism of Italian intellectuals derives from their isolation from the general public – especially from the working class, which has little access to higher education. Like many of his generation, Negri rejected his colleagues' accommodation with state power even as he continued to use the educational institution as his base of operations. In France, Michel Foucault served as a role model for such activity; his appointment to the Collège de France in 1971 coincided with the broadening of his involvement with the Prison Information Group and other militant organizations. As director of Padua's Institute of Political Science, Negri staffed it with like-minded young theorists who were doing collective interdisciplinary research and were also politically active in the movements that emerged from the experiences of the sixties. His colleagues included labor historian Sergio Bologna, multinational theorist Luciano Ferrari Bravo, and materialist feminists Alisa Del Re and Mariarosa Dalla Costa. Together they established a militant counter-institution within the university, one that attracted a broad audience of students and workers to its courses. The institute also published radical periodicals and book series in collaboration with Feltrinelli and other leftist publishers, allowing its members to intervene in theoretical debates outside the university as well. Negri's book *Marx beyond Marx* exemplifies the paradox of this period: it is the transcription of a graduate seminar on revolutionary agency given at France's most prestigious institution of faculty training, the ENS. After Negri and his colleagues were arrested, their writings and university courses were treated as evidence against them – hence the epithet *cattivo maestro*, which was applied to many of them, though most consistently to Negri. In addition to its denotative meaning, "wicked teacher," the phrase also connotes "evil genius" or arch-villain, and "Pied Piper" or misleader of young people.

After his arrest and during his imprisonment, while he was awaiting trial, Negri recognized that the generative paradoxes that energized his earlier career were no longer functional. He was almost totally isolated, cut off both from the academic world, which had provided him with a stable institutional base of operations, and from the militant world, in which he found a broad field for political action. Consequently he had no choice but to embark on a monumental effort to clear the ground for a new start. Unexpectedly and in quick succession, he wrote three books of metaphysical, theological and literary analysis that articulated his new credo: *The Savage Anomaly* (Negri 1991) on Spinoza, *The Labor of Job*, written in 1982, published in 1990 (Negri 2009b), and *Lenta ginestra* (*Gentle Broom*), written in 1983–4, published in 1987: Negri 2001) on the poet Giacomo Leopardi. These works served notice that Negri was now ready to engage paradox directly, through the letter and spirit of his writings, and not primarily in the form of what Jürgen Habermas would have called the "performative contradiction" between his institutional position and his militant activity – which defined the earlier phases of his career. When he returned to political philosophy with 1992's *Il potere costituente* (*Insurgencies: Constituent Power and the Modern State*) (Negri 1999), the transition was, in effect, complete: his focus shifted from an ungainly alternation between analyses of the historical ideologies of the capitalist state and local modes of organization available to new social subjects, to a consistent engagement with the historical possibilities of the revolutionary process. He theorized this through the irreducible antagonism between constituent and constituted power, which forms the basis for all his later work, including the theory of Empire. At the same time he found a way to meld the poststructuralist critique of the autonomous human subject with an anti-essentialist conception of collective agency – "the multitude" – which allowed him to escape the political aporias of deconstruction and postmodernism.

The chapters that follow argue that we can best grasp these constitutive paradoxes by approaching Negri as a type of thinker who might superficially seem to be very different from the Marxist radical and from the postmodern metaphysician, who define his popular reception: the Renaissance humanist. Although there is little that Negri has written directly on Renaissance humanism (and that little came relatively late in his career), almost all his works take Renaissance humanism as their pre-text, in the sense that they situate their subjects "after the Renaissance," in historical relation to the crisis and blockage of Renaissance humanism's most radical social, political and scientific project. What is that project, according to Negri? In the chapter on the great Renaissance humanist Niccolò Machiavelli in *Insurgencies* Negri writes: "What is the Renaissance? It was the rediscovery of freedom and, with it, of the virtue of constructing, of inventing: at the same time it was the discovery of the possibility and the capacity of accumulating" (Negri 1999: 76). In *Empire* Negri and Michael Hardt write that, between 1200 and 1600,

[h]umans declared themselves masters of their own lives, producers of cities and history, and inventors of heavens. They inherited a dualistic consciousness, a hierarchical vision of society, and a metaphysical idea of science, but they handed down to future generations an experimental idea of science, a constituent conception of history

and cities, and they posed being as an immanent terrain of knowledge and action...In those origins of modernity, then, knowledge
shifted from the transcendent plane to the immanent...(Hardt and
Negri 2000: 70–2)

This account of the Renaissance, though not unprecedented,
emphasizes not the revival of classical learning that gave the period
its name, but rather the innovations that the liberation
from the metaphysical, social and political constraints of the
overlapping ideologies of transcendence made possible in Europe.
Perhaps the most important arena of innovation was in human
subjectivity, which came to be seen as malleable after centuries
of theological and metaphysical fixity. Contemporary critics of
Enlightenment humanism often forget that one of the fundamental
insights of Renaissance thinkers like Giovanni Pico della Mirandola
was the notion that human subjectivity was not fixed and
inalterable, but rather a potentiality that could be constructed and
reconstructed, as it took new forms in response to new conditions.
Hardt and Negri paraphrase the teaching of these thinkers as
follows: "Through its own powerful arts and practices, humanity
enriches and doubles itself, or really raises itself to a higher power"
(p. 72).

But, in Negri's view, the Renaissance humanist project was no
sooner articulated than it was corrupted from within. As he notes
in that same passage from *Insurgencies*, "through accumulation
fortune was built, and fortune so established opposed virtue – the
dialectic revealed itself through this negativity of the result" (Negri
1999: 76). The victory of the capacity for accumulation characteristic of the Renaissance – accumulation of power, wealth and time
– over the capacity for free human self-(re)construction laid the
groundwork for the triumph of capitalism and marked the first
manifestation of the crisis that would block the completion of the
humanist project. Fortune, Machiavelli's concept of objectified
human labor or constituted power, gained the upper hand over
that of virtue – that is, living labor or constituent power. Out of this
triumph of fortune emerged the dominant philosophies of modernity on which Negri's early work was focused: those of Descartes,
Kant and Hegel. Negri goes on to insist:

The only possibility of resisting this perversion of the development
of virtue and its dialectic is the foundation of a collective subject that
opposes this process, who tries to fix the accumulation not of fortune
but of virtue. Who will be able to do it? Only in the forms of democ-

racy and of the government of the multitude will this project be conceivable. (Ibid.)

This revival and re-constitution of the Renaissance humanist project is not only Machiavelli's aim but also, in Negri's view, Spinoza's, Marx's, and ultimately Negri's own. This alternative line of philosophical descent constitutes a counter-modernity that contests the closure of the dominant line of modernity.

The antagonism between virtue and fortune is the source of Negri's thesis of the two modernities, which constitutes the wellspring of both his theoretical work and his militancy.

> What does this thesis assert? At the end of the humanist revolution of the Renaissance – which constituted the first modernity proper – the Counter-Reformation blocked the development of thought as well as the structure of property at one and the same time (and, under this respect, the Counter-Reformation thereafter influenced and even included also much of the Protestant Reformation). Between the sixteenth and the seventeenth centuries, in other words, we witness a general refeudalization of society in all of its main aspects... [T]he reactive blockage of the Counter-Reformation, on the one hand, posited itself as a second and rightful modernity, and, on the other hand, was never able to erase that other, prior, and alternative modernity completely. The revolutionary energies of that first modernity lived on and found their theoretical expression in the Spinoza–Marx line of thought. (Casarino and Negri 2008: 79–80)

Modernity as Negri understands it is not merely a philosophical or aesthetic category but also a historical and political one:

> just as there are two different genealogies of thought when it comes to the articulation of modernity, there are also two distinct genealogical lines when it comes to democracy: on the one hand, what you might call the Hobbes–Rousseau–Hegel line, and, on the other hand, the Machiavelli–Spinoza–Marx line – in which one could also include Nietzsche perhaps. The point is that the latter series of thinkers developed the concept of democracy not at all as a specific form of government among others but as the form of living together that constitutes the condition of possibility of governing tout court. (P. 103)

The Hobbes–Rousseau–Hegel line of democracy emphasizes the irreversibility of the transfer of sovereignty from individuals to the state and thereby leads inexorably to the foreclosure of real democracy by juridical procedure, legislative representation and executive delegation, while the Machiavelli–Spinoza–Marx line strives to shatter that institutionalization and to reactivate the sovereignty of the social collective. Thus the unfulfilled promise of Renaissance humanism, an alternate or counter-modernity, is what draws together Negri's diverse philosophical monographs, his organizational writings and his militancy into a coherent project of revolutionary transformation.

To understand how controversial and untimely this project actually is, let's take a moment to examine the current of contemporary philosophy in which Negri's work is most commonly and appropriately contextualized: anti-humanism. Contemporary anti-humanism comes both in a Marxist form and in a phenomenological form, corresponding to the two major traditions that contribute directly to Negri's own work and to the two principal modes of reception of his work. Virtually all the major thinkers who represent both forms trace their methods and problematics back to Martin Heidegger's rejection, in his 1947 "Letter on Humanism," of Jean-Paul Sartre's claim that humanism constituted the necessary horizon of thought and action for the postwar world (see Sartre 2007). Heidegger sees Sartre's work as merely the most recent version of the same static humanism that has dominated Western thought in various forms since the Renaissance; and he insists that,

> [h]owever different these forms of humanism may be in purpose and in principle, in the mode and means of their respective realizations, and in the form of their teaching, they nonetheless all agree in this, that the *humanitas* of *homo humanus* is determined with regard to an already established interpretation of nature, history, world, and the ground of the world, that is, of beings as a whole. Every humanism is either grounded in a metaphysics or is itself made to be the ground of one…(Heidegger 1947: 280)

This means that, for Heidegger, all humanisms, including Sartre's, are modes of thought that do not question their fundamental assumption of a universal human essence, which – in a more or less alienated form, depending on the version of humanism in question – remains actually or potentially present in thought and action. Humanism is thus another name for what Heidegger's most innovative follower, Jacques Derrida, will call "the closure of the metaphysics of presence," which defines Western philosophy from Plato to the twentieth century. As another disciple of Heidegger, Gianni Vattimo, puts it, "humanism is the doctrine that assigns to humanity the role of the subject, that is, of self-consciousness as the locus of evidence, in the framework of Being as *Grund*, or, in other words, as full presence" (Vattimo 1988: 43–4).

Derrida would ultimately bring against Heidegger the same charge that Heidegger brought against Sartre and the metaphysical tradition. Through a deconstructive critique of the history of phenomenology, Derrida finds an overt essentialism of the human not merely in Heidegger's predecessors Hegel and Husserl, but also in Heidegger himself. For Hegel, as Derrida shows, "[c]onsciousness is the truth of man, phenomenology is the truth of anthropology. 'Truth', here, must be understood in a rigorously Hegelian sense. In this Hegelian sense, the metaphysical essence of truth, the truth of truth, is achieved" (Derrida 1982: 120). For Husserl, "[t]ranscendental phenomenology is... the ultimate achievement of the teleology of reason that traverses humanity. Thus, under the jurisdiction of the founding concepts of metaphysics, which Husserl revives and restores... the critique of empirical anthropologism is only the affirmation of a transcendental humanism" (p. 123). Despite Heidegger's critique of these versions of metaphysical humanism, a critique to which Derrida's own is deeply indebted, Derrida reveals Heidegger's project to be "a kind of re-evaluation or revalorization of the essence and dignity of man. What is threatened in the extension of metaphysics and technology... is the essence of man, which here would have to be thought before and beyond its metaphysical determinations" (p. 128). Unlike elsewhere in his work, Derrida's conclusion in this case is not derived from careful analysis of footnotes, asides or other "marginal" moments, but from Heidegger's own frank admission that his thinking is "'humanism' in the extreme sense," carried out "as no metaphysics has thought it or can think it": "It is a humanism that thinks the humanity of man from nearness to being" (Heidegger 1947: 294) and thus falls within the very closure that it criticizes.

Heidegger does not recognize this irreducible humanist/metaphysical residue within his own project of thinking; so, in response to Sartre's proposition that contemporary philosophy must retain the essential humanist assumption, Heidegger asks instead: "should thinking, by means of open resistance to 'humanism,' risk a shock that could for the first time cause perplexity concerning the

humanitas of *homo humanus* and its basis?" (p. 296). That is, should
thinking interrogate and ultimately reject the humanist assumption
of a universal essence of humankind? For the most important continental thinkers of the last half of the twentieth century, the answer
to that question was an emphatic "yes." The first to join the chorus
was Jacques Lacan, whose synthesis of Freudian psychoanalysis
and Saussurean linguistics constitutes one of the fundamental axes
of poststructuralist thought. In the second year of his influential
seminar, Lacan denounced humanism in far more inflammatory
terms than Heidegger had:

> Every time there's been a revision of the discourse on man, we have
> difficulty imagining what happened, because the gist of each of
> these revisions is always deadened, attenuated, with time, in such a
> way that today, as always, the word humanism is a bag in which the
> corpses of these successive disclosures of a revolutionary point of
> view on man must slowly rot, piled one on top of the other. (Lacan
> 1988: 208)

For Lacan, Freud's "revision" lies in his focus on how the unconscious de-centers the self-conscious subject of the phenomenological tradition. Like Heidegger, Lacan traces the problem of
self-consciousness as presence back to Descartes and his influential
claim of the immediate certainty of the cogito ("I think, therefore I
am"): "the philosophical *cogito* is at the center of the mirage that
renders modern man so sure of being himself even in his uncertain-
ties about himself, and even in the mistrust he has learned to
practice against the traps of self-love" (Lacan 1977: 165). The cen-
teredness of the cogito constitutes the essence of the human and
the basis of all philosophical anthropology, against which Lacan
positions Freud's innovation and his own analytic practice: "Hegel
is at the limit of anthropology. Freud got out of it. His discovery is
that man isn't entirely in man. Freud isn't a humanist" (Lacan 1988:
72). And neither is Lacan, who views the mid-century shift from
Freudian models focused on the unconscious to a more positivistic
ego psychology as a regression back to the same kind of uncritical
humanism that Heidegger resisted in Sartre.

The Cartesian cogito is also a privileged point of polemical reference for Michel Foucault, who launched the argument of his *History
of Madness* against the exclusions that constitute the cogito and
thereby inaugurated a systematic project that occupied his entire
career. In a later interview he expansively and polemically defined

the humanism that his work intended both to historicize and to dismantle:

> By humanism I mean the totality of discourse through which Western man is told, "Even though you don't exercise power, you can still be a ruler. Better yet, the more you deny yourself the exercise of power, the more you submit to those in power, then the more this increases your sovereignty." Humanism invented a whole series of subjected sovereignties: the soul (ruling the body, but subjected to God), consciousness (sovereign in a context of judgment, but subjected to the necessities of truth), the individual (a titular control of personal rights subjected to the laws of nature and society), basic freedom (sovereign within, but accepting the demands of an outside world and "aligned with destiny")...The theory of the subject (in the double sense of the word) is at the heart of humanism and this is why our culture has tenaciously rejected anything that could weaken its hold on us. (Foucault 1977: 221–2)

Like Heidegger, Foucault emphasizes the metaphysical continuity of the essential subject between the different modes of humanism and calls upon the resources of critical thought to break that continuity, as he announces in the famous conclusion to *The Order of Things*: "One thing in any case is certain: man is neither the oldest nor the most constant problem that has been posed for human knowledge...As the archaeology of our thought easily shows, man is an invention of recent date. And one perhaps nearing its end" (Foucault 1970: 386–7).

Foucault's critique of the humanist subject fits into the phenomenological wing of anti-humanism as a result of its focus on the continuity of subjective interiority, from the Cartesian cogito to the subjects of modern disciplinary institutions like the clinic and the prison; but its historical, or rather archaeological/genealogical, orientation also provides a point of contact with the Marxist wing of anti-humanism, best represented by Louis Althusser. Like Lacan, who locates a radical alternative to humanism in Freud's work, Althusser finds in Marx a method of escaping from the impasses of humanist subjectivism. According to Althusser's reading, Marx rejects two interdependent and essentialist postulates of humanism:

> If the essence of man is to be a universal attribute, it is essential that *concrete subjects* exist as absolute givens; this implies an *empiricism of the subject*. If these empirical individuals are to be men, it is essential

that each carries in himself the whole human essence, if not in fact, at least in principle; this implies an *idealism of the essence*. (Althusser 1969: 228)

While the young Marx, still under the sway of Hegel's anthropology, deployed these postulates in his early critical works, the mature Marx, who emerged from the epistemological break inaugurated by the "Theses on Feuerbach" and *The German Ideology*, abandoned them in order to found a theoretical practice based not in the subject but in the masses. This is the sense in which Althusser defines history as a "process without a subject." Thus Althusser insists that,

> *theoretically speaking*, Marxism is, in a single movement and by virtue of the unique epistemological rupture which established it, an anti-humanism and an anti-historicism. Strictly speaking, I ought to say an a-humanism and an a-historicism. But in order to give these terms all the weight of a declaration of rupture which far from going without saying is, on the contrary, very hard to accept, I have deliberately used this doubly *negative* formula (anti-humanism, anti-historicism)...(Althusser 1970: 119)

This aspiration to an effective "rupture" with humanism is common to all the philosophers under discussion here, and this list could be extended to include Jean-François Lyotard, Pierre Bourdieu and others.[6] Among them, Negri is just as much of an anomaly as his beloved Spinoza was in the seventeenth century.

Humanism after the Death of Man

In the face of such a broad and influential consensus, how can Negri maintain his commitment to Renaissance humanism? Yet he does, despite direct attacks on his work from both Derrida and Lyotard. The former accuses him of being "confined, out-of-it-in-it, within the walled perimeter of a new ontological fatherland, a liberated ontology, an ontology of self-liberation" that remains essentialist (Derrida, in Sprinker 1999: 261),[7] while the latter dismisses him as a nostalgic humanist intellectual:

> The promise of emancipation was rekindled, championed, and expounded by the great intellectual, that category born of the Enlightenment, defender of ideals and the republic. Intellectuals of

today who have chosen to perpetuate this task in ways other than a minimal resistance to every totalitarianism, who have been imprudent enough to nominate the just cause in conflicts between ideas or powers – the likes of Chomsky, Negri, Sartre, Foucault – have been tragically deceived. The signs of the ideal are hazy. A war of liberation does not indicate that humanity is continuing to emancipate itself. (Lyotard 1992: 96)

The key to Negri's intransigence in the face of such attacks from the most influential contemporary thinkers lies in the double historical displacement that he carries out. First of all, his conception of humanism derives from – and is rigorously historicized within – the moment of its greatest critical force, the Italian Renaissance itself, while the conception shared by the majority of poststructuralists dates from the fossilization of humanism into an ideology, in Descartes' later rationalism and in the Enlightenment idealism that followed from it. Even in Foucault's famous disagreement with Derrida over the status of madness in the West, the two philosophers did not dispute the Cartesian moment as the historical point of origin for their analyses. Second, Negri recognizes that humanism in the present must be modified for new social, political and technological conditions, including – most prominently – the accomplished critique of essentialist humanism itself. In *Empire* he and Hardt call their re-evaluation of Renaissance humanism a "humanism after the death of Man," humanism *after* anti-humanism:

This anti-humanism...need not conflict with the revolutionary spirit of Renaissance humanism...In fact, this anti-humanism follows directly on Renaissance humanism's secularizing project, or more precisely, its discovery of the plane of immanence. Both projects are founded on an attack on transcendence...Anti-humanism, then, conceived as a refusal of any transcendence, should in no way be confused with a negation of the *vis viva*, the creative life force that animates the revolutionary stream of the modern tradition. On the contrary, the refusal of transcendence is the condition of possibility of thinking this immanent power, an anarchic basis of philosophy: "*Ni Dieu, ni maître, ni homme*" ["No God, no master, no man"]. (Hardt and Negri 2000: 91–2)

In Foucault's terms, Negri criticizes and rejects the static, essentialist version of humanist subjectivism in favor of radically new modes of human subjectivation, which are being constructed in the present. This immanent, constructivist interpretation of Renaissance humanism is the pre-text, the antecedent, of all of Negri's work as a philosopher and historian of philosophy, as well as the regulative framework of all the stages of his militancy, from the fifties to the present.

In the first phase of his work as an academic historian of philosophy (examined in chapter 2), he traces the consequences of the crisis of Renaissance humanism backwards, through the heroic figures of idealism, from Hegel to Kant to Descartes: Descartes' philosophy offers a "reasonable ideology" for regenerating the development of the bourgeoisie during the period of absolutist reaction against the political insurrections of the radical Reformation (insurrections that were inspired by the implications of humanist thought), and Kant and Hegel refine that ideology in the legal and political arenas over the course of the consolidation of capitalism and of the absolute state across Europe, especially in the aftermath of the French Revolution. This period of Negri's work, carried out individually in pursuit (at least initially) of a professorial career, constitutes a negative basis for his thought – the thorough study of the enemy, which is necessary in order to find ways to defeat him – and it also positions him in intellectual proximity to the great Hegelians and sometime Marxists Georg Lukács and Theodor W. Adorno.

In the next phase Negri's work shifts into an affirmative mode, though not within the discipline of philosophy or history of philosophy; rather, the negative lessons of his first phase of development provide him with tools that he can use on the terrain of direct political action, as chapter 3 shows. Moving out of the university, he begins to work collectively, not only on research projects but also on organizational problems of the workers' movements to which he was drawn. He brings his deep historical understanding of the mutations undergone by the capitalist state and its ideology over the course of their constitution to bear on the struggle against the Italian state in the present; but even there, in the midst of intense partisan polemics and of the most contemporary forms of antagonism, the framework of Renaissance humanism emerges clearly. In the preface to his 1975 pamphlet *Proletarians and the State*, he insists: "Materialism is in no way a historical and political conventionalism, but rather the always new flavor of reality, not sixteenth-century mechanism but rather humanist realism...as Marx...emphasizes several times..." (Negri 2005: 120).[8] Negri's critics in this period are legion, but the most cogent are his comrade

Sergio Bologna and the English socialist Alex Callinicos, whose critiques identify Negri's most original claims as well as his most tendentious ones. Of course, the crudest critique of his work in this period was also the most effective in blocking his project: the Italian state's charges of armed insurrection and terrorism.

In the imposed solitude of prison and exile, Negri's approach to Renaissance humanism changed dramatically: if both in the first and in the second phase of his career it had served as a negative foundation for his critique of, and struggle against, the modern state, in the third phase, which opened in 1981, it became an affirmative project of reconstructing the revolutionary subject and finding "alternatives to modernity" (the original Italian subtitle of *Insurgencies*) within modernity itself. This project, examined in chapter 4, would ultimately expand to encompass a near-total revisionary history of modern political philosophy, culminating in 1992 with *Insurgencies* (Negri 1999) and setting the stage for the fourth phase of Negri's career, which was centered on the theorization of Empire and of the multitude. The first fruit of this new perspective was *The Savage Anomaly*, originally published in 1981 (Negri 1991), which opens with an evocation of Spinoza's humble optical workshop (and, by implication, Negri's own prison cell) as an extension of the humanistic workshop from which the multiple practices of counter-modern immanence emerged:

> The workshop of the humanist no longer has an artisanal character. Certainly, a constructive spirit animates it, that of the Renaissance. But already we find such a difference, here, now, in the manner of situating oneself before knowledge, of fixing the constructive horizon of thought...Here instead, in Holland, in Spinoza, the revolution has assumed the dimensions of accumulation on a world scale, and this is what constitutes the Dutch anomaly: this disproportion between the constructive and appropriative dimension. (Negri 1991: 7)

Thus Machiavelli's insight concerning the struggle between virtue and fortune returns to the fore in new historical conditions, which demand that new forms of subjectivity and resistance be constructed. Through engagements with the Book of Job and the poetry of Leopardi, Negri traces a counter-history of modernity and postmodernity that allows him to identify the fissures that split what Heidegger and Derrida define monumentally as the "era" or "closure" of metaphysics, and to find in those fissures the seeds of a "time-to-come" ["*a-venire*"], a virtuous future that would rupture the long history of fortune or constituted power.

  With the publication of *Empire* in 2000, Negri became once again an intellectual celebrity, as he had been at the time of his arrest in 1979 and of his exile in 1983, and he did so through a return to his preferred mode of subversive work: collective, or rather collaborative. His paradoxical self-reinvention, abetted by Michael Hardt, coincided both with a rising level of public interest in issues of economic globalization and with the resurgence of transnational movements of resistance to globalization, both of which found in his "humanism after the death of Man" productive ways of comprehending and engaging the new world order. In his influential 1991 book *Postmodernism, or, The Cultural Logic of Late Capitalism*, Fredric Jameson had challenged Marxist critics to offer a practical "cognitive map" of late capitalism that would allow self-reflexive postmodern culture to be historicized and resisted (Jameson 1991: 51–2, 415–16); Negri and Hardt responded to Jameson's challenge with the concept of Empire, the de-centered structure of governance that underpins capitalist globalization. Rising up against Empire is the multitude, the fount of constituent power and the basis for all political collectivity, both before and beyond the capitalist nation states. The multitude, a term derived from Spinoza, materializes Negri's lifelong effort to theorize and produce the subject of what he had years earlier called, in defiance of Althusser, "Marx's collective humanism" (Negri 2005: 114 n. 6). Chapter 5 relates both Empire and the multitude to Negri's longstanding concerns with the state form and with revolutionary subjectivity, to the flowering of a broad set of movements contesting capitalist globalization, and to a number of critiques offered by both sympathetic and rival leftists.

***

A note before we begin to examine Negri's career in detail: because this book is intended to encourage English-speaking readers to engage directly with Negri's work (and not to serve as a substitute for such engagement), it consists largely of close readings of his writings, focusing mainly on those that are available in English translation. Because Negri's style is often dense, allusive, abstract and/or difficult, I have chosen to cite and explicate substantive passages from many of his books in order to offer the reader a primer in understanding his prose. However, several of Negri's most important works – primarily his early books on Hegel and on Kantian jurisprudence and his later book on Leopardi – are not yet available in translation, so I have provided more extensive analyses of those works in order to offer a comprehensive account of Negri's intellectual and militant development. Conversely, the sheer quantity of Negri's publications during every period studied in this book means that a few significant works, including some that may be well known to readers, had to be passed over in order to preserve the balance between breadth and depth of analysis that an introductory volume must present. Throughout the book I have also provided accounts of what seems to me to constitute the most acute and productive criticisms of Negri's work; but because his work has intervened in such widely disparate areas of scholarship and militancy, the amount and form of that criticism vary equally widely from period to period. Negri's early works in the history of philosophy provoked a few highly specialized scholarly responses, while his collaborations with Hardt have inspired critiques and appropriations from a much broader range of readers and disciplines. My discussions of Negri's critics in the chapters that follow reflect this unevenness. Lastly, in response to those readers who may accuse me of producing an account that is too linear and neat, I would argue that some demonstration, or at least assumption, of the intellectual coherence of a thinker's work is the precondition for any more discontinuous or nonlinear account. In short, the story that this book tells about Negri is not the only story that can be told about him and his work, but it seems to me the most useful one at present.

2

A Critical Genealogy of the
Modern State – In Reverse

Although Negri did not hit upon the thesis of the two modernities, one constituent and progressive and the other constituted and static, until his work on Descartes in the late sixties (Casarino and Negri 2008: 57), he laid the groundwork for it in his earliest writings on Hegel and post-Kantian juridical philosophy during the late fifties. Indeed his early work can best be understood retrospectively, from the viewpoint established in *Political Descartes*; so in this chapter we will work backwards, to trace the emergence of Negri's historiographical method and his thematic focus on the capitalist state. For Negri, both Hegel and the Kantian formalists define their projects against the challenge posed to philosophy by the French Revolution, that ambivalent triumph of the bourgeoisie and capitalism; but they are really the heirs to Descartes: "Descartes's reasonable ideology extends from the classical age through the Enlightenment and up to the Revolution. The Revolution, as it were, completes its design" (Negri 1970b: 325). What does this mean? Negri specifies:

> From Leibniz to the thinkers of the Enlightenment and to Hegel we witness the problem progressively being defined, just as it had progressively established itself in Descartes…Metaphysics continues to provide the metaphor for the emergence of the bourgeoisie as a class, the allusion to a project of reconquering a lived essence, of realizing a willed revolution. Metaphysics thus becomes more and more clearly the metaphor of the political demand to reconquer the world

for the mode of production, to reconquer the state for society, to reconquer power for the bourgeoisie. (P. 315)

Thus Descartes articulates the ideology for a bourgeois conquest of the state that only comes to fruition in the wake of the French Revolution. He establishes the poles of a dialectic that only Hegel, via the mediation of Kant, can resolve: it begins in the separation of the bourgeois subject from the external world of the absolute sovereign; it develops into the Kantian antinomy of reason and history, which vexes the late Enlightenment; and it finds resolution in Hegel's dialectic of the absolute subject and the popular state. The German philosophers thereby relay the force of Descartes' thought to the nineteenth century and complete the philosophical legitimation of the modern capitalist state form. In this way Negri's early studies trace the inception and culmination of bourgeois political ontology in reverse chronological order.

Despite the remarkable degree of coherence that Negri's intellectual trajectory shows over the course of his career, this trajectory is also significantly marked by discontinuities and reversals – of sequence, perspective and judgment. The reversal of chronological sequence is linked to another discontinuity, which is the most important of all, for it was the one that set him on course toward the radical rethinking of communist theory and practice for which he is now renowned. Although he came from a left-wing family, his own political philosophy remained largely unarticulated in his writings until well after the start of his scholarly career. His early training focused on philosophy of law, and during his early adulthood he kept his academic work separate from his political activities, which were affiliated with the Italian Socialist Party. His earliest writings, which we will examine hereafter, make few overt references to Marx and major Marxist thinkers like Lenin and Gramsci (by that time the latter was revered as the patron saint of the Italian Communist Party and was ritually invoked by party ideologues in ways that Negri found reductive and offensive). Not until 1961, when he had been teaching at the University of Padua for several years, did Negri finally take the time to read Marx. He undertook this reading on the advice of his senior co-editor on the board of the radical journal *Quaderni rossi* (*Red Notebooks*), Raniero Panzieri, and as part of the outreach to factory workers to which his rising political consciousness had led him. This transformational experience would establish the pattern for Negri's entire career: every important intellectual development in his thought would arise from work that was as militant as it was scholarly, and as collective as it was singular.

The consequences of the encounter with Marx were immediate and massive. Negri reconceived his entire intellectual itinerary and re-aligned his research program. His books on German historicism, Hegel and Kantian jurisprudence, which had originally arisen out of his scholarly focus on legal philosophy and its impact on political reform, were re-imagined as stages of an archaeological reconstruction of the development of the modern state, from the crisis that ended the Renaissance to the stabilization of the nation state in the nineteenth century. These excavations in the history of philosophy would lay the groundwork for Negri's studies of Keynes, the welfare state, capitalist planning and crisis management that we will examine in chapter 3, which in turn formed the basis for his theorizations of militant worker organization during the seventies. The most obvious sign of this systemic re-orientation of his thought is the eight-year gap between the publication of *Alle origini del formalismo giuridico* (Negri 1962) and Negri's next book, *Political Descartes* (Negri 1970b) – by far the longest interval between books in his career. Only with the publication of the Descartes book did the contours of Negri's critical genealogy of the modern state and of the philosophies that had legitimated it become apparent. By that time he had found a way to unite his academic work in political philosophy with his militant efforts in the factories of Venice and Turin.

Before we begin our chronologically reversed analysis of Negri's early writings in the history of philosophy, we must establish the sequence of their composition and grasp its underlying evolutionary logic. Although Negri began a thesis on Hegel while studying in France in 1954, the dissertation he submitted for his doctorate focused on the German historicist school of the nineteenth and early twentieth century and had chapters on Wilhelm Dilthey, Ernst Troeltsch, Max Weber and Friedrich Meinecke.[1] A relation of reciprocity, if not a dialectic, linked the two projects, which were published in quick succession: in Negri's view, the work of the historicists constituted a formalization of Hegel's innovative philosophy of right and the state – a formalization that corresponded to the institutional stabilization of the bourgeois state over the course of the nineteenth century. Negri simply followed the trail backward from Meinecke and Dilthey to Hegel.[2] The recognition of this relationship set the young Negri on the trail of the emergence of Hegelian philosophy out of its own precursors: the Kantian jurists. The overall achievement of these three early books can be defined as a "thick description" of the philosophical transition between the Enlightenment and European Romanticism, a transition that corresponded to the political one, marked by the French Revolution, between eighteenth-century absolutism and nineteenth-century republicanism. But this achievement posed a new analytical challenge: how was the prior consensus between Enlightenment rationalism and monarchical absolutism established? This question led Negri to Descartes and the transition from monistic Renaissance humanism to dualistic rationalism. By this point Negri's method had developed into a more sophisticated form of "biographical materialism" that could tease out not only the influence of philosophical schools in rivalry with Descartes, but also issues of class position and political geography that overdetermined his thought. Just as Marx wrote in the *Grundrisse* that human anatomy provides the key to the anatomy of our ancestors the apes, so Negri's mature work provides the key to understanding his early work.

Descartes' Reasonable Ideology

Negri's study of Descartes is the first of his writings openly to manifest his claim that "every metaphysics is in some way a political ontology – as has been clearly demonstrated by Machiavelli, Spinoza and Marx (and, after them, was the basis for the broad philosophical consensus that runs from Nietzsche to Foucault and Derrida)" (Negri 1970b: 317). As we will see, his previous studies of Hegel and of Kantian juridical philosophy had focused on the political aspects and implications of major philosophers' systems of thought and had insisted on a continuity, both in method and in results, between their political writings and their metaphysical writings; but they had not explicitly equated metaphysics and politics. Put another way, his previous works had respected the disciplinary demarcations of philosophical scholarship more fully than his mature work would. In large part this was the result of the maturation of what Matteo Mandarini and Alberto Toscano call his "anti-deterministic, 'biographical' and agonistic concept of historical materialism" (Mandarini and Toscano 2007: 1). This method enables Negri to see unexpected links between the thinker's historical context and his thought, "[b]ut what is particularly fascinating is the way that the links are made: how metaphysical problems are shown to be immediately political, and political tasks are sustained through the development of a metaphysics" (p. 3). This "biographical materialist" methodology began from the assumption that "a thought is (always) constituted and defined through choices and breaks, that it is all the more significant to the extent that it is able to control and subsume the different and, at times, contradictory historical articulations of a period, as well as the movement of subjects that in this period sought and/or constructed hegemony" (Negri 1970b: 318–19). This genealogical conception, which owes a debt to Nietzsche as well as to Marx, goes beyond the conventional Marxist method of situating influential persons at the cusp of transitions within, or between, modes of production – a method that too often deploys crudely mechanical definitions of those modes and deterministic presuppositions regarding the logic of transition. Instead Negri situates Descartes in the midst of a number of scientific, metaphysical, religious and political camps whose conflict defined on the one hand the collapse of the Renaissance humanist project of reconstruction of the world and the self and, on the other, the emergence of monarchical absolutism – which would hold political sway over Europe until the revolutions of the eighteenth and nineteenth centuries.

Unlike most critical interpreters of Descartes' thought, who treat it as separable from the specifics of its historical context, Negri sees Descartes as passionately involved in the great debates of his day, especially the political ones. Indeed Descartes' thoroughgoing adherence to the social, political and scientific problematic of the early 1600s and his engagement with the real issues of his day provide a key to reading his work in a rigorously historical fashion.

> We are unable to call this total, critical adherence and this general dimension of the appreciation of the surrounding reality by any other name than 'political', especially if we consider the intimate dialectic between theoretical moment and practical perspective which it involves...he is 'political' above all because in these years – from the 1500s to the 1600s and in France in particular – in a situation of radical alternatives and of profound reflection on the historical events of the time, it is the moment of politics which internally tends to confer meaning upon all others. (Negri 1970b: 89–90)

If Descartes' work is "overdetermined" – to use Louis Althusser's term for the overlap of distinct forces and forms of causality and constraint that give a historical event its unique dimensions – then politics is the "determination in the last instance," which crystallizes those forces into a specific shape. In Negri's view, then, the only convincing way to follow the internal development of Descartes' writings is to relate them to the social movements and polemics that, in the seventeenth century, cut across the disciplinary boundaries scholars take for granted today. The result is similar to what Althusser and his followers call a "symptomatic reading" of ideological form.

Negri consistently defines the power of Renaissance humanism in terms of the latter's radical monism: as a consequence of its insistence on a profoundly univocal conception of being shared by the human soul and its environment, humanism immersed humanity into the world and promised to reconstruct both along parallel progressive lines. This is what Negri means by the "freedom" that Renaissance humanism promoted. The young Descartes is a late product of this humanist adventure and remains committed to its project for the rest of his career, though never more directly than near its beginning, when he proposed to delineate a completely new science of absolute knowledge: "The *scientia penitus nova* [completely new science] is science that traverses the world and nature *iuxta sua propria principia* [according to its own principles]. It is a science in which the humanist faith in discovery and reconstruction, in the radical renewal of the world, is fully unfolded" (Negri 1970b: 44–5). For Renaissance humanism, the scientific inquiry into the functioning of the world was inseparable from the political and social project of reconstructing the world according to the results of that inquiry. Bertolt Brecht's Galileo speaks for this dual effort when he insists:

Our new art of doubting delighted the mass audience. They tore the telescope out of our hands and trained it on their tormentors, the princes, landlords and priests. These selfish and domineering men, having greedily exploited the fruits of science, found that the cold eye of science had been turned on a primaeval but contrived poverty that could clearly be swept away if they were swept away themselves. (Brecht 1994: 108)

The scientific revolution and the Reformation are the two most powerful fruits of the Renaissance project; but, as we have seen, both also lead to the project's crisis. The Reformation not only frees the monarchs from the pope and the merchants from their former marginal positions; it also inspires more radical movements, which question and reject the economic and religious basis of social hierarchy itself – including peasant uprisings, apocalyptic sects like the Anabaptists and so on. The scientific revolution threatens the existing hierarchy in a related way, by eroding its fixed conceptual basis, even as it creates new technical powers of uneven accumulation on a massive scale.

Descartes' family were *robins*, "men of the robe" – which was the class of professional administrators that emerged as the bourgeoisie began to consolidate itself through the political and legal institutions of the late Renaissance. "A new class comes to recognize itself in the discovery of freedom and, in so doing, is emancipated. The *robins* interpret, for France, the general significance of the bourgeois revolution which, having it roots in the humanism of the Italian city states, will affect the whole of Europe" (Negri 1970b: 94). The humanist *robins* provided the fledgling bourgeoisie with specialists in the discourses of law, politics and administration who allowed it to establish influence over the monarchical states in which it took root. The role of these specialists was to intervene within institutions so as to establish the autonomy of bourgeois interests as part of the general project of class hegemony against the traditional medieval defense of monarchical power. The interests of the bourgeoisie and of the *robins* briefly converged with those of the more radical peasant movements in the critique of medieval absolutism, but they soon diverged when the peasants' and the sectarians' demands began to threaten the security of bourgeois property. Fortune, then, began to eclipse virtue.[3]

The Thirty Years' War, in which Descartes served as a mercenary, put an end to the linear development of the Renaissance humanist project and re-asserted the authority of the monarchs and churches over the rising bourgeoisie. The struggle against the peasant uprisings and radical egalitarian sects forged an alliance between the old royal courts and aristocracy on the one hand and the bourgeoisie on the other. Instead of an open field of endeavor subject to a single universal set of laws that science can derive and apply, the world was re-distributed among the forms of power that were initially shaken by the Renaissance project: the court and the aristocracy, abetted by the churches, reclaimed the state apparatus, leaving the marketplace to the bourgeoisie. Galileo's condemnation, trial and recantation of his Copernicanism demonstrate this to all the intellectuals and reformers of Europe.

> Descartes had seen the world in the same way as Galileo: the wondrous unfolding of divine laws immediately comprehensible to man, the macrocosm homogeneous with the microcosm – this was a sci-

entific fabric that practical hope latched on to. Practical hope was then immediately revolutionary. It was certain of its strength and happy to contemplate its own triumph. A memory of freedom, of its heroic development. No longer. (Negri 1970b: 144; see 71–4, 140–7)

With this the bourgeoisie's aspiration to a revolutionary role comes to an end. As Negri says, "The Renaissance world is shattered. Universal discontinuity takes the place of universal continuity. Radical contingency takes the place of the ubiquitous necessity of the Renaissance world. The reversal could not be more complete" (p. 107).

This reversal results in what Negri sees as a situation of radical separation between the bourgeoisie's sense of its own identity – as the progressive class of merchants who have brought immense new accumulative powers under human control – and its claim to political hegemony over society and the state: the latter is foreclosed even as the former expands. Thus the displaced *robin* Descartes can only experience the Renaissance humanist hope as a utopian nostalgia that the political events of the early seventeenth century make impossible to realize. His initial project, then, cannot simply perpetuate the Renaissance method but must instead produce the conditions for restoring that method. His early work aspires to be

> the refinement of the general humanist model of the construction of knowledge, a refinement elicited by the need to render the model workable, to make it confront the world and to verify it in this relation. This project could be realized only by winning back humanist heroism in all its mythical originality. (P. 61)

His project constitutes a frank recognition of the crisis of the bourgeoisie: "Descartes's crisis is truly the crisis of the century, the individual facet of a collective drama" (p. 113). The crisis marks the failure of the bourgeois revolution to attain hegemony, and "The historical substance of the failure of the bourgeois revolution mutates and is fixed in the philosophical form of separation" (p. 153). Absolutism cuts off the bourgeoisie – and the *robins* – from influence over the state. But this is not a return to a feudal model of fixed estates. This new or remodeled "[a]bsolutism is born of the lack of pursuable alternatives for men who had set their sights on revolution" (p. 128), and it is based on a new dualism of political and economic power.

The blockage of his Renaissance-inspired philosophical project, the restriction of his bourgeois world to subjective interiority and productive engagement with the world through manufacture, drives Descartes to profound introspection, conceived of not as a purely personal reaction to events but as a means to find a resolution to the intolerable tension of the separation in which he and his class were forced to exist. The *Discourse on Method* can therefore be read, Negri insists, as the first *Bildungsroman* of bourgeois thought (p. 156). This is not a hyperbole: Negri reads the *Discourse* very carefully to demonstrate exactly how, "[t]hrough his own history, Descartes exemplifies the defeat of Renaissance man. He follows the path leading from the joyous, spontaneous participation in the life of science and the world to one's separation from the world...and from the exaltation of spontaneity to the recognition of organization" (p. 159). Essence, the interiority of the subject, is blocked from expanding its existence "horizontally," into and over the world, and can seek consistency and direction only within itself and its "vertical" relation to God. The most famous sentence from Descartes' *Discourse, Cogito ergo sum* ("I think, therefore I am"), emerges from Negri's reading as an ontological anchor for the bourgeois self in its separation from the world and from the state: the self-certainty of the statement connects the subject to God and establishes a basis for infinite subjective autonomy in a situation of real political impotence.

The *malin* ("malicious demon") that deceives the bourgeois subject about the world is consequently the figure of the prince or sovereign, to whom the subject concedes that bewitched world – the realm of politics and the state. "Descartes describes the political world in the vocabulary of absolutism: a fully sovereign will, inscrutable in its majesty, which simply owes its capacity to legislate to its arbitrary power...and this will is binding, we cannot avoid subordinating all social obligation to it" (pp. 179–80). On this basis Descartes' "reasonable ideology" begins to arise, although Negri is quick to note that

> we still do not have here an ideological conception of the I completely separated from the ontological discovery of the I. In sociological terms we could say that here the consciousness of the bourgeois I still expresses the consciousness of autonomy and not the full-blown consciousness of organization...Nevertheless, the qualitative leap has been accomplished, the mature philosophy and the ideological path are opened up. (P. 172 n. 165)

Autonomy of the bourgeois subject is the precondition for his or her organization of production and of what will come to be called "civil society" into a long-term project of state conquest. Negri points out that "the specificity of Cartesian thought derives from this contradiction: the deeper the dualism, the more organized becomes this urge to overcome. Not in utopian daydreaming, which either forgets or wishes to obscure the initial situation of scission, but operationally, methodically: to control and possess the world..." (p. 207). The poles of this dualism – essence and existence, individual and world, reason and history, subject and state – are precisely the antitheses of the dialectic that will emerge from Kantianism to define Hegel's solution to the contradiction.

The reasonable ideology is further developed in Descartes' *Meditations* – in which, according to Negri,

> political meaning can be recognized at once: the active and independent subject is characterized by its confrontation with the bewitched world of absolutism; the productive form of this separate existence projects its own class essence in the shape of absolute autonomy; the impossibility of politically possessing the world, of remaking it as real from its current bewitched state, is registered, but it is accompanied by the hope... that the productive, social and cultural hegemony of the bourgeois class will find in absolute mediation the capacity to rebuild the world. (P. 228)

A step forward is taken here in the recognition that the key to the realization of this hope is the will, which for Descartes means "the internal productivity of thought" through which "existence can project itself" (p. 218). The will constitutes the basis and motor of truth "only to the extent that truth is the productivity of the subject's unfolding" (p. 220). The external world of the sovereign cannot simply be seized, since it is "not a reality of which we could gain possession, but a reality that must be produced" (p. 226). Thus Descartes' metaphysics is a logic of production, of manufacture, that must transform the existing world by creating its own conditions of rule. The ultimate result will be "the image of a thoroughly artificial world... of craft and industry. Within this horizon, individuality indefinitely interprets its own infinite productive power... Its separate value must be sought in the human capacity to produce" (p. 299). This image clearly alludes to the Renaissance project of virtue, but at the same time it translates it into immediately accumulative terms – that is, into fortune.

Productivist logic defines the "new science" that Descartes was forced to develop in the face of the blockage of Renaissance science caused by the re-assertion of absolutism. But, Negri asks, can this dualistic "new science" really call itself a science? Can it really claim to succeed and supplant the monistic Renaissance project?

> It is not a science especially in its opening to the world of subjects, sociality, history. It is not the mirroring of reality. It is not the analytical reconstruction of a separate world. What is it then? It is a fiction, what today we would call an ideology. A reasonable ideology that spreads out over the space of the crisis of the world of the 1600s...
> (P. 241)

As an ideology, it contends with the other ideologies of its day: libertinism, Hobbes' mechanistic dualism (pp. 229–39), the quietist withdrawal of Jansenism (pp. 262–7) and other forces. So what is it that, for Negri, gives the historical advantage to Descartes? What makes his ideology materially productive and determining for the next two centuries?

The final stage of Descartes' work, in Negri's interpretation, constitutes an effort to realize the reasonable ideology:

> The projection of the bourgeois essence in time must become real; that is, it must be articulated within history. Ideology must pass into politics. The project that had been presented...now needed to be verified. The reference to time could not remain hypothetical, it had to become living experience. (P. 256)

The separation of individual, subjective essence – the *cogitans* – from worldly existence – the realm of the sovereign and the state – was experienced as a deprivation, a foreclosure of the Renaissance project that was imposed within historical time. That foreclosure must be overcome and the project re-proposed in and through time. The infinity of subjective essence and its divine authority will only conquer the external world of the state though the indefinite duration of historical time. This "militant" or "activist" aspect

> is the sign of the historical significance of Descartes's thought because it captures the effective problem of the century, that of giving form to that spontaneous emergence of individuality – more precisely: of realizing the pressing need of the bourgeois class to reconnect its existence to a project of development. (P. 272)

Bourgeois individuality can only define itself as the productivity of the subjective will, which in turn can only be expressed within the constraints of a dualist metaphysics that presents fundamental class conflict in the form of the development of production – that is, of manufacture, industry and trade. Descartes addresses many parties in his attempt to realize his thought: the Jesuits, the Dutch universities, the Parisian scientific community, the Swedish court. All reject him, because they are committed to different philosophical–political programs. At last he turns to the only party left him: the literate public.

By addressing his *Principles of Philosophy* to general readers, Descartes translates his ideology into a technics, a metaphysics of the technical (and technological) invention of a new world for the bourgeoisie to dominate. The value of this new world is to be found in work:

> The bourgeois experience of work, of manufacture, is expressed here... with all the intensity it is capable of. Once again a concept that had already been expressed in Descartes's youthful experience – work as a product of universal mathematics – is disinterred, renewed and inverted: universal mathematics is a product of work. (P. 299)

This step in the development of the reasonable ideology finally provides a point of contact with reality precisely in the central bourgeois practice of manufacture – the site where "universal mathematics" or scientific inquiry and human labor intersect. It makes economic development the motor of the project to wrest political control of the state from the sovereign, thereby overcoming the dualism in which the cogito is trapped and re-activating the unified project of Renaissance humanism, though in sharply different fundamental terms. This is the key to the success of the reasonable ideology.

> The fact is that this Cartesian project is really adequate to the public it is addressed to, more than any other historical project produced by his century. And it is adequate precisely to the extent that it is ambiguous, to the extent that it affirms the insuppressible class reality of the bourgeoisie, grasping its heavy destiny of defeat, and yet attempting a reconstruction within this very separation. (Pp. 295–6)

The ambiguity of the Cartesian project stems from its focus on the reconquest of sovereignty through the indefinite – the time of history in which the technical and institutional reconstruction will take place. Although this is not yet a philosophy of history, it is the metaphysical precondition for one and, as such, it lays the groundwork for Hegel's apotheosis of bourgeois subjective history two centuries later.

Negri's analysis demonstrates how Descartes' reasonable ideology constituted "an attempt to mediate between [the] two modernities" (Casarino and Negri 2008: 57), between Machiavelli's virtue and fortune as they were understood by the emergent bourgeoisie. "[I]n Descartes, as in Machiavelli, we encounter the generalization of the meaning of the end of the humanist revolution and of the necessary rescaling of bourgeois action in these new conditions. But the aim and the objective remain" (Negri 1970b: 252). Although Machiavelli's defense of constituent virtue was more far-reaching and radical, a fact that will become more significant to Negri later in his career, Descartes' project was the more immediately effective. The centrality of his thought in the evolution of European philosophy – which inversely parallels the misrecognition of his role in the development of modern politics – is the most significant symptom of that effectiveness.

Despite its breadth and originality, Negri's reading of Descartes has been virtually ignored by English-language scholarship, largely because his political reading refuses to acknowledge the conventional disciplinary boundaries between "metaphysics" and "political philosophy." A telling example of this refusal to read Negri can be found in Quentin Taylor's essay "Descartes' Paradoxical Politics," which is one of the few English-language studies that even mention *Political Descartes*. Taylor surveys Descartes' political views as they appear explicitly in his writings, in an effort to understand why "the Revolutionaries of 1789 acknowledged Descartes as a forerunner" despite his "markedly conservative, even reactionary" political ideas (Taylor 2001: 76). After examining all of Descartes' overtly political remarks, Taylor draws no meaningful conclusion beyond noting that the fact that "the French Revolutionaries embraced him as an enemy of tyranny and a friend of freedom is ironic indeed" (p. 103). Even though he cites Negri's book as one of the "two most comprehensive studies" of "Descartes's politics and the political implications of his philosophy" (p. 77 n. 4), he finds no continuity between Descartes and the Revolution – which is the opposite of Negri's conclusion. How is this possible? The answer, first of all, is that Taylor, like many Anglo-American philosophers and historians of philosophy, implicitly accepts the contemporary division of intellectual discourse between metaphysics and political philosophy and simply fails to look for political implications in most of Descartes' major writings. Second, when he looks at Descartes' overtly political statements, he takes them at face value and makes only limited attempts to reconstruct their polemical context and potential audience. Not only does his analysis ignore the possibility of a symptomatic reading such as Negri's; it seems unacquainted with the most basic presupposition of ideology critique, which can be summed up in Marx and Engels' caustic jibe:

> Whilst in ordinary life every shopkeeper is very well able to distinguish between what somebody professes to be and what he really is, our historians have not yet won even this trivial insight. They take every epoch at its word and believe that everything it says and imagines about itself is true. (Marx and Engels 1998: 70–1)

Even though Taylor read Negri's study, he could not assimilate it to his own analytical assumptions.[4]

In Italy, however, *Political Descartes* was widely read and generated more controversy than one might expect from such a specialized work. As Negri notes in his 2004 postface: "The book came as a surprise both to academics, for its choice of subject (what could a Marxist do with Descartes?), and to my comrades in the movement (why is Negri wasting his time on Descartes?)" (Negri 1970b: 317). At least one reader had a foot in both camps: Negri's longtime friend and sometime ally, the philosopher and militant Massimo Cacciari (who later served as mayor of Venice), wrote a scathing review of it in *Contropiano*, the journal that he and Negri founded and co-edited before Negri resigned from the board. Cacciari singles out Negri's focus on Descartes' humanist nostalgia for particular criticism, and insists instead on Descartes' affirmation of the emerging sciences – he views Descartes as providing a rationale not for political impotence but for technical mastery: "Abandoning the Renaissance myth doesn't mean abandoning the hope of possessing and dominating, but instead renewing it, grounding it on entirely new, *more powerful* [*potenti*] logical terms" – which means techno-scientific terms (Cacciari 1970: 377, my translation). As befits his Heideggerian orientation, Cacciari reads the subject in Descartes not as the emerging bourgeois self, and thus as a historically situated and overdetermined class subject, but rather as "the very metaphysical subject of modernity, hollowed out and calculating" (Mandarini and Toscano 2007: 19):

not subjectivity in the sense of activity forming–organizing experience but rather in that limited to "interiority" – separation is already
defined in terms of a reduction to the I as seat and center of freedom
and order that is definitively emancipated from the *adequatio* of the
classical episteme...Here begins the story of "nihilism" in Heidegger's sense...[a]nd on this basis the form of subjectivity as possibility and will to power is constructed...(Cacciari 1970: 380, my
translation)

For Cacciari, Descartes inaugurates the "closure of metaphysics"
and installs the subject of monolithic, abstract, dehistoricized
humanism against which critical thinkers from Marx and Nietzsche
to Derrida and Foucault will struggle, as we saw in chapter 1.
Clearly this approach is antithetical to Negri's project – not only in
Political Descartes but also in the works leading up to it and following it, as we will see. It also opens up a radically different political
line, which explains why their collaboration on *Contropiano* fell
apart: Negri's notion of the class-specific subject form coincided
with his militant emphasis on self-valorization, on the autonomous
development of working-class needs, desires and values separate
from and antagonistic to the value system of capital, while Cacciari's totalizing notion of the dehistoricized modern humanist
subject led him to emphasize the measure of technical mastery over
the productive process and hence to a politics of engagement with
political management through the existing party system. In short,
Negri's interpretation of Descartes was in line with his extra-parliamentary militancy, which attacked the Italian Communist Party
(PCI) as well as the Italian right, while Cacciari chose to join the
PCI in order to take charge of the management of production on
behalf of the working class (see Mandarini and Toscano 2007:
15–21).[5] We will examine this development of Negri's work in
chapter 3.

Kant and the Formalists

It is difficult to imagine a more specialized book than Negri's study
of Kant's influence on the philosophy of right[6] in the years between
the culmination of critical philosophy and the emergence of its
most profound successor, Hegel – a period of only thirteen years.
Aside from Kant himself, almost all the figures whom Negri exam-
ines are largely unknown today, and his argument relates to few

well-known doctrines or perspectives in the history of philosophy – unlike his work on Descartes, which treats well-known issues from unexpected perspectives, and his Hegel book, which parallels the analyses of Georg Lukács and Theodor W. Adorno.[7] Nevertheless, *Alle origini del formalismo giuridico: Studio sul problema della forma in Kant e nei giuristi kantiani tra il 1789 e il 1802 (At the Origins of Juridical Formalism: A Study of the Problem of Form in Kant and the Kantian Jurists Between 1789 and 1802*: Negri 1962) is an anticipatory sequel to *Political Descartes* and a "prequel" to Negri's Hegel book. It attempts to reconstruct the philosophical and ideological context for the development of the young Hegel in terms of a dialectic between the conceptual form of right and its institutional practice in the judicial system and in the state. As such it can most fruitfully be read as an early example of the form of analysis that Stephen Paul Miller calls "micro-periodization": the critical effort to reconstruct the defining characteristics of a short but crucial transitional period in political or cultural history. This book enriches Negri's project of explicating Hegel's thought as being the result not of individual genius but rather of a broad movement in European culture that owes its ultimate genesis to Descartes' reasonable ideology. As Negri described his overall project much later,

> What interested me was the formation, the coming-into-being, of the dialectic. The main thesis of my book on the young Hegel was that political thought had been central and fundamental in Hegel's formation: the critical question was to understand how Hegel had confronted the various forms and modes of Kantian formalism. In Kant, the law is defined as a form that organizes certain social relations. In Hegel, this form becomes a transformation: at the same time that it organizes these various elements, it transforms them and raises them to a higher level... What interested me was to ascertain what kinds of alternatives had emerged within Kantianism, understood as that absolutely central site in which all the political–philosophical – and hence also juridical – currents of the time had converged. What I started excavating within Kantianism, therefore, were the various ways in which the philosophers of law – and especially the practical jurists who directed and shaped the massive codifications that were taking place at the time – interpreted the Kantian form, that is, the juridical qualification of social facts. (Casarino and Negri 2008: 47–8)

But Kant does not represent a beginning *ex nihilo* any more than Hegel does; Kant's philosophy emerges from the crisis of the late

German Enlightenment, which was forced to confront the antinomy of reason and history that it had inherited from Wolff's rational theology (Negri 1962: Ch. 1). This antinomy is simply a
differential repetition of Descartes' polarity between the autonomous rational subject and the bewitched, irrational world of the
absolute sovereign that we just explicated; Descartes' derivation of
subjective autonomy from the internal relation to God is also a
crucial source of rational theology. Thus Kant's challenge is inherited from Descartes, although Negri does not note that fact in this
book, and Kant's solution will constitute an important moment in
the realization of the reasonable ideology.

Negri's thesis is simple to state but extraordinarily difficult to
follow. Essentially he argues that each of the different currents of
juridical and political philosophy that emerged from Kant's critical
model can be traced back to one of the conflicting modalities of the
concept of form to be found in Kant's own texts. As Antonella
Guaraldi put it in a perceptive review of the book (which is almost
certainly the first account of Negri's thought to appear in English),

> Kant has both a critical and a metaphysical ideal, and this duplicity
> is found in the ambivalence of the idea of form, conceived from one
> point of view as a condition of critical research and from the other
> point of view as constitutive of metaphysical reconstruction. Cor-
> responding to this double conception of form is the ambiguous
> conception of freedom which Kant uses in legal philosophy[:] [o]n
> one hand...freedom as autonomy of mind, and to this conception
> of freedom there corresponds the conception of form as constitutive
> of objectivity...But on the other hand...freedom as independence,
> and...to this conception of freedom there corresponds the concep-
> tion of form as a "rational structure, as a registration of relation of
> wills." (Guaraldi 1965: 135, citing Negri 1962: 74)

Kant's two concepts of freedom are collapsed into one another by
subsequent juridical formalism; the melding of the objective
freedom of thought with the subjective freedom of will reifies the
antinomy into the closure of bourgeois individualism. From this
viewpoint, the development of post-Kantian juridical philosophy
before Hegel constitutes a decomposition of the Kantian system,
an unraveling of Kant's resolution to the antinomy of reason and
history and a reduction of his thought to sheer formalism, defined
"as the dualistic ordering [*assetto*] of philosophical analysis, as the
accentuation of the rational element of validity in the face of
the irrationality of history and value, as the attempt to found the

horizon of scientificity in purely logical or methodological terms" (Negri 1962: 3, my translation). In order to prove this hypothesis, Negri divides his subject into four parts, which are organized chronologically: an introductory examination of the multiple functions or modalities of form across Kant's entire critical philosophy, followed by three sections focused on the major currents of Kantian philosophy of right before the appearance of Hegel, namely subjective idealism, objective idealism and historicism. Our discussion here will not trace the many local complexities that Negri explicates in order to advance his analysis; we will focus instead on the aspect of juridical formalism that offers the clearest points of connection between the Cartesian reasonable ideology and Hegelian dialectics: the relationship between individual right and the state.

Kant claimed to resolve the various versions of the dualism between reason and history through the distinction between noumenon and phenomenon, between the unknowable thing-in-itself and the knowing subject's construction of objectivity according to his/her own epistemological capacities. Such epistemological construction constitutes the genesis of form in Kant's metaphysics. In the course of the highly technical opening discussion, Negri identifies five different conceptualizations of form in the Kantian corpus:

- form as the precondition of objectivity, in the Transcendental Aesthetic of pure reason and the phenomenology of practical reason;
- form as subjectively and teleologically constitutive of objectivity, as the rational, goal-oriented activity of the thinking subject faced with the world in the original Analytic of pure reason and the early theorization of ethics;
- form as objectively, systematically constitutive of objectivity in a self-contained, non-relational sense, in the revised Analytic of pure reason and the Analytic of practical reason;
- form as the index of the dialectical relation of theory and practice, in the Dialectic of pure reason and in the writings on history and public right;
- form as conformity to objectivity in the sense of cultural tradition, in the doctrine of right (see Negri 1962: 89–90).

Each of these modes of form is structured dualistically, and therefore can be mapped onto the founding dualism of reason and history inherited from Descartes. The schools of juridical formalism that follow Kant will grant conceptual priority to one or more of these modes, according to the requirements of their individual class interests and corresponding legal projects.

Although Negri makes comparatively little effort to situate historically or socially the modes of form that he finds in Kant, as he would do with the stages of Descartes' philosophical project and as he had done in a preliminary way with Hegel's development, his explication here shares with those other projects an extraordinary sensitivity to the internal differences that fissure even those schools of thought that aspire to the strictest systematic coherence. What Kant held together by means of the intense architectonic rigidity of his logic would soon fall apart under the combined pressures of profound historical rupture and antagonistic class interests. The characteristics of Kant's "Copernican Revolution," however, correspond remarkably to the features of the French Revolution:

> [D]id not the French Revolution, whose development parallels that of the critical revolution, pose the very same questions on the political plane that the Kantian philosophy had tried to answer? Did not the Revolution destroy the *ancien régime*, the eudemonistic absolutism of the eighteenth-century state, just as Kant dissolved the absolutist metaphysics of rationalism? ... The translatability of philosophical and political languages seems almost perfect. (Pp. 101–2, my translation)

This correspondence dovetails with Negri's insistence, discussed above, that the French Revolution "completes the design" of Descartes' reasonable ideology. All three events – the reasonable ideology, the Copernican Revolution and the French Revolution – are expressions of the same conceptual matrix at different stages of its development, and all the schools of juridical formalism will have to be measured against those events.

The school of subjective idealism emerged earliest and dominated the German philosophical scene between 1792 and 1795. Its major representatives – Beck, Reinhold, Löbel, Schmid and others – are almost all forgotten now. Although all the currents examined in *At the Origins of Juridical Formalism* are defined by their specific definitions of form, the subjective idealist current has resulted in a concept of right that must be called formalist to the highest degree. According to Negri, the concept of form distinguished by the authors of this [*sc.* the high formalist] current is that of form as constitutive of objectivity in subjective–idealist terms. This current claims that it is possible to understand right according to a purely formal schema, according to an abstract calculus on the basis of certain conceptual presuppositions, first among them the concept of freedom as individual independence... [I]t leads to an extreme legalism and at its limit ends up transforming the philosophy of positive right into a methodology of juridical science. (P. 112, my translation)

Among the most important presuppositions underlying the conception of this school are those of a strict separation of right and law from morality, which results in a positivist conception of right in opposition to natural right, and of the abstract forms of the legal or juridical person and the contract. The legal or juridical person is essentially the hypostasis of the bourgeois individual subject whose "independence" is defined in economic terms, by his property or possessions – in other words, the subject of C. B. Macpherson's conception of "possessive individualism," which appeared in print at virtually the same moment as Negri's study.[8] This person then enters into contracts with other similar persons, on a footing assumed to be equal (that is, free of class differences) and guaranteed by the state as the regulator of formal right.

The state so conceived is the *Rechtstaat* or the liberal state of right, which administers a form of right that is

essentially command and coercion... to guarantee its efficacy: the compossibility of arbiters becomes real only when coercive power [*potere*]... is transferred and consolidated into a general coercive force that supports and defends the freedom of the individual universally, within the limits posited for the intersubjective relationship. (P. 156, my translation)

The state's job is to impose abstract equality on subjects so as to reduce their conflicts to logical unity and thereby to secure a formal space for the accumulation of property. The presupposition of hypostatized bourgeois subjectivity with property as its foundation leads to a purely positivist concept of right and abstract legalism as the dominant mode of jurisprudence. As Negri writes, "the exaggeration of formalism to its metaphysical limit paradoxically impinges, in the science of right, on its opposite, that is, it tends to be converted into an extreme positivism, understood no longer simply as the approach or theory of positive law but as nothing more than an apology for it" (p. 189, my translation). Such exaggeration justifies Negri's labeling of this school as "high formalist." In other words, this current of thought offers a powerful legitimation of existing bourgeois legal practices without providing tools or leverage for the critique or transformation of those practices, in response to inequalities of class, gender, ethnicity and so on.[9]

However, its original inspiration was the polemic against monarchical absolutism, which took natural right as its founding ideology. In natural right theory, the legal system strives to reflect, however imperfectly, the demands of morality, and therefore it is open to critique and modification from that perspective. At the same time, natural right theory preserves the centrality of absolute monarchy through its appeal to the divine origin of the moral order, and therefore it stood in the way of the bourgeois conquest of the state. "Within the ideology of juridical legalism a force that rejected the absolutist structure of political power and the monopolistic regime of economic organization began to organize itself" (p. 194, my translation). The subjective idealist school was initially sympathetic to the revolutionary movements in France; but, with the radicalization of the Revolution, the German high formalists moderated their position to one of political reform, with the aim of establishing a secure liberal state. Ultimately they colluded with the *ancien régime* to establish a strong state in defense of bourgeois property and individual liberty:

> individualistic demands, with objectively revolutionary content, were proposed tactically in reformist terms...[and] proceeded by means of a series of proposals that did not affect the substance of the organization of power...A new alliance of the absolutist State and the bourgeoisie was thereby sanctified. (P. 197, my translation)

This result parallels the accommodation between the rising bourgeoisie and the absolutist state that Descartes' reasonable ideology was meant to facilitate and represents a further elaboration of that ideology's focus on historical development.

A violent self-contradiction emerged, however, within the high formalist current, between its defense of the abstract bourgeois individual and its defense of the state. This self-contradiction, exemplified in the writings of the most prominent subjective idealist, Wilhelm von Humboldt, can be understood in terms of the two parties to which the formalists opposed themselves: the absolute monarchy, which had to be constrained from interfering in the bourgeois marketplace, and the radical democrats, who emerged from the objective idealist current of Kantianism (we will examine it hereafter) and who had to be prevented from flattening the hierarchical class structure over which the bourgeoisie had only recently and precariously established control. As Negri puts it, "the two fundamental themes of liberal polemics were on the one hand the struggle against princely absolutism and on the other the struggle against democratic ideology" (p. 207, my translation), which means that

> this simultaneity... of the apology for individuality and for the State – always here understood as the German State in which the forces of the bourgeoisie had obtained adequate recognition – can be explained solely from the ideological and political viewpoint, which held that the bourgeoisie needed a strong State and coercion in order to consolidate its own position...But undoubtedly there is a profound contradiction between the individualistic demand and the apology for the State... (Pp. 213–14, my translation)

The model of the state that emerges from the subjective idealist camp is one that cannot help but reveal its fundamental irrationality – the unacknowledged class antagonism at its heart, which results in "the definitive unsustainability of the relation between the procedure of rational connection of parts and the irrational whole they comprise, which demonstrates the implicit irrationalist resolution of the entire system that results" (p. 217, my translation). Thus the old antinomy between reason and history re-emerges from its temporary Kantian balance, marking the overall failure of the high formalists.

The second camp, that of objective idealists such as Maimon, Erhard, Tieftrunk and others, who dominated the scene from 1795 to 1797, also opposed the despotic absolute state of the eighteenth century, and for a time its juridical theories and projects resembled those of the subjective idealists, despite being based on a different reading of Kantian form.

> The interpretation of the concept of form on which [these] authors insist is that of form as constitutive of objectivity in objective–idealist terms; here the concept of freedom is restored to autonomy. The reconstruction of the universe of right undertaken by this current will thus have a character that is not so much formalist as objective and metaphysical: thought will not merely reconstruct the general theory of right in force but also constitute its real systematic weave. (P. 113, my translation)

Unlike the subjective idealists, the objective idealists defined freedom not in the bourgeois terms of independence predicated upon property ownership, but in terms of political autonomy, understood as "equality, participation and community" (p. 259, my translation). In addition, they did not seek to legitimate or justify the existing legal order but to rebuild it systematically from the ground up. Their focus on concrete conditions led to a recognition of the hierarchies and inequalities within social and political life that the abstractions of the subjective idealists had obscured.

The objective idealist definition of freedom as equality resulted in a conception of the state that was radically different from the liberal moderates' state of right. The objective idealists adopted Kant's suggestion, made in "Perpetual Peace," that history could be considered the measure of freedom's forward progress, and consequently they demanded a state form that would accelerate that progress.

> The most advanced theme in the political and juridical polemics of this current was the representation of the ideal of the cosmopolitan State of perpetual peace... [T]he ideal of perpetual peace foresees... not only a type of international organization but also a certain type of organization internal to individual States; the discourse involves problems of the reform of the absolutist State and implies the decisive taking of positions on the most varied arguments: against slavery, for the universality of voting rights, on the legitimacy of the right of resistance of subjects with regard to the sovereign, against the death penalty... (P. 237, my translation)

This cosmopolitan or "ethical" state (p. 270) would not be the coercive regulator and defender of the abstract equality of economic subjects, but rather an organic community, understood "as the condition and at the same time the realization of the freedom and equality of citizens" (p. 269, my translation).

The highest development of this objective idealist current appears in the philosophy of Fichte, whose work on state and right most clearly prefigures Hegel's. Fichte argues that

> the rational necessity at the basis of right is the necessity of social existence. He must consequently demonstrate the necessity of the social as necessity of reason, he must see how the position of the I in the system of reason implies on the practical plane a reaction of the not-I – that is, other "I"s, society – in order to institute free reciprocal causality of the I on nature and society. (P. 304, my translation)

Fichte raises the idealist philosophy of equality and community to the highest level it will attain, and he does this by setting up a dialectic between subjects through which they realize their own autonomy. This realization is right itself, which is posited as the condition of an egalitarian society:

> Such a discovery of rationality and freedom outside me is therefore the condition of a first synthesis of the I with the other rational, free and finite beings that constitute society, and this first concrete synthesis is represented by right...Right makes social life possible and thereby constitutes the first degree of the practical expansion of the I. (P. 306, my translation)

Nevertheless, Fichte too attributes a crucial role to the state as an agent in this process of realization, and thereby he perpetuates the legacy of Cartesian ideology:

> [H]e foresees a mediation of totality and individuality that cannot be left to spontaneity, to the unitary dialectical resolution of the two elementary terms, but must be based on a third element, superior to the first two, that is to say on a form that does not run through the relationship but institutes and prefigures it. In this organic conception, the concept of the State, in its compactness and solidity, is absolute and necessary...(P. 323, my translation)

The state is the instrument, or agent, that rationalizes history by enabling the synthesis of totality and individuality; therefore control of the state remains an essential goal for Fichte and his party, even if the purpose behind it is the advance of freedom.

The objective idealists' conception of history as the progress of freedom, derived from Kant, led them to embrace a broadly democratic ideology, which would have been called Jacobinism in France; Negri had already used this term to describe Hegel's political sympathies in his earlier study. The German Jacobins came into direct conflict with the liberals over the degree of freedom the state should promote.

> The democratic ideology...provides either a definition of freedom as autonomy (against the empirical and formalist reduction of freedom to individual independence) or an organic conception of the totality as the goal of the realized process of freedom. With regard to autonomy, the productivity of the idea of freedom, it establishes the universal extension of this idea to individuals by virtue of

> the concept of equality and to the totality by virtue of the concept
> of community. (Pp. 256–7, my translation)

Thus objective idealism pursued a project of reconciling the antithetical claims to freedom of all individuals on the one hand and
of the entire community on the other; that is, it attempted to resolve
the antinomy of reason and history by universalizing rational right
and thereby extinguishing the irrationality of history in the universal ethical state.

The objective idealists' enthusiasm for the French Revolution
never moderated into the cautious reformism of the liberals; indeed
it intensified over the course of the last decade of the eighteenth
century.

> Consequently, as had happened in the Jacobin phase of the French
> Revolution, German Jacobinism supported the people's right to
> revolt and insurrection against any political power that violated the
> most fundamental of the fundamental rights of man, the right to the
> management of power [*potere*], to freedom and equality. (P. 269, my
> translation)

The objective idealists went even further, to the point of "insist[ing]
on the necessity and the opportunity to diffuse the principles of the
French Revolution and the possibility of their application in other
European countries" (ibid.). This development, which we might
call the "rational imperialist" phase of German Jacobinism, was the
logical culmination of its universalizing project: the imperative to
spread the ethical state, otherwise known as the rational state or
Vernunftstaat, across Europe, in order to replace the particularist
imperialisms of the existing absolutist monarchies.

With the ultimate triumph of anti-revolutionary forces – the
liberal formalists and the reactionary historicists (whom we will
examine next) – in Germany and much of Europe, the Jacobins'
project of a broadly democratic state became unrealizable, and they
retreated into purely theoretical celebrations of democracy. The
objective ideal of freedom became a utopian prison of popular
energy, and its thinkers lost themselves in spiritualist compromises
and magical solutions to material problems. As Negri says,

> objective idealism was in this sense not so much a sign of the crisis
> of the times – in the equivocality and duplicity of its constitutive
> elements – as the prison in which the freshest, liveliest and healthiest
> energies of the German people and culture were confined. (P. 278,
> my translation)

The very radicalness of the objective idealist position isolated it within the German philosophical and political landscape; but its dogged persistence in passing the white light of intersubjective autonomy through the prism of the rational state led it to re-inscribe the antinomy that it so forcefully sought to overcome.

The third and ultimately triumphant current of Kantian formalism in the philosophy of right prior to Hegel was the historicist reaction, represented by Brandes, von Gentz, Hugo and others.

> The concept of form that distinguishes [the historicists] belongs to Kantian aesthetics, form as the condition of objectivity, but with a singular tendency to be interpreted ever more explicitly in terms of the *Metaphysics of Morals*, where form is reduced to mere conformity with positivity. Rationality, according to these authors, exists in reality, innervating the historical tradition and juridical habit...
> (P. 113, my translation)

Essentially, the reactionary historicists began where the liberal high formalists ended up: in the frank assertion of the unsurpassability of the national tradition of positive right. The historicists predictably viewed the entire revolutionary movement and its sympathizers as terrorists from the very beginning. Unlike the liberals, who abandoned the Revolution when it became too radical for their class interests, the historicists ruled it out of bounds immediately: its ends may have been just, but its choice of means invalidated it. This view was part of a trend that was widespread throughout Europe:

> the process of democratic evolution from the kingdom to the republic...came to be described as the evolution of a terroristic and despotic movement, and the action of the armed French in defense of free republican institutions and a new political framework was presented as an example of a dangerous imperialist involution of the Revolution itself. (P. 330, my translation)

The threat to bourgeois stability and independence that the liberals or formalists registered in legalistic terms is here presented, in historicist terms, as a pathological deviation from the cultural tradition of the people. Since the Revolution could not be made to conform to the bourgeois conception of history as the conquest of the state in the name of the economic right of individuals, it could only be condemned.

Historical experience, conceived of as a closed circle of repetitions or habits and embodied in national traditions, becomes the only possible source of right for this current. By this definition, the Revolution is not part of history but an exception to it – one that must be brought back into the circle as quickly as possible. Negri asks:

> Why not consider the revolutionary events also as historical events, thus as the fount of a new history?...[R]eactionary thought folds back on itself, refuses to extend the sense of history from past to present and assumes accents of mere conservation...[culminating in] a conception of man and his freedom not as historical activity but as products of history, as the simple mechanical stratification of various levels of experience, all past and not present. (P. 338, my translation)

And, as Negri writes,

> to the conception of freedom as ethical principle and aspiration of men, and as such the motor of history – a conception that supports the systematic and metaphysical formativity of critical idealism – is opposed an institutional conception of freedom in the new formalism, nourished by reactionary thought. (P. 350, my translation)

Thus the historicists' institutional notion of freedom constitutes the determinate negation of the objective idealists' autonomous notion.

Historicism borrowed from Edmund Burke's absolutist conservatism, but it developed in new, specifically German directions. The denunciation of the French Revolution as abstract and contagious led ultimately to the celebration of mere order as an ethical concept and as the foundation of right. As Friedrich von Gentz argued, "order is the highest ethical concept since on it, and only on it, can right be based" (p. 344), therefore "the true foundation of social life is order in the double sense, of self-consistency in social ethicality and its self-foundation on the one hand and of correspondence to historical tradition and its course on the other" (p. 346, my translation). Right is here equated with the abstract institutionalization of freedom in the order of the state, whose authority resides in the historical life of the people. "Right, therefore, is first and foremost institutionalized freedom" (p. 356, my translation). This is the most strident panegyric to the state that we find in the entire panorama of Kantian juridical philosophy:

The State in fact represents the totality of institutionalized freedom, and therefore the totality of right...Right thus organizes the multiform life of society in which it is immersed, but this organization is summed up in the State as the auto-foundation of the totality itself; right covers a vaster range than that covered by coercion, but the latter surreptitiously succeeds in characterizing right – in the Statism in which the doctrine concludes – under the form of authority, coercion extended and legalized by the State; and ultimately right represents freedom in history but only in the mode in which freedom is already realized in history, in its immobile figure as mere factuality of which the State is product and guarantor. (P. 361, my translation)

The "immobile figure" of which Negri writes is the figure of the *Volk* – the "people" conceived of as a primordial and unchanging linguistic and cultural unity, the definition of which excludes not only other peoples and nations but also its own internal fractures and possibilities of transformation (with the signal exception of economic development): "The substantial unity that presides over the constitution of the concept of the people is thus an eternal metaphysical power [*potenza*] that expresses itself through infinite individual manifestations" (p. 373, my translation). The state emerges organically from the people and then forms and defends it – primarily from historical change. The apotheosis of the *Volk* as a form of habit or static repetition here turns into an almost perfect apology for revived absolutism, going far beyond the compromises of the liberal high formalists.[10]

At this point the historicists abandoned the basic terms of the Kantian system, but no more so than the idealists had done. In all three cases, "the overcoming of form derives in fact...from its absolutization," for "the absolutization of form leads to the parallel absolutization of matter, the empirical world: the absolute is the synthesis, the immediate coincidence in the absolute of the two terms whose duality the critical philosophy had initially marked as antinomian" (p. 378, my translation), namely reason and history. The attempt to use Kant's critical philosophy to resolve this stark dualism that the Enlightenment inherited from Descartes ultimately fails because the critical philosophy fails to develop an adequate conception of transformation, and thus an adequate conception of historical development.

It was immersed in a profoundly contradictory reality, however, between absolutism and liberalism, between liberalism and

> Jacobinism, between Jacobinism and reaction...In this situation
> juridical formalism consolidated itself as ideology...[H]ere the
> center of the evolving process of reason was no longer represented
> by the diversity and contradictoriness of the contents but by the
> identity and homogeneity of the form, here everything is contorted
> and corrupt: as a result of the formalist refiguration of right and the
> State, Jacobinism was sterilized, liberal thought compromised with
> the *ancien régime*; in a word, legality was made into legalism, the
> ideology of juridical positivism. (Pp. 387–8, my translation)

Only the dialectical current that emerged out of Kantianism after 1800 – that is, Hegel – would find a solution to the antinomy by "grasping the revolutionary significance of the immersion of reason in history" (pp. 113–14, my translation), transforming it into a dynamic dialectics of right that would serve as the functional ideology of maturing capitalism throughout the nineteenth century and beyond.

Hegel and beyond

Negri's first major publication was an analysis of the emergence of dialectical thought out of the young Hegel's political theory: *Stato e diritto nel giovane Hegel: Studio sulla genesi illuministica della filosofia giuridica e politica di Hegel* (*State and Right in the Young Hegel: A Study of the Enlightenment Genesis of Hegel's Juridical and Political Philosophy*, 1958). In this book, which George Steiner (1984) saluted as one of "the most useful elucidations" of the young Hegel's writings (p. 22 n. 1), Negri began the methodological exploration that would become characteristic of all his work in the history of philosophy: as he would later do with Descartes, Spinoza and Leopardi, he situated Hegel at the cusp of a major intellectual and political transition between two historical periods – in this case the Enlightenment and Romanticism. This move is similar to an established practice in Marxist historiography of locating the historical significance of "great men," whether they are artists like Shakespeare, statesmen like Napoleon or philosophers like Hegel, in their engagement with major social and political processes of transition between modes of production or significant moments therein. But Negri does not adopt this method uncritically and without profound modification. He evades the deterministic deployment of historical periodization that dominated Marxist analyses before and after the Second World

War by emphasizing the progressive and materialist elements of Hegel's emerging philosophy of right that laid the groundwork for his mature idealism, and he complicates the mechanistic conception of base–superstructure relations by deploying a preliminary version of his "biographical materialist" method. This method reaches maturity in Negri's books on Descartes and Spinoza, but we can see aspects of it emerging already in his book on Hegel.

Negri presents his study as an attempt to go beyond the sterile opposition between right-wing interpretations of Hegel that emphasize the pole of totality in the fundamental logic of his dialectic and identify it with a hypostasized vision of the state and liberal interpretations that emphasize the pole of individuality and hence relativize the state (Negri 1958: 7–8). Although Negri situates his own interpretation of Hegel in relation to a third line of descent – the Marxist one – he has also admitted that he had not yet engaged Marx's own writings at the time when he was first working on Hegel, not even the *Critique of Hegel's Philosophy of Right*, which might have been most pertinent. This lacuna might account for the surprisingly affirmative account of Hegel that Negri's book contains, one that often seems closer in spirit to Georg Lukács' pre-Marxist writings like *Soul and Form* or *Theory of the Novel*, or to Theodor W. Adorno's many sympathetic studies of Hegel, than to Negri's own later work. As Negri puts it in his introduction, "Hegel never closes down his theoretical horizon but rather opens up and leaves open a problem that, with the scrupulousness of a phenomenologist, he cannot conclude wherever historical experience presents demands [*istanze*] or problems that outline tasks but offer no definitive truth" (p. 12, my translation). The language of openness and problematization applied here to Hegel will remain an important part of Negri's theoretical vocabulary, although he will change its referents drastically as the years pass. Far more fully than Lukács, Negri would break with Hegelianism after his reading of Marx in the early sixties.

Nevertheless, at this point in his development Negri was working not under the aegis of Marxist historiography per se, but under the not entirely compatible influences of Lukács' sympathetic interpretation of the early Hegel (in *The Young Hegel* (Lukács 1975), published in full in 1954) on the one hand and, on the other, of the analyses of Jean Hyppolite, an acknowledged mentor of Michel Foucault and Gilles Deleuze who had overseen Negri's doctoral research during the period of his fellowship in Paris (Casarino and Negri 2008: 45). The incompatibility of the two versions of Hegel he was trying to synthesize presages Negri's ultimate break with Hegelianism, as we will see. Lukács' interpretation of Hegel, elaborated in his Russian exile during the thirties, follows straightforwardly from the traditional humanist conception of subjective alienation contained in the influential *History and Class Consciousness* of 1923 (Lukács 1971). As Eugene Lunn (1982) has noted, "[t]hroughout his career, Lukács criticized capitalism largely from the perspective of an aesthetic and ethical humanism and idealism, rather than in terms of social and economic inequalities or the political powers of corporate wealth" (p. 110). This humanism and idealism were drawn from the German Romantics, especially Goethe and Hegel, as well as from the revolutionary bourgeoisie of the late eighteenth and early nineteenth centuries. Stanley Mitchell has pointed out that, in his literary criticism as well as in his political writings, Lukács worked to establish what amounts to an "'essentialism' or 'anthropologism'" that viewed "the course of history as a battle between human wholeness and the successive modes of alienation introduced by the different divisions of labor" (Mitchell 1972: 149–50). This aspect of Lukács' interpretation appealed somewhat to Negri's predisposition toward Renaissance humanism, but his emerging materialist methodology would not permit him to follow Lukács' nostalgic humanism too far. Even at this early moment, Negri's humanism is already implicitly a constructivism, as his interpretation of Hegel will suggest and as his studies of Kantian formalism and Cartesian ideology have clarified.[11]

The influence of Hyppolite allowed Negri to begin moving beyond Lukács' perspective on Hegel and planted the seeds that would eventually grow into his engagement with French poststructuralism. As Leonard Lawlor puts it,

> Hyppolite's non-reductionistic interpretation of the relation between the phenomenology and the logic effectively ended the simple anthropological interpretation of Hegel popularized by Kojève before World War II. Because of Hyppolite, no reading of Hegel would be able to push man up to the immodest position of being the Absolute, the end of history, the source of nothingness. (Lawlor 1997: viii)

In this regard, Hyppolite helped free Negri from the orthodoxy of essentialist humanism that dominated European academic philosophy and political science – as well as Marxism – before and after the Second World War, just as he had helped free other major thinkers of the period. In an early book review, Gilles Deleuze lauded Hyppolite for positioning himself "against all anthropological or humanistic interpretations of Hegel" (Deleuze 1954: 194), while Michel Foucault paid homage to Hyppolite in his inaugural presentation to the Collège de France, "The Discourse on Language":

> If...more than one of us is indebted to Jean Hyppolite, it is because he has tirelessly explored, for us, and ahead of us, the path along which we may escape Hegel, keep our distance, and along which we shall find ourselves brought back to him, only from a different angle, and then, finally, be forced to leave him behind once more...[H]e wanted to turn Hegel into a schema for the experience of modernity...and he wanted, conversely, to make modernity the test of Hegelianism and, beyond that, of philosophy. (Foucault 1972: 235–6)

Both aspects of Hyppolite's teaching that Foucault highlights would prove crucial to Negri's own effort to escape Hegel, in his mature as well as in his early work.

While Lukács centered his examination of the young Hegel on "the relations between dialectics and economics" (to quote the subtitle of his book), Negri focuses his on the role that legal and political philosophy played in the emergence of Hegel's mature thought. Indeed, despite the disagreement over humanism noted above, Negri's book may fruitfully be approached as a complement to Lukács', in that both view Hegel's early years in Stuttgart, Tübingen, Bern and Frankfurt as formative of the system that later reached fruition in Jena and Berlin.

> In fact, in the youthful phase of his thought Hegel elaborates the dialectical method and defines the categories of ethical life above all by means of the enquiry into political themes, by qualifying such concepts in a phenomenological sense; and whoever forgets this character of Hegel's thematic formation runs the risk of reducing the mature system to a mere game of formal logic, and consequently of no longer understanding the evolving continuity of his philosophy. (Negri 1958: 270, my translation)

This caution against an uncritically formalist reading of Hegel is one that Negri himself would follow in his next book on the Kantian jurists; the task he sets himself, rather, is to historicize Hegel's development of dialectics. Having just completed his own training as a philosopher of law, Negri views Hegel as himself a philosopher of law or right whose most original and influential insights arise from the context of his studies in the history and philosophy of right.

In order to explain the development of Hegel's philosophy of right, Negri must first place him in an appropriate historical context, which is that of German Enlightenment rationalism culminating in Kant's critical philosophy. As we know, Kant defined the moral law not in terms of its content but in terms of its form, and that form is universality: the "categorical imperative" demands that a moral or ethical prescription can only be affirmed if it can be adopted without contradiction by all subjects, universally. Thus, for Kant, morality is essentially a logical form, and therefore practical reason is prior to, and determinant of, pure reason. Out of this notion of the necessary universality of the moral law, some of Kant's formalist followers (the objective idealists, as we saw above) deduced a corresponding conception of the institutional framework that would be necessary to implement it: the *Vernunftstaat* or rational state, whose structure would be as universal as its legal contents. As a logical corollary of Kant's reasoning, this notion of the rational state might seem no more disturbing than Plato's ideal republic; but, as one of the culminating points of the political thinking of the late German Enlightenment, it exercised a profound philosophical influence on revolutionary ideology in the late eighteenth century – an influence that paralleled the practical influence of the French Revolution itself. To many politically committed rationalists such as the objective idealists, the concept of a universal rational state seemed to demand realization in all the nation states of Europe. The outbreak of the French Revolution was widely viewed by sympathizers as the beginning of an era of universal revolution, in which the rational-state model would spread from France to the other imperial powers of Europe. This leads to what Negri calls, in Kantian fashion, a new "antinomy" or near-contradiction between – on the one hand – the universalizing mission of Enlightenment rationality and the state form in which it culminates and – on the other hand – the proto-Romantic particularism of the primordial cultural–linguistic communities – essentially the existing nations re-imagined as *Kulturstaaten* – that rise up in opposition to the imperialist ambitions of the rationalists (or perhaps it would be better to say the rationalist justifications of the new imperialists, in contradistinction to the particularist ideologies of the established

imperialists). The most intransigent representatives of this opposi-
tional perspective were the historicists discussed earlier.

In contrast to Lukács, Negri consistently describes Hegel as a
Jacobin, a sympathizer of radical revolution; but Hegel's enthusiasm for rationalist imperialism had sharp limits in Negri's view.

> On the one hand ... the Enlightenment antinomy is revealed in the
> bloody crisis of the Terror, on the other in the clash between French
> imperialism and German nationalism; in any case it is the same divi-
> sion, in which the objective necessity of the revolution is opposed to
> the feeling of individuality of persons and peoples. It is plausible
> that, in this situation characterized by the uncertainty and fluidity
> of events, Hegel would have been involved in the crisis: whereas his
> political radicalism seems to be inflamed as regards the anxiety for
> action, in parallel fashion it is calmed in the political substance it
> expresses, and the young Hegel shows himself to be more attentive
> to the modality than to the ends of revolutionary action, to the juridi-
> cal forms of the realization of principles than to mere ideological
> declamations. (Negri 1958: 182–3, my translation)

This careful navigation between the terms of the antinomy characterizes what Negri calls "the drama of the young Hegel," who
"continually strives for a mediation between individuality and
rationality, past and present, positivity and revolution" (p. 122, my
translation). Hegel's Jacobin sensibility led him to critique the existing German state and to demand democratic reforms in a direction
that was broadly congruent with the revolutionary ideology of the
rational state, but also more tightly focused on constitutional issues
of right. To this end he studied the German Constitution itself, in
order to determine both the limitations of the existing state order
and their underlying causes. He concluded by denouncing, in
Negri's words, the "despotic character ... of the constitutional
formula as well as the degrading and mystifying justification of the
system," which he attributed to "three fundamental aspects, namely
political individualism, economic privatism, and juridical formalism ... [that were] each the effect of the others and all the cause of
the disaggregation of the state totality, of the expulsion of spirit
from the juridical formula" (pp. 260–1, my translation). All three of
these aspects, which had been functional elements of the German
state for decades, if not for centuries, took on new importance in
the context of universal rationalism: their realized abstraction
would lend itself too readily to the despotism of the *Vernunftstaat's*
abstract reason. In Hegel's view, Germany was "no longer a state"

but merely a collection of isolated parts interacting mechanically, and the further development of Kantian formalism in the philosophy and practice of law would only exacerbate its tendency toward dissolution.[12]

Hegel refuses to adopt either term of the antinomy and instead proposes a synthesis of the terms that, for Negri, constitutes the first deployment of the dialectical procedure that would become Hegel's most profound contribution to philosophy:

> To the theory of *Vernunftstaat* that in the Enlightenment antinomy of rationality and individuality absolutized the first term and to that of the *Kulturstaat* that introduced mediation only to confound it in the vision of a happy ending of history, Hegel substitutes the positive ideal of the *Volksstaat*, in which totality and individuality are connected and individualized universality gains strength. (P. 121, my translation)

The *Volksstaat* ("popular state") overcomes the antinomy between the universal rational state and the particular cultural state by grounding itself neither in abstract rationality nor in an unmediated cultural tradition of political orthodoxy, but rather in the right of a people that is conceived of democratically, as the totality of individual reasons working toward their own collective historical realization together. The derivation of this concept from Fichte's thinking, discussed earlier, should be clear. Hegel thereby mediates and synthesizes the formalist positions of the objective idealists and of the historicists. In the popular state

> the people regained the sense of their right, since they knew that sovereignty could only derive from it, that only the totality is universal and has power [*potere*]; and right could be founded solely on this nexus that connects it to the whole. In summary, right, in order to remain intact and not to decline into a mere form, into the fixing of private economic and pre-constituted egoistic relations, must be the right of state, guaranteed by the State for the totality of citizens. (P. 264, my translation)

The popular state avoids the pitfalls of imperialistic abstraction and unreflective tradition, both of which constitute "mere forms" of the state that divide the people into atomized classes and private life the better to rule them despotically. Hegel's conception melds the identitarian essentialism of the historicist definition of the *Volk* with the transformative openness to historical innovation that characterizes the objective idealist school. It constitutes a model of the state form that corresponds to the bourgeois project: one with fixed borders, both geographical and demographic, but with a flexible – dialectical – internal structure, which draws its motive force from historical change yet constrains that change within the limits defined by technical and economic development. The popular state will be the form of the bourgeois reconquest of political sovereignty, the realization and surpassing of Descartes' reasonable ideology.[13]

For Negri at this early point in his career, Hegel's solution to the antinomy has a certain unexpected appeal:

> [T]he popular state…does not involve an ideal of the totalitarian state, since the state assumes no transcendence in relation to individuals; it is an optimistic mediation, a full integration. Thus, since totality and universality are equivalent, the state arises entirely in the course of ethical demands, not indiscriminately and not having ends in itself, but in terms of natural law and revolution, freedom and equality, and gradually independence. (Ibid.)

The popular state was for Hegel the logical outcome of the revolutionary dialectic set in motion by the conflict between the Enlightenment's demands for universal rationality and the emerging Romantic emphasis on the specificity of individuals and peoples. As Negri interprets it here, this state constitutes the institutional realization of an immanent, historical and constructive humanism, and not of a transcendental anthropology. This conception could only have emerged from a dialectical approach to the philosophy of right as it stood at the end of the eighteenth century.

> The fact that Hegelian thought is situated at the limit of the Enlightenment and on the threshold of Romanticism, in its effort to bring diverse intuitions to unity, is particularly confirmed in the Hegelian meditation on right…On the one hand Hegel accepts the natural-law position that the historical validity of right is conditional upon its adequacy to the rational idea of right itself, but on the other hand he sees the idea unfolding in history and therefore is led to identify the rational idea with the reality of the fact of right, thereby making the postulates of historicism his own. (Pp. 277–8, my translation)

The position of natural law finds its most influential expression in eighteenth-century absolutism, as we have seen, while the pole of individuality of "persons and peoples" finds its expression in historicism. Hegel's conception of the popular state subsumes both and thereby overcomes the antinomy that emerged from the competing philosophies of right, to spur a series of open political and social struggles that defined the transition to the Romantic period.

The emergence of the concept of the popular state offered not only the solution to the Enlightenment's antinomy between universality and individuality, reason and history, but also a methodological template the range of which Hegel would soon begin to broaden. According to Negri, this first successful usage of the dialectical procedure set the stage for the development of Hegel's larger system of philosophy:

> the dialectic, intended to mediate individuality and rationality, historicity and universality, those extremes of the old Enlightenment antinomy... gradually reveals its objectivity, becomes the key to historical interpretation, and when it is subsequently discovered to be the nexus of destiny and freedom, it manifests its operative and perfectly humanist essence: history is destiny as accomplished reality, as past, and it is freedom as reality yet to be accomplished, as future, and at the limit of past and present, theory and practice, man freely constructs his own destiny. And if in destiny an indestructible community of memory is established among all men... the freedom that sets up and transforms history is still open to the bonds of human solidarity. The popular state is the substance and motor of the dialectical procedure, all other themes – alienation, positivity, freedom, destiny – revolving around this center. (P. 265, my translation)

Dialectics becomes the master key to history, one that can overcome all obstacles to affirm even the identity of predestination and free will. This remarkable conclusion of Negri's analysis almost appears to situate him in the neo-Hegelian camp, which was hegemonic in pre-War Europe, including in Italy. As he explained in his contemporary essay on Dilthey, while the neo-Hegelians of the early twentieth century "considered Hegelian thought in its methodological aspect, thus as a key to the interpretation of the world," the historians of the Hegel revival "viewed it in an ideological perspective as the representative of a historically determined culture. Whereas for the neo-Hegelians Hegel's philosophy was a beginning, for the historians it was an endpoint, indeed the definitive endpoint of bourgeois Christian metaphysics" (Negri 1959: 135, my translation). Negri would soon come to view Hegel as the culmination and, in at least a logical sense, as the endpoint of the dialectical tradition of modern sovereignty that runs from Descartes, Hobbes and Rousseau to the present – a tradition that Negri would engage polemically throughout his later career, up to and including *Empire*. However, to the extent that his synthesis realized and transcended Descartes' reasonable ideology to become the new ideology of the triumphant bourgeois state, Hegel was also the start of a new period in capitalist development; this may account for the tone of approval in Negri's assessment. As he noted much later, "my first attempt at a critique of Hegel in the early 1960s had not been very well defined and articulated" (Casarino and Negri 2008: 58).

Negri followed up his study of the early Hegel with a pair of translations of key works from the end of that period: "The Scientific Ways of Treating Natural Law, Its Place in Moral Philosophy, and Its Relation to the Positive Sciences of Law" and the "System of Ethical Life" (both written in 1802–3), which were published in 1962 (see Hegel 1962). These works are among the most difficult and controversial in Hegel's corpus, and Negri's effort to translate them for the first time into a foreign language (English-language editions did not appear until the 1970s) confirms his claim that he had studied Hegel "really well" (Casarino and Negri 2008: 43). But, by the time these translations appeared (in a book series edited by the well-known scholar of Renaissance humanism Eugenio Garin), Negri was already beginning to rethink the premises of his Hegelian interpretations as a result of his first readings of Marx. The sympathetic tone and open-ended conclusions of Negri's first engagement with Hegel would not remain unchallenged by his later analyses. Indeed, *State and Right in the Young Hegel* and the two translations form a foundation for Negri's later work that is negative much more than it is positive. As Negri has said of his early career, Hegel "was the pivot, the great passage – and I would have to reckon with him and struggle against him in later years" (ibid.).

That struggle can be traced in the only other critical study of Hegel that Negri has ever published: the essay "Rileggendo Hegel, filosofo del diritto" ("Re-Reading Hegel, Philosopher of Right") (Negri 1970a),[14] where Negri radically inverts his own early reading of the openness of Hegel's dialectical system, demolishing not only Hegel's philosophy of right but also his own youthful understanding of it in the process. This re-interpretation of Hegel was published in the same year *Political Descartes* appeared, and it was motivated by the same intention: to break with the dominant tradition of the philosophy of modernity, especially its conception of politics and the state. The simultaneous appearance of these two texts confirms our hypothesis of the radical re-orientation of Negri's overall perspective following his encounter with Marx and constitutes a self-criticism of his prior scholarly work in the history of philosophy. In this essay Negri takes up once again Hyppolite's interpretation of Hegel as the defining thinker of modernity (an interpretation emphasized by Foucault), but only to invert it. Negri begins peremptorily, asserting that "Hegel's *Rechtsphilosophie* is perhaps the primary philosophical text of modernity...Hegel the philosopher of right is, from this point of view, a totally contemporary author" (Negri 1970a: 254, my translation).[15] In this context, modernity in the singular refers to the triumph of the linked forces of capital and of the dialectical lineage of sovereignty; Negri identifies his own project not with this modernity or postmodernity but, as we will see in chapter 4, with the anti- or counter-modernity of Machiavelli, Spinoza and Marx.

Hegel's doctrine of the popular state, far from being the ethical, non-transcendent and hence non-totalitarian structure that Negri celebrated at the end of *State and Right*, is here denounced as the instrument of dialectical transcendence and capitalist control par excellence:

> Subordination, the reality of the State, is ontologically immanent in the dialectical process that constitutes it, it is present in the moment of social cooperation and gives it its determinate being. Labor is the foundation of the State, it is the foundation of all legality insofar as it is matter submitted to the control of the State. Control over living social labor is the labor of the State. (P. 259, my translation)

By this time in his development Negri had abandoned the idealist language of abstract right – which, even in the tradition of natural right, was never accessible except in the alienated form of juridical rights – and he had replaced it with Marx's central concept of "living labor," the real activity of living bodies and minds. Labor, not the contractual delegation of abstract popular right, is the constitutive foundation of the state, but the state constantly seeks to transcend its foundation by exercising command over it.[16] In this regard Negri can accurately describe Hegel as the ultimate "philosopher of right, as the philosopher of the bourgeois and capitalist organization of labor" (p. 261, my translation).

The dialectic here is no longer the instrument that transcends the opposition between the rational and the real, the universal and the individual, or destiny and freedom, but simply the tool that imposes the relationship of exploitation upon the laboring subjects of capital:

> if the real is labor, if the rational order is "capital," if the relationship between cooperation and subordination, between particular and universal is the State, then the State is development, capital necessarily in development. The State as capital is the State as development. Power [*potere*] is exercised in development, by means of development. The State is a dynamic institution that views right as the development of action determined within the framework of society, in such a way as to relate all social action to the overall set of determinations of the given rational order. (Pp. 261–2, my translation)

This is essentially the same dialectic that Negri had described in quasi-utopian terms at the conclusion of *State and Right*; but he evaluates it from the opposite perspective – the workers' perspective – and not from the viewpoint of the state itself, which Hegel had implicitly adopted. From the workers' perspective, the state is the essence of capitalist domination and, as such, remains exploitative whether it is controlled by the bourgeoisie or by a socialist technocracy. Here Negri is also attacking Cacciari's decision to join the PCI and through its electoral success to oversee state control over development – a decision that stemmed from his disagreement with Negri's account of the Cartesian project and of its ultimate Hegelian payoff. For Negri, the only solution to the Hegelian transcendence of the state – which has infected the traditional labor movement just as badly as it has infected the capitalist class – is the refusal of work, which "for the first time . . . shatters the substantial definition that ties [labor] to the state; in refusing itself [labor] presents itself altogether as the refusal of the state and posits itself as the collective agency [*impresa*] of freedom" (pp. 268–9, my translation). The refusal of work, which we will examine in chapter 3, is the practical means of escape from dialectical negation and its infinite recuperative power – the refusal of work is non-dialectical antagonism.

Much later, Negri summed up the evolution of his relationship with Hegel and with dialectics as follows:

> [H]ere was this thing called the dialectic: sometimes it worked; and yet some other times it seemed to be a false key, a false solution. It opened any door – and only a false key opens all the possible doors . . . It lacked radical antagonism. In short, Hegelianism was

reactionary. But it was so precisely because it was reactive with respect to real and important matters – which is why I have always believed that it is only from reactionaries that one learns what is most fundamental. Even though it annoyed me, I continued to use Hegelianism because it was a philosophy of modernity. What made me suspicious of Hegelianism eventually was the fact that it lacked any internal obstacles; rather, there were only limits that could always be overcome. It was extremely difficult to bring practical materiality back into these philosophical schemata. (Casarino and Negri 2008: 46)

Only in the wake of his participation in the collective editorial work of *Quaderni rossi*, his reading of Marx and his engagement with the factory workers' movement in the Veneto did Negri find a way to bring "practical materiality" back into the philosophical schemata he had studied earlier. In the concept of an antagonistic relationship with dialectical synthesis – a concept derived from the practice of worker militancy – he found a way to escape from Hegel that was just as successful as the ways that Deleuze and Foucault found. The key insight of his early work remains the concept of political ontology as concrete, historical practice:

When capital constitutes the political as the domination of one class by another, metaphysics is affected by both poles of the relationship: it is the forces in struggle that assume the sense of a metaphysical tradition and oppose it to another one…A metaphysics, distinct metaphysical positions and the alternatives they represent are the most concrete of historical objects. They are "concrete" because they are swollen with antagonisms and possibilities. (Negri 1981: 290, cited in Mandarini 2009: 72)

3

Workerism between State and Party

Throughout the first phase of his career, when he was publishing scholarly studies of canonical continental philosophers and of their relationship with the bourgeois state, Negri was also becoming increasingly involved in the politics of labor in the Veneto, the region around his home base of Venice and Padua. During the sixties his publications reflect the intensifying polarization of his intellectual life: in the eight years that separated *At the Origins of Juridical Formalism* and his Hegel translations from *Political Descartes*, he alternated between writing scholarly reviews of academic philosophy books for specialized journals and writing and editing political newspapers and journals for the working class of the Veneto. He was leading a double life, though not a clandestine one. His university colleagues knew of his militant work, and his fellow militants knew of his scholarly work; but neither side could see the relation between those poles. As he notes in the postface to the English edition of *Political Descartes*, that book "came as a surprise both to academics, for its choice of subject (what could a Marxist do with Descartes?), and to my comrades in the movement (why is Negri wasting his time with Descartes?)" (Negri 1970b: 317). He was struggling to find a way to apply his scholarly understanding of law and the biographical–historical method he was developing in his academic studies to analyses of the present that could serve the interests of the workers with whom he was allied.

As we noted in chapter 2, Negri's belated reading of Marx added a powerful new ingredient to his analytical approach and served as a catalyst for the major shift his thinking and militancy underwent in the early sixties. He had become a communist early in life, primarily through the influence of his family and through his experience of living on a kibbutz during a year in Israel; but he became a Marxist considerably later, after spending his early adulthood in the orbit of the moderate Italian Socialist Party. As he admitted in a recent interview: "In reality, by 1964 I had barely finished reading Marx...I read Marx thoroughly only around the age of thirty" (Negri 2009a: 121–2, my translation), in the context of a workers' reading group that Negri, his wife Paola Meo and Massimo Cacciari had organized in Porto Marghera at the urging of Raniero Panzieri. That reading re-oriented him, but not all at once. In the same interview he notes: "The essay on 'Labor in the Constitution' is therefore the first product of Toni Negri as a Marxist – and, if you like, as a 'workerist'" (p. 122, my translation), though it was not published for a dozen years. That essay, which uses an explication of the Italian Constitution to investigate the legal mechanism by which the working class is constrained within capital, constitutes the bridge between his early work in the philosophy of right and the writings on working-class subjectivity, organization and resistance that would preoccupy him, with few exceptions, until his arrest in 1979.

"Labor in the Constitution," originally written in 1964 (see Hardt and Negri 1994), takes as its point of departure the first article of the 1948 Italian Constitution, which declares that "Italy is a democratic republic founded on labor." The essay seeks to determine how labor was formalized as the conceptual and productive basis for an advanced capitalist nation. Negri proposes that, in order to meet the growing insubordination of the expanding and unruly working class after the war, capital must itself collectivize – it must become collective social capital – and it must control labor by abstracting it as fully as possible, by turning concrete labor into abstract labor not only conceptually (as the science of economics always has) but materially. This is the intent Negri discerns in the language of the Italian Constitution, its "constitutionalization" of labor: the democratically empowered "people" must be defined and ultimately subordinated as workers or, more precisely because more abstractly, as labor-power.

> Labor-power, which appears as a social totality, is configured as the people within the mechanism of the reproduction of capital: the people are labor-power constitutionalized in the State of the factory-society. As labor-power, the people therefore come to be called to

participate in the production of the social product, organized in the general process of capitalist production in society; equally they are subordinated and forced to yield to the demands of social accumulation, and thus the continual reproduction of the relationship of waged labor. At this level of capitalist organization, the people, as social labor-power, are thus called upon to manage their own social exploitation, to guarantee the continuation and reproduction of the general movement of accumulation. (Hardt and Negri 1994: 80)

This demystification of populist legal language as a mode of subjective interpellation into ideology (a "call to participation" that anticipates Althusser's argument in "Ideology and Ideological State Apparatuses" by several years) contradicts Negri's earlier enthusiasm for Hegel's popular state and prefigures the critique of the concept of the people, which underpins Hardt and Negri's definition of the multitude in *Empire*.[1] For Negri, the self-exploitation of workers as constitutionally acknowledged labor-power represents not a subversion of capital but rather the final absorption of the unions' and left parties' reformist socialism into a socialized, yet still exploitative, capitalism. As he notes: "The 'democracy of labor' and 'social democracy' both reside here: they consist of the hypothesis of a form of labor-power that negates itself as the working class and autonomously manages itself within the structures of capitalist production as labor-power" (p. 62).

Negri concludes his juridical analysis of the Italian constitutionalization of labor in aggressively affirmative terms for working-class struggle, setting a tone that will be found throughout his mature work, whether philosophical or political:

[T]he growth of capitalist accumulation had unified society around labor-value, but had done so around its two extremes, concreteness and abstraction. The entire juridical system of the contemporary State was born to resolve this determinate opposition. The antagonism between concrete labor and abstract labor needed to be transformed into contradictions, and the entire path of contemporary juridical thought is oriented toward determining the specific mediations of these contradictions...The entire movement of the construction of the model of the State of labor...can now be seen in its inverted form: where there is unity we can see contradiction, and where there is contradiction we can see antagonism. (P. 134)

In other words, the function of the constitution is to define a conceptual and legal framework – the "democratic republic founded

on labor" – through which to redefine labor's fundamental antagonism or incompatibility with capital as an abstract mirroring, as a
hierarchical mechanism or as a mere logical contradiction. Contradiction is dialectical, Hegelian, and therefore subject to synthesis
and accommodation, while antagonism is non-dialectical, differential, and remains incapable of accommodation within capital. If the
implications of this are not clear enough to the reader, Negri spells
them out, and in so doing he marks the distance that his encounter
with Marx has carried him from his youthful Hegelianism even
more starkly than his 1970 essay on Hegel would:

> The dialectic is finished. Hegel is dead. What remains of Hegel is
> the self-consciousness of the bourgeois world. The bourgeois world
> is dialectical and cannot but be dialectical. But we are not. The
> workers' critique is not today the restoration of the dialectic, but
> rather the discovery of the terrain and the form of the conflict.
> (P. 135; translation modified)[2]

If we wish to follow Negri onto the terrain of non-dialectical class
conflict, we must first grasp what "workers' critique," or more
precisely "workerist critique," really is.

The Workerist Matrix

To understand the emergence of Negri's militancy and its impact
on his theoretical work, we must understand the historical and
intellectual context in which both developed. That context was
defined by *operaismo* – "workerism." In conventional Marxist
polemics, workerism is generally a derogatory term, used to
denounce a crude and exclusive devotion to the industrial working
class on the part of certain leftist thinkers and organizers. In postwar
Italy, however, workerism was the name adopted by an innovative
approach to Marxist theory and practice that first appeared among
the contributors to the dissident socialist journal *Quaderni rossi* (*Red
Notebooks*), which was organized by Raniero Panzieri. A leading
member of the Italian Socialist Party (PSI), Panzieri was disturbed
by the distance that was growing between the Italian working class
and its institutional mediators – the Italian Communist Party (PCI)
and the PSI, which had the largest membership of all the left parties
in Europe, as well as the unions – in the wake of both parties'
abandonment of anti-capitalist confrontation and worker militancy

in favor of electoral participation and political alliance-building on the terms of the Italian Constitution of 1948 (see Togliatti 1979). By the late 1950s, that distance was threatening to throw these institutions into crisis.

> If the crisis of the organizations – parties and union – lies in the growing difference between them and the real movement of the class, between the objective conditions of struggle and the ideology and policy of the parties, then the problem can be confronted only by starting from the conditions, structures and movement of the rank-and-file. Here analysis becomes complete only through participation in struggles. (Panzieri, quoted in Wright 2002: 21)

This programmatic statement already contains in embryo the central methodological innovation of Italian workerism, on which all of its participants would, in different ways, rely: the empirical study of class composition. As an analytical concept, class composition has two poles: technical composition, which is the set of social and disciplinary relationships and skills that the labor process imposes on workers in a specific historical conjuncture, and political composition, which is the form of worker organization that corresponds to and struggles with the technical composition.[3] In essence, Panzieri and his collaborators argued that only by investigating the experience of work both objectively and subjectively could labor organizers and workers' parties find effective ways to unleash the pent-up power of the growing working class.

The Italian working class was indeed growing rapidly, as the "economic miracle" of industrialization accelerated after the collapse of Fascism (see Ginsborg 1990: Ch. 7); but Italian social science was largely unprepared to analyze it, so the workerists (like the Frankfurt School Marxists) looked to American empirical sociology for methodological inspiration. The most important proponent of class composition analysis was Romano Alquati, whose sociological studies of the structure of work at FIAT, the largest Italian auto manufacturer, and at Olivetti, the business-machine manufacturer, appeared regularly in *Quaderni rossi* and in its successor journal, *Classe operaio* (*Working Class*) and were later collected in the book *Sulla FIAT e altri scritti* (*On FIAT and Other Writings*) (Alquati 1975). Like Theodor W. Adorno, however, the Italian workerists were aware that the sociological techniques they were borrowing had developed in the context of capitalist efforts to control workers and thus were hostile partisan instruments, despite their appearance of academic neutrality. To combat this covert methodological bias, the workerists explicitly acknowledged the proletarian partisanship of their inquiries, which they called *inchieste operai*, "workers' inquiries" (see Wright 2002: 21–5). Such partisanship was not merely a matter of good intentions; it also expressed itself directly in the most explicit and basic assumption of all workerist research, which has come to be called "the workerist hypothesis." The most concise and influential statement of that hypothesis was written by the Marxist philosopher Mario Tronti in his manifesto "Lenin in England," which appeared in the first issue of *Working Class* in January 1964 and was later collected in his influential book *Operai e capitale* (*Workers and Capital*) (Tronti 1971):

> We too have worked with a concept that puts capitalist development first, and workers second. This is a mistake. And now we have to turn the problem on its head, reverse the polarity, and start again from the beginning: and the beginning is the class struggle of the working class. At the level of socially developed capital, capitalist development becomes subordinated to working class struggles; it follows behind them, and they set the pace to which the political mechanisms of capital's own reproduction must be tuned. (Tronti 1964: 1)

The workerists' assumption of the practical priority of working-class activity was a rebuke not only of capitalist ideology, which attributed all creativity and organizational agency to capital and treated workers as passive instruments to be commanded, but also of the dogma of the institutional left, which similarly attributed agency and organization to the union and the party, while granting the workers themselves only spontaneous and transitory initiative.[4]

Along with Alquati and Tronti, Negri was among the young leftists whom Panzieri recruited for *Quaderni rossi*, though their collaboration would only last for two years, until the younger workerists broke with their elders and established their own journal, *Classe operaia*. Despite this split – and later ones – Negri would continue to insist on the centrality of the partisan study of class composition for any genuinely revolutionary movement, for example in the postscript to *Crisis of the Planner-State*, published in 1974:

> This working class needs to be studied and analyzed, with a view to grasping its new being and the new structure of needs brought

about by the fact of being proletarian within capital's *Zivilisation*. The new structure of needs is a determinate ontological level within the dialectic of the wage; today it is essential that we succeed in grasping this determinate level – in its formal and real dimensions, in its temporal and spatial dimensions, and in its dimensions of consciousness and consumption. The fixing of determinate quantities of the wage has provoked changes in the quality of life of the proletariat and thus changes in mass needs and forms of behavior. The accumulation of experiences of struggle has redefined the workers' interest in subversion…The theory of proletarian organization must always move within a continual re-elaboration of the phenomenological analysis of the structure of the workers' needs. (Negri 2005: 45–6)

Negri embraced the workerist concept of class composition because this concept confirmed and extended the constructivist conception of human subjectivity that had begun to emerge from his historical studies. He saw class composition as an essential tool for the re-establishment of an immanent humanism of the sort he would ultimately identify with both the Renaissance and the post-structuralism of Michel Foucault and Gilles Deleuze.

His conception of contemporary class composition can best be grasped through a *"historical typology of the forms of organization* of the working class, in relation to different political compositions" (p. 95), which begins with the Russian Revolution and its effects on the capitalist world.[5] The period from 1917 to 1929 was dominated by capitalist efforts to block the spread of the Soviet model by means of an attack on the composition of the class. The early Soviet model had succeeded in Russia because Lenin and the Bolsheviks had built their conception of the party on the composition of the Russian industrial working class (which, despite superficial differences, was similar to the composition of the industrial working class in other countries).[6] That class labored in factories filled with relatively simple machines, which needed trained operators and caretakers to keep them functioning. The professional skills of the leading factory workers gave them leverage over the factory because they could shut it down whenever they pleased, and capital could not keep it running without them. The "professional workers," as Negri called them, played a leading role not only in the production process but also in the organizational process of the Soviets – in their political structure, the Soviets reflected the functional structure of the factories, demonstrating the workerist insight that political class composition developed in relation to technical class composition. Just as the factories depended on technically sophisticated workers to oversee the production process undertaken by the masses of unskilled laborers, so the Soviets depended on the oversight of Lenin's "professional revolutionaries" to guide the actions of the proletarian masses (pp. 11–13, 95–6). The subject form common to both professional workers and professional revolutionaries was marked by sophisticated technical training, by an "aristocratic" attitude toward the untrained workers whom they led and by an existential asceticism that complemented the gratifications of their productive and organizational labor itself.

Capital responded to this challenge by restructuring the production process: advanced machines that needed no skills in order to be operated were introduced, thus destroying the leverage exercised by the professional workers. The workers were "deskilled," in other words their skills were deprived of function – and of differential wage value and control over the production process – by the new machines, which any worker, regardless of skill, could learn to operate quickly. At the same time the Fordist approach to income was gradually generalized: in place of the liberal commonplace that dictated a ruthless reduction of wages in order to increase profits, automaker Henry Ford's insight that paying workers enough to allow them to consume would expand the overall market, and thus would increase profit, took center stage. The two innovations destroyed or "decomposed" the technical class composition on which the Soviets were erected, undermining their political efficacy. The demise of the professional worker marked not the end of working-class struggle, however, but the mutation of class composition – the birth of the mass worker as a result of Keynesian policies of aggregation of capital for purposes of state planning. Indeed, planning at the state level, primarily through the monetary policy of central banks and through the development of welfare protections such as the US New Deal, provided the framework for this effort to reintegrate the working class within capitalism (Negri 1988: 13, 33). The minimal differentiation of skills among mass workers was counterbalanced by the sheer number of workers necessary for the large-scale commodity production required by Fordist wage policies – more consumers demanding more goods meant more workers who were themselves consumers. The mass worker soon found political expression in the trade unions and parliamentary parties, either socialist or communist, which attempted (with limited success) to articulate his growing wage demands within the system of planned capital. These wage demands reflected a broadening range of class needs, amounting almost to a class hedonism that contrasted markedly with the asceticism of the professional worker, which threatened to destabilize the capitalist system anew (Negri 2005: 96–9).

Thus far Negri's analysis of class composition largely matched the conception of his workerist colleagues; but disagreements emerged over how best to go beyond the reformist political organizations of the mass worker. The split mentioned earlier between Panzieri on the one hand and Negri, Alquati and Tronti on the other arose over this very issue. As the labor historian Sergio Bologna, who was also involved in *Quaderni rossi* and later workerist publications, explains:

> Panzieri's political objective was to produce a shift "within" the workers' movement, [especially] the PSI (where he had been a member of the Central Committee) and the PCI; on the other hand, the others wanted to create a new movement that could develop in the post-communist era and to experiment with a new way of doing politics with the working class. At this point Toni Negri's role became central and decisive. More than anyone else, he had the "will" to undertake such a project and he tried hard to convince Panzieri... that his path was the right one to take. (Bologna 2003: 98–9)

Classe operaia was the first result of that new path; but further splits followed that pushed Negri far from the Italian political mainstream and marked him as the most original, influential and controversial thinker outside the traditional party system. In 1969, as Negri and other workerists were founding the radical worker/student alliance Potere operaio (Workers' Power) to contest the PCI's collaboration with capital, Tronti and other prominent workerists like Massimo Cacciari decided that the PCI, despite its strategy of electoral accommodation and compromise, offered the best possibility for realizing the political potential of the mass worker, so they joined the PCI in the ultimately vain hope of transforming the party from within. Their justification for doing this lay in their notion of the "autonomy of the political" – the idea that the political sphere was independent of the economic and social spheres and therefore had its own internal logic, which permitted political representatives (like the PCI) to act without coordinating their activities with the needs of their constituents.[7]

Negri's path was different, and it followed from his unique take on the workerist hypothesis of the working class' priority in driving

– and ultimately in overcoming – capitalist development. He was one of the first theorists to register agreement with Tronti's original formulation; in "Labor in the Constitution" he wrote:

> [T]he relationship between capitalist reformism and workers' struggles...is a double movement: on one side, capital, with its primary goal of politically combating the working class, has to make itself open to concessions that organize the working class (as labor-power) internal and homogeneous to the process of social production; on the other side, the working class, while conceding to capital the partial and transitory moment of economic affirmation, always recomposes that moment later in the continuity of its own political reunification and in the next bid at revolutionary power, always within but always beyond the single determinations of development. The double relationship between capitalist reformism and workers' struggles, therefore, is born within capital. It imposes on capital a continual process of restructuring, designed to contain its negation. (Hardt and Negri 1994: 60)

Expressed less concisely than Tronti's version, this statement amounts to the same point. In the late sixties and seventies, however, Negri would go beyond this partisan hypothesis to assert a stronger program for workers' inquiry, which he called "the method of the tendency." His extension of the workerist hypothesis foreclosed any possibility of joining the PCI, and the organizational models he proposed first to Potere operaio and later to the groups that made up the area of *Autonomia* reflect this fact.

The clearest articulation of the "method of the tendency" appears in the middle of *Crisis of the Planner-State*, originally published in 1971, Negri's first attempt to propose rules for the development of a new model of working-class organization outside the PCI, the PSI and the unions.

> The tendency is in no sense a necessary and inevitable law governing reality. The tendency is a general schema that takes as its starting point an analysis of the elements that make up a given historical situation. On the basis of that analysis, it defines a method, an orientation, a direction for mass political action... The tendency is the practical/theoretical process whereby the workers' point of view becomes explicit in a determinate historical epoch... it represents an adventure of reason as it comes to encounter the complexities of reality, an adventure of reason that is prepared to accept risks: in fact, the truth of the tendency lies in its verification. (Negri 2005: 27)

In *Marx beyond Marx* Negri calls this focus on the tendency *"communism in methodology"*: "it is not simply what permits a passive construction of the categories on the basis of a sum of historical acquisitions; it is above all what permits a reading of the present in light of the future, in order to make projects to illuminate the future" (Negri 1984: 49). Negri attributes this method to Marx, Lenin, Mao and other communist thinkers who strive, not for a disinterested "objective" knowledge that neutrally describes a state of affairs, but for a situated, overtly partisan knowledge that engages a state of affairs in order to modify it. Like workers' inquiry, the method of the tendency is a militant epistemology that produces knowledge of, by and for workers. On that basis,

> analysis of the tendency can uncover in the past (precisely as their presupposition) those objective antagonisms that today the class standpoint wants to extol. Thus we can confirm in the past the changing mechanisms of control and the recomposition of the dialectic of capital which today the class viewpoint seeks to destroy. (Negri 2005: 28–9)

But the method of the tendency is also an "adventure," almost a mode of prediction or prophecy. It re-reads the past in order to imagine action in the present that will open up new possibilities for the future. It identifies trends and transformations that may appear minor or trivial but that actually represent fundamental alterations in how the social order works, alterations that will spread and reconfigure the entire order. Marx's focus on industrial labor – in his day a demographically small and geographically limited part of overall capitalist production, but one that would soon restructure all other production in its image – is the best example of this method at work. If the workerist hypothesis articulated a historical demand that the past and present be understood as the result of working-class activity, then the identification of the tendency constituted a speculative and anticipatory demand for the class to project its organization into the future. Negri felt that this method made revolution possible by giving the working class an analytical and performative advantage over the conservatism of capital; and he continues to apply it in his work with Michael Hardt on Empire and the multitude.

On the basis of this method, Negri would argue by the mid-seventies that the mass worker, too, was being decomposed by capitalist restructuring, just as the professional worker had been at an earlier stage. The new technical class composition that he saw emerging, which he called the social or socialized worker [*operaio sociale*], could not organize itself in the party and union forms that had, however inadequately, represented the mass worker; it required radically new forms, which Negri struggled to theorize. As the name suggests, the socialized worker is defined by the general socialization that characterizes contemporary capitalist production: s/he works collaboratively, by means of intricate communications networks, to produce not only commodities but also the tissue of social life itself. The mass worker had been relatively homogeneous, not just in terms of skill level but also in terms of gender, ethnicity, sexuality and other variables, which came under increasing scrutiny in Italy during the seventies. For Negri this meant that the new composition, the socialized worker, must be conceived of as radically heterogeneous. Sections of the feminist movement, for example, criticized the sexism implicit in the mass worker, his exclusionary union organization, hierarchical party organization and unacknowledged dependence on the unpaid labor of women, who were excluded from the factory labor force. Feminists also attacked some of the basic assumptions of classical Marxist theory, such as the definition of productive labor, which limited it to factory labor that produced commodities and relegated the "reproductive" domestic labor most often undertaken by women – not just childbearing and rearing, but also the labor of restoring the productive capacity of male workers – to the margins of political activity. In her influential pamphlet *The Power of Women and the Subversion of the Community*, Negri's colleague at the Padua Institute of Political Science, Mariarosa Dalla Costa, was the first theorist to demonstrate that "the extraction of surplus value could occur outside the sphere Marx had designated as the direct process of production" (Wright 2002: 134–5).

Although other workerists such as Sergio Bologna resisted and criticized it as incoherent or unfounded,[8] Negri's heterogeneous and communicational concept of the socialized worker found some empirical confirmation in the forms that capitalist restructuring took in the early and mid-seventies. The large factories, sites of effective worker resistance and of increased wage demands during the sixties, were shrunk by the outsourcing of productive functions to small contractors, many of them women working at home. Class composition was changing geographically as well as demographically. At the same time productivity increases were imposed that depended on a more intensive and extensive socialization of workers – continuing education to support flexible employment, social services to support labor mobility and state welfare to support long periods of unemployment, for example – and these further eroded the boundary between factory and society. The exploitative structure of the factory had begun to spread to all areas of social existence – a phenomenon that Tronti had called the social factory:

> At the highest level of *capitalist development*, the social relation becomes a *moment* of the relation of production, the whole of society becomes an *articulation* of production; in other words, the whole of society exists as a function of the factory and the factory extends its exclusive domination over the whole of society." (Tronti, quoted in Wright 2002: 37–8)

The rising wage demands of the organized workers – which Negri saw as an expression both of working-class intransigence regarding the exploitation of surplus labor and of the widening array of class needs that were coalescing into an autonomous workers' value system – were simultaneously producing inflation and stagnation, thereby further reducing the capital's rate of profit. At the same time new forms of resistance, unprecedented in the history of class struggle – such as the self-reduction of prices by workers, or the outright refusal of work – were proliferating.[9] These facts gave rise to two workerist questions, or rather two ways of asking the same workerist question – one that would dominate Negri's political analyses during the seventies: What were the contours of the socialized worker's technical composition? And what form of organization would constitute an adequate political composition, a "party," for the socialized worker?

Workers' Power and Autonomy

With the founding of Potere operaio in 1969, Negri's analytical and organizational work began to focus on the above two questions, and he continued to engage them after the organization dissolved in 1973 and while the more heterogeneous set of groups called Autonomia coalesced over the next several years. On the eve of his arrest in 1979 he had still not found a satisfactory answer, in large part because the social and political situation in Italy mutated continuously throughout that period and, like other militants, Negri struggled to keep up with it. He was not the only one to propose organizational models for the new class composition; he wasn't even the most influential of those who did.[10] But he was perhaps the most audacious, both in the intensity of his arguments and in the abrupt changes of direction he took. It is also important to recall, as Michael Hardt notes, that

> Negri was very conscious of his role as an intellectual within the movement and accordingly he attempted to integrate the principal terms and ideas that were general in the movement into his own discourse, in order to situate and evaluate them within a coherent theoretical framework...His works lose their scholarly tone and formalities such as footnotes disappear completely; rather, they aspire toward the collective voice of political programs, continually proposing "our immediate task." (Hardt 2005: 8)

In this section we will not follow all the borrowings from the movement and all the changes of direction, nor will we examine every aspect and implication of his ideas. As in chapter 2, we will focus on the aspects of Negri's organizational work that connect most clearly to his lifelong humanist project: first, the characteristics of the emerging subject form that Negri called "the socialized worker" and its relation to the new form of the capitalist state and, second, the proposed forms of political organization that would permit the socialized worker to combat that state form successfully. Along the way we will encounter key concepts that continue to guide Negri's thinking, such as the real subsumption of labor within capital, as well as elements of his arguments that would lead to his arrest on charges of terrorism.

For Negri, the point of departure for workers' struggle at the end of the sixties and the beginning of the seventies was defined by the crisis of the "planner-state," which had emerged from economist John Maynard Keynes' response to the Soviet challenge and to the Great Depression. Those events demonstrated that capitalism was no longer an absolute horizon or an inevitable future, and the working class realized that it could step outside that horizon. It could assert its autonomy from capital, while capital could not free itself from its reliance on the working class' labor-power. "What was new, and what marks this moment as decisive," Negri writes in his 1968 essay "Keynes and the Capitalist Theory of the State Post-1929," was the recognition of the emergence of the working class and of the ineliminable antagonism it represented within the system as a *necessary feature of the system which state power would have to accommodate*... Working-class political revolution could only be avoided by recognizing and accepting the new relation of class forces, while making the working class function within an overall mechanism that would "sublimate" its continuous struggle for power into a dynamic element of the system. (Negri 1988: 13)

If it wished to accomplish this sublimation, the state could no longer stand by and allow the development cycle to operate as it had under the laissez-faire regime of classical liberalism; instead, the state must adopt the role of planner, guaranteeing the continuing compatibility of capital and labor. Keynes' project, therefore, would be the construction of a new model of equilibrium that would restore capital's faith in the future by fixing the future in the present. The only way for this to be accomplished is for the state to intervene directly in the economy. As Negri puts it: "The state has to defend the present from the future. And if the only way to do this is to project the future from within the present, to plan the future according to present expectations, then the state must extend its intervention to take up the role of planner" (p. 25). Control over the working class is accomplished through the manipulation of effective demand, which is linked to employment and wage levels and must be maintained in dynamic equilibrium with aggregate supply in order to forestall economic collapse. This method required the continual expansion of the Fordist wage regime, which the New Deal accomplished on a national scale in the US.

Keynes' planner-state was intended to avoid crises altogether, but both Marx and the Austrian economist Joseph Schumpeter recognized that as a utopian dream. A more practical approach would be to expect crisis within the cyclic development of the system and to use it to accelerate restructuring. As Negri noted in "Marx on Cycle and Crisis," published in 1968, for Schumpeter "[d]evelopment is struggle; it is a restructuring of power-relations; and it must necessarily pass via a moment of direct conflict – the crisis – to end with capital's victory over its opposing forces" – the working class (p. 55). Crisis is provoked by innovation, which destroys whatever equilibrium has been achieved because such equilibrium leads inevitably to the destruction of profit as a result of rising wage demands and the falling rate of profit. The planner-state must incorporate such crisis into its planning in order to preserve capitalism; it must become a crisis-state.[11] Marx offers an even more comprehensive model through his law of the tendency of the rate of profit to fall. The working day is divided into the period of necessary labor, in which the costs of the worker's needs are met by the wage, and the period of surplus labor, in which the worker produces profit for capital by working beyond the value of the wage. Marx's law states that the rate of profit, which is the proportion between surplus labor and necessary labor, tends to fall because the struggles of the working class compel capital to reduce the overall amount of labor it purchases by replacing workers with machines. But machines, as fixed capital, do not produce profit, so by reducing the amount of profit-producing labor (variable capital) employed, capital reduces its rate of profit even as it attempts to preserve it by reducing the loss caused by strikes and other forms of worker antagonism. Development, then, is driven by "a conflict between two strategies: the strategy of the working class, which advances from the level of mere subsistence to the point of limiting profits by increases in the necessary wage; and the strategy of the collective capitalist obliged to respond in strategic terms to this working-class attack, and thus to mobilize capital's entire political and economic potential for this conflict" (p. 67). The working class' strategy is to increase the level of necessary labor by claiming an ever greater share of profit even as the rate of profit drops as a result of the technological means employed to dismantle working-class power over production. These two forces drive the law of value, which subordinates necessary labor to surplus labor, into general crisis; and the crisis-state must attempt to re-impose the law of value, by force if necessary.

Thus the form of the state has changed, and the old Leninist illusions about taking it over must be abandoned in favor of the plan to smash it. Even if the working class managed to conquer the crisis-state, all this would mean is that the class would exploit itself, paradoxically realizing the promises of the Italian Constitution, because the law of value and the law of the wage are built into the crisis-state as the means of development that it exists to impose. The only way the working class can defeat the crisis-state is to destroy the wage relation and the law of value that underpins it; and the only way in which Negri imagines that the working class can succeed in this project is that of organizing itself so as to increase and rigidify its wage demands still further. His 1971 pamphlet *Crisis of the Planner-State* (re-issued with a postscript in 1974) and the 1973 essay

"Workers' Party against Work" begin from this hypothesis and attempt to derive organizational principles for Potere operaio from it. In "Workers' Party," however, he turns for the first time to a Marxian concept that will be as important to the development of his later work as the workerist hypothesis is: the transition from the formal subsumption of labor within capital to its real subsumption. "Marx generalizes the distinction between absolute and relative surplus-value to the point of describing two important phases in the subsumption of labor under capital. It is through these phases, the first 'formal' and the second 'real,' that we can witness a progressive subordination of the labor process to capital's command" (Negri 2005: 57–8). Absolute surplus value is the value produced by labor simply by extending the amount of labor time; this reaches its limit quickly, since workers cannot work without interruptions for rest and recovery – what Marx calls time for reproduction. Relative surplus value, on the other hand, is the value that is produced by reducing the proportion of necessary labor to surplus labor during the fixed working period, so that more time is spent producing surplus value. Capital relies on pre-capitalist forms of labor until they reach the point at which no further absolute surplus value can be wrung from them, and at that point it begins to restructure the labor process in order to maximize efficiency and productivity so that workers can create more value during the same time period, and therefore capital can extract more surplus value and thus more profit from their labor. This transition marks the passage from formal subsumption, in which capitalism is merely a profit-making shell around traditional labor practices, and real subsumption, in which labor processes – and the workers who perform them – are remade according to the norms of capital itself.

In order to make labor more productive, capital encourages it to socialize – first within the factory, by means of an increasingly rationalized division of labor or specialization of tasks (Taylorism), and later outside the factory, by means of a growing network of interlocking associations and enterprises that provide training, support and leisure for workers. As capital carries out this task, it also fosters relations of mutual activity and interest among distinct categories of workers. The result is a situation in which the border between factory and society is not rigid – Tronti's vision of the social factory is realized. Capital does this in order to increase the productivity of labor and thus to increase the relative surplus value it produces; but every increase in productivity makes the next increase harder to accomplish, because the development of large-scale industry makes *the proportion of neces-sary labor to surplus-value produced* (that is, the degree of productivity of necessary labor) *an insignificant relation because of the small amount of necessary labor and the mass of capital, of dead labor, that is accumulated against it…As a matter of fact, the theory of the tendency of the rate of profit to fall is nothing but the historical extension of this first fundamental consideration of the inevitable contradiction that pits living labor against dead labor within that elementary unit of analysis (and exploitation) which is the working day.* (Negri 2005: 61–2)

This situation produces a further paradox that capital cannot escape: it constantly presses to reduce the amount of necessary labor – but it does so by encouraging the development of abilities in the working class that it must then constrain and repress in order to preserve its control over production. Thus the transition to real subsumption compels capital to press simultaneously and contradictorily for a higher (social) value of labor and for its devalorization.

The tactic that has brought capital to this crisis is working-class appropriation, the demand for wages and consumption beyond the capacity of the system to generate them out of the profits of surplus labor. Since "[a]ppropriation is…the recognition that the forms of production are increasingly moving from a state of *contradiction* with the social forces of production into a state of *antagonism*," this means that class struggle "must necessarily be developed on the terrain of generalized appropriation, the mass management of an assault on social wealth as something that should be regarded as our own" (p. 31). The tactic and goal of the new class composition is not the dialectical apotheosis or redemption of work preached by the socialist tradition and the Italian Constitution, but rather the refusal of work.

> Workers imagine their life not as work but as the absence of it, their activity as free and creative exercise. We are talking about the massive flight of productive labor from factory work toward the tertiary or service sectors. We are talking about the spontaneous refusal to accept the rules of training for abstract labor and appren-ticeship to unmediated labor. All of this is displayed at the level of spontaneity, as an implicitly subjective characteristic, as a general tendency toward the workers' refusal of work… (P. 75)

The workers want more, and they refuse to accept the austerity measures being imposed upon them.

Generalized appropriation and the refusal of work constitute the mass pole of proletarian action, but in *Crisis of the Planner-State* Negri insists that it must be guided by the other pole – the vanguard pole comprised of organized workers in the large factories:

> The vanguard has to prove capable of interpreting and directing the mass will to appropriation against the enterprise, against the factory-command over the class. These two moments cannot be separated, nor can they be merged: both of them must be present within the overall movement, playing specific roles and recomposing themselves through insurrectional action led by the vanguards. Any separation of these two moments must prove disastrous. Action by the vanguards alone is empty; action by the mass organisms alone is blind. But it is equally dangerous to attempt to merge the two moments into unified mass vanguards. (P. 34)

The mass pole must coordinate its appropriative demands, which throw Keynesian mechanisms of proletarian sublimation out of proportion, with the focused violence of the factory vanguards, which attack the bosses wherever command is most direct and intense. This concept of the party cannot be a revival of the Bolshevik model, but must instead use Leninist analytical principles to invent a new form of vanguard party, which reflects the increasingly socialized class composition of the mass worker.

Two years later, the upshot of "Workers' Party against Work" was somewhat different. The increased socialization of labor beyond the factory walls means that "we can now state that the concept of the waged worker and the concept of the productive worker tend toward homogeneity" (p. 79) and that many categories that would have been "unproductive" from a Marxist or Leninist viewpoint are now definitely productive, as the work of Dalla Costa (among others) had proven. Nevertheless, this gesture of inclusion is counterbalanced by Negri's re-assertion that even this expanded notion of proletarian subjectivity is structured by a polarity that re-introduces hierarchy. There is still a Leninist vanguard that must lead the struggle, and "the vanguard that is capable of doing this is once again the *working class of the large factories*, which is the privileged subject of exploitation and at the same time the effective agent of the devalorization of labor and profit" (ibid.). The redefinition of productive labor has consequences, however, for the conception of the party that Negri is proposing here. First of all, the industrial working class is no longer coterminous with the party structure, and it no longer imposes itself as a strict model of class identity, from the top down, as the Bolshevik model did. Instead, working-class organization must emerge immanently and spontaneously from the interactions among the many instances of worker subjectivity that have become directly productive under the conditions of real subsumption, even if that immanence and that spontaneity are ultimately overtaken by the strategic transcendence of the industrial working class. The factory workers' wage struggle is the linchpin of the new organizational proposal, just as it was two years earlier. That struggle continues to coordinate the various mass practices of appropriation and refusal of work that spread out from the epicenter of the industrial factory throughout the diffuse "social factory." But at this point Negri's new conception of the party contradicts his earlier proposal: whereas in 1971 he wrote that it was "dangerous to attempt to merge the two moments into unified mass vanguards," now he "must insist on the concept of the *mass vanguard* ... The concept of the party of the mass vanguards is that of the *unification between the struggle for the wage and the revolutionary struggle for power*" (pp. 85–6).

It is difficult to assess what effect this party model would have had in practice, since it never fully coalesced. The closest the movement came to realizing it, in Negri's view, was during the occupations of the FIAT Mirafiori plant near Turin in March 1973, when the factory workers outmaneuvered their union representatives and "turned the indefinite-term strike into an armed occupation" (Negri 1979: 61; translation modified). Even there, however, the workers did not succeed in communicating their struggle to the "city-factory" of Turin itself. On the theoretical plane, the logical paradox of "mass vanguards," which might be glossed as "leaderless leadership," would appear to move the proposition out of the realm of party politics altogether; but Negri saw the matter differently. The party's task was not representation or transcendence, but rather differentiated articulation and continuity of struggle. "[W]e *propose to start using the term 'party' again* ... [b]ecause in Marx and in Lenin, in the most profound reality of class composition, 'party' basically means two things to the working class. It means *independence of the proletariat as organization* and *uninterrupted revolution*" (Negri 2005: 83–4). The party is a relay and intensifier of action, primarily from the factory workers to the diffuse proletariat outside the factory; but, in the interest of socialization, Negri concedes that a relay in the reverse direction might also be conceivable.

Negri's paradoxical model of a party of mass vanguards was never realized, largely because the organization for which he proposed it, Potere operaio, voluntarily dissolved a few months after "Workers' Party against Work" was published in 1973. The tension between Workers' Power's privileging of the workers of the large factories and its efforts to reach out to the new, diffuse and non-traditional workers tore it apart, forcing Negri to return to more theoretical analyses of the conditions of struggle that emerged during the seventies. These analyses laid the foundation for his involvement with the more de-centered collection of radical movements that would define the "area of Autonomia." His 1975 comparative analysis of "Communist State Theory" (in its Soviet, structuralist and Frankfurt School versions) concluded, unsurprisingly, that only the workerist approach adequately acknowledged the agency of the working class in bringing about a rupture of the state. Negri's verdict on the structuralist argument between Marxist sociologists Nikos Poulantzas and Ralph Miliband regarding the "autonomy of the political" was particularly pointed:

> "[T]he autonomy of the political" is presented again, not as a dia-lectical nexus between productive forces and capitalist arrange-ments of production, but rather as a "third level" located between the other two...the very theoretical objective of the analysis – iden-tifying the relative autonomy of the State with respect to other regional terrains (the economic terrain in particular) – remains mys-tified since the relative autonomy is presupposed so as to constitute the result of the analysis. (Hardt and Negri 1994: 150)

The autonomy of the political is predicated on the theoretical repression of the link between workers' struggles and political institutions. Negri was not merely pointing out a logical flaw in these analyses, since the concept of the autonomy of the political was at that very moment splitting the Italian workers' movement. The apologists of this autonomy, like Negri's onetime comrades Cacciari and Tronti, had opted to join the PCI in order to influence its policies and, to do so, they were compelled to acknowledge the growing distance that separated the PCI's positions from those of the radical workers. They justified their support for the Party pre-cisely by means of the autonomy of the political, which authorized the Party to pursue its overall political goals by any means neces-sary – even means like the Historic Compromise (to which we will turn shortly), which imposed hardship and persecution on large sectors of the working class that the Party claimed to represent.

The next phase of Negri's scholarly investigation, in the 1975 essay "The State and Public Spending," focuses on an area that has

grown so large since the New Deal period that it has come to dominate the state's functions; hence the phrase "welfare state." Public
spending, which conventional economics and traditional Marxist
theory treat as unproductive because it does not constitute a direct
investment in commodity production, is an aspect of the expanded
notion of productive labor that Negri began to outline in "Workers'
Party against Work." It grows as the socialization of the working
class grows, and in fact socialization both draws upon and drives
public spending. Since socialization for the purpose of increased
productivity is the goal of state intervention in planned economies,
whether Keynesian or Soviet, public spending constitutes the lifeblood of the crisis-state in its effort to spread the logic of the factory
over the whole of society. As Negri says, "public spending represents the cash flow of the factory-State" (Hardt and Negri 1994:
188), in which the state apparatus has been subordinated to the
needs of the corporations.

As a consequence of the state's subordination, its spending constitutes an extension of the wage: the corporation pays a factory
wage, while the state pays a social wage.

> The factory wage and the social wage are two poles of the figure in
> which the working class is mediated and subsumed in the social and
> State figure of capital. Capital tends to separate itself into two figures,
> to play the factory wage as an element of the legitimacy of the capi-
> talist State against the emergence of the productive unity of social
> labor. (Pp. 192–3)

Thus the working class must launch a struggle on two fronts:
against the factory and against the state. "Recognizing society as a
factory, recognizing the State as a boss, destroying the fetish of
productivity as legitimation, and bringing legitimation back to the
comprehensive needs of the proletariat is, at any rate, today's subversive task" (p. 193). Negri identifies several important new tactics
that were emerging from the Italian struggles in which he was
deeply involved. The first and best known is self-reduction: the
direct appropriation of goods and services by workers, who pay
what they see fit for those things rather than the price set by the
market. Throughout Italy during the mid-seventies, workers practiced the self-reduction of grocery prices, public transit fares and
movie ticket prices (among other things). This tactic of struggle,
which blurs the distinction between the factory wage and the social
wage, is only possible on account of the high degree of socialization

that links the mass workers of the large factories and the diffuse proletariat of the cities. As such, Negri insists, "[s]elf-reduction is the last, highest form of the struggle of the mass worker, and the first figure in which the social re-appropriation of wealth is determined on the basis of the new proletarian subject of the class struggle – the negation and sublation of the mass worker" (p. 211; translation modified). That sublation or self-overcoming of the mass worker is the subjective form that Negri will call the "social" or "socialized" worker, the immediate precursor to the multitude. Negri's focus on the organization of the socialized worker coincided with his involvement in Autonomia operaio (Workers' Autonomy).

Unlike the early workerist movement, centered around journals like *Quaderni rossi* and *Classe operaia*, and unlike organizations such as Potere operaio, centered around the factories and schools of the Veneto, Autonomia had no center, either geographically or conceptually. Some critics described it as an archipelago – a dispersed set of small groups that shared only a few general features; but a more affirmative description might call it a "movement of movements," not unlike the struggles over globalization today. The most common contemporary term was simply the neutral "area." However one describes it, Autonomia lacked the stable structure of more traditional political organizations, and along with structure it also lacked clear points of origin and end. Soon after the composition of "Capitalist State Theory" and of "The State and Public Spending," Negri recast parts of the arguments advanced in these pieces, in an effort to intervene into the organizational processes of Autonomia. Just like "Workers' Party against Work," *Proletarians and the State*, published in 1975, takes as its point of departure the actualization of Marx's prediction regarding the declining rate of profit that results from the increased use of fixed capital and attributes it to the working class' success in appropriating an increasing share of the surplus value it produces – which it does through the factory wage and through the social wage of public spending.

Negri's aim in *Proletarians and the State* is to interrogate the "Historic Compromise" proposed between the old adversaries the PCI and the center-right Christian Democrats, in an effort to engineer a stabilization of worker demands on the one hand and increased worker participation in governing on the other – that is, participation mediated by party and union representatives. The alliance was promoted by participants as an innovative moment both in Italian and in global politics: as the first practical initiative taken by the Eurocommunists to assert their autonomy from Moscow and to demonstrate their commitment to pluralist parliamentary democracy, it represented the very model of the autonomy of the political and of its promises. For Negri and his allies, however, the Historic Compromise

> *proposes the same model of the Planner-State,* the model of the workers' co-participation in the exploitation of workers and the apology for work as a proposition of socialism – the same model, we are saying, *that has been defeated by the workers' struggles in all the countries of advanced capitalism these last forty years.* (Negri 2005: 136)

Far from being a measure of the originality and contemporaneity of the official labor movement, the Historic Compromise was a clear indication of its capitulation to, and collaboration with, capitalist technocracy in that it required the PCI to police dissident elements to its left, specifically the workerists and autonomists.

The autonomy of the political as a concept and the compromise based upon it were false and misleading because they were premised on the persistence of the category of civil society that could operate independently of the state, which according to Negri no longer exists: "To the extent that the realization of profit devolves upon the state, civil society disappears. It dissolves not because the categories of revenue and unemployment disappear, but because their characterization is referred directly to the state" (p. 139). Thus the claim that PCI representatives of the working class require tactical autonomy in order to further the class' interests collapses not because the political sphere is epiphenomenal, but rather because its logic of separation and representation has become impossible. The state no longer stands opposed to – and above – civil society, but absorbs it completely. The subordination of the state to private corporations demonstrates it. There can be no more mediation or delegation to political representatives, because there is no longer a space of delegation – only direct, unmediated confrontation between the state and the insurgent working class.[12]

In an important review of *Proletarians and the State,* Negri's university colleague Sergio Bologna found this analysis of the autonomy of the political troubling for several reasons. First of all, in asserting the impossibility of the autonomy of the political, Negri overlooked the possibility that the PCI was not claiming that autonomy as a transhistorical given, but was rather attempting to construct it as a viable framework within which to implement its own reformist policies. That is, the autonomy of the political was not a precondition of the Historic Compromise, but an intended consequence of it, and as such it must be combated with different tactics from those that Negri proposes (Bologna 2005: 41–2).[13] More importantly, the representational logic underpinning the autonomy of the political also underpinned Negri's own activity as an organizational theorist for Autonomia; so, if his critique is correct, then his own work is just as untenable as the Historic Compromise itself. As Bologna acidly puts it:

> If it is true that the relationship between the "socialized" worker and the party is different, if it is true that civil society no longer exists, if it is true that the theory of consciousness is different, then why continue to pursue the worn-out trade of the theoretician or ideologue? This form of political discourse is obsolete; this millenarian language is so infuriating; this autonomy of the theoretician should be combated, precisely as a negation of a "general theory." (Pp. 46–7)[14]

As Negri's efforts to synthesize the incommensurable shifts of the movements became increasingly tortuous, this indictment would be progressively harder to ignore.

Nevertheless, if Negri is correct and the autonomy of the political has become untenable, this implies that the class' own organization must dispense with all relations of representation as well. This is where the proletarian party comes back into Negri's analysis.

> "The party," if one still wishes to call it that, is in this case something other than a vanguard on the march: *it is the motive force of the transformation of a system of mass struggles, it is the organ of the mass political reappropriation of power, against wage labor, as an invention of communism.* (Negri 2005: 153)

The party must coordinate the emergence of linked struggles out of the diffuse instances of re-appropriation that spring up across the entire social field, both inside and outside the factory. Unlike "Workers' Party against Work," *Proletarians and the State* does not fall back upon the Leninist model of the factory workers' vanguard role in party organization. At the same time as it struggles against capital and its state, the workers' party must also continue to struggle against work, and thus against any hierarchical claim – not just from factory workers, but also from the party itself – to represent the class. Various tactics are available to the party, but its overall strategy must be one of unification of productive labor through an intransigent demand that necessary labor should be expanded so as to block the divisions that capital and the state strive to re-impose within the fabric of the proletariat. The goal of the class, then, is

> the *dictatorship of the proletariat*, that is, the direct appropriation of the productive forces by the workers, the destruction of the capitalist mediation of the socialization of the productive forces, and the trans-fer of the material legitimation of the management of power from the parties to the organs of proletarian democracy. (P. 158)

All the institutions of representation and delegation, from tradi-tional left parties and unions to the state itself, must be destroyed in order for this project to come to fulfillment.

The Italian proletariat has to invent a new party form, which should be capable of responding to the new tactics of capital, par-ticularly to its efforts to divide and conquer. In the face of this need, the new party must be conceived of as inclusively as possible in terms of the new class composition, which extends far beyond the traditional strongholds of wage labor.

> The *marginal disarticulation of the proletariat* ... requires an interven-tion able to clarify, in every single aspect related above all to the youth proletariat and schooling, to the female proletariat and domes-tic labor, and to unemployed labor-power and the mechanisms of marginalization, the inherent nature of the disarticulations of the unitary process of proletarianization and their necessity from the standpoint of accumulation. But here, perhaps the most important element of the inquiry consists in the political characteristic of the process: out of proletarian marginalization emerge new needs that are irreducible to the demands of wage labor. (P. 169)

Intervening in this situation is the function of the party, which must accelerate the consolidation of the new, fully socialized class com-position. This is one of the few points in Negri's political essays where his implicit humanism returns to prominence – for example in his account of the unorganized or "lumpen" proletariat:

> the "lumpen" are the true bearers of those "human values" that fill the mouths of socialism and revisionism. With this difference: they are not bearers of values that take the form of an "originary and

generic essence," but rather *Träger*, the bearers and transmitters of struggle. (P. 170)

Consistently with the viewpoint of his studies in the history of philosophy, Negri still sees humanism as the historical constructivism – in this context, the constructivism of struggle and antagonism – that he first located in the radical strains of the Italian Renaissance. This conception continues to define his version of Marxism to this day. As he wrote in the preface to the second edition of *Proletarians and the State*, "[m]aterialism is in no way a historical and political conventionalism, but rather the always new flavor of reality, not sixteenth-century mechanism but rather humanist realism...as Marx...emphasizes several times..." (p. 120).

In their effort to struggle together, workers faces huge obstacles – not only from capital, but also from the historical parties of the official labor movement, which Negri fears are likely to be more brutal in repressing the extra-parliamentary movements that they claim to represent than the parties of the extreme right.

In the very short term, the failure of the reformist prospect launches another round of the most brutal repressive action against the class...This action is taken particularly against those spaces and forces that the critical self-realization of the Historic Compromise sees forming on its left wing, and thus against the party of workers' and proletarian autonomy. (P. 164)

This warning proved to be especially prophetic for Negri himself. The PCI unleashed a campaign of intense repression against the movements to its left, as a way of demonstrating, in the eyes of its intended allies in the Christian Democratic Party (DC), its commitment to public order; and, after the failure of the Historic Compromise to bring the PCI into government, it retaliated against perceived leaders of the extra-parliamentary left, like Negri, through the one branch of government on which it had an influence: the judicial system.

Having analyzed formally and conceptually, in "Labor in the Constitution," the paradox of labor in the Italian Constitution of 1948, Negri next recognized the need to bring that analysis up to date and to assess the changes to the constitutional synthesis imposed by the acceleration of the workers' struggles during the intervening years. "Toward a Critique of the Material Constitution," originally published in 1977, can be read as a sequel to, or even a rewriting of, "Labor in the Constitution."[15] Where the earlier essay focused on the mode of production of juridical right instead of that of the workers' organization, the later text takes up the challenge of organization on terms that Negri had developed more recently. He begins his revision with the peremptory claim that

> the political event of the Constitution of 1948 is now over...The Constitution is no longer the law of all laws: laws proceed by themselves, following the pace and coherence of the constitution of a new structure of political power. A *new regime* is taking shape day by day and a *new material constitution* is arising. (P. 180)

Although in that earlier essay he had noted the distinction between the written or formal constitution (the textual object of study for philosophers of right, the "law of all laws" controlled by legislators and judges) and the material constitution (the constantly changing set of social, productive and reproductive relations that are the object of struggle of collective subjects), he did not emphasize it because at that point the logical distinction had not yet developed into the practical disjunction – or antagonism – that workers' struggles in the sixties revealed.

The fundamental change that Negri identifies at the root of the obsolescence of the old constitution is the radical polarization of the subjects in struggle: capital and labor-power. Whereas earlier capital could functionally incorporate labor-power into relations of exploitation through market mechanisms (the wage and the blackmail threat of exclusion from the market), this is no longer possible. Capital had previously functioned by getting members of the working class to participate in capital's own process of valorization as participants in consumption, the point in the cycle that realized value as profit. However, with the advent of an increasingly rigid level of necessary labor, proletarian consumption no longer acts to valorize capital, but instead creates its own circuits of valorization. The working class realizes itself, valorizes itself, on the terrain of reproduction – the terrain of its own immediate needs and desires, not those of capital. This is the chief qualitative result of the overall unification of labor that increasing socialization has encouraged. The complex of factors that Negri identifies points to a fundamental transition in worker struggle and in capital's attempt to contain and subordinate it: a shift in focus from the sphere of production to the sphere of reproduction – specifically, the reproduction of the working class itself. The omnipresence of antagonism in the sphere of production – the large factories, the small workshops, unemployment and so on – drives capital to seek control over the still atomized sites of proletarian reproduction: the home, the school, places of leisure. However, those sites have already been subjected to the general logic of capitalist labor relations, as part of the real subsumption of labor within capital. Consequently, *"the terrain of reproduction is dominated by the antagonistic categories of production and the process of production does not disappear in the commodity* but re-emerges in all of its elements" (p. 190) – most importantly, the element of struggle. Capital cannot escape from the antagonism it has itself produced by shifting the field of action, nor can it abandon its relationship to its opponent. "If the constitution of the capitalist state changes materially, this is due to the fact that the state, faced with this impending struggle, must nevertheless always take on a corresponding process of the *constitution of the insubordinate proletarian subject"* (p. 198).

As a consequence of the generalized socialization of labor necessary for increasing its productivity, reproduction of labor-power takes place practically everywhere and supports itself through the rigidity of necessary labor in the directly productive sectors and through public spending in the indirectly productive or socialized sectors. For capital to respond to a generalization of resistance, it must unify its command in the state, but it must also spread its control over the whole area of reproduction, that is, over the whole of society. "The state is the party, the party dictatorship of capital. Administration is the exercise of will of the bosses' state" (p. 206). As Negri argued earlier, it can only administer by dividing the unity of labor-power into new hierarchies; constitutionally speaking, then, the state must abandon the juridical logic of formal equality that legitimated it during the earlier history of bourgeois dominance. *"The state founded on the crisis of the law of value assumes the rule of inequality as the explicit content of its political will"* (p. 208). Such open inequality can only be enforced by means of violence. We will return to this shortly.

Although it is constructing its own sociality independently of the state, the radical workers' movement cannot rely solely on that diffuse condition. Instead it must generate a focus of power equal and opposite to that of the state administration, if it is to resist the violent imposition of inequality. That focus is the party, according to the equation that views "the *state* as the *party of capital* and the *party* as the *state of the working class,* or, rather, the anti-state of workers' power" (p. 215). As Negri had argued before, the new party cannot be a representative body because the class composition will not tolerate delegation of its power in any way – since power is the substance of its subjectivity and the goal of its activity. *"Proletarian independence, self-valorization, counterpower: these are successive and highly integrated levels – they are faculties that a new composition of the working and proletarian class shows to be different yet complementary moments of its own subjectivity"* (p. 216). To acquiesce to party representation would be to affirm its objectivity, its dependence on capital, when the point is to negate that objectivity in all its forms and in a non-dialectical way. *"Any determinate class composition is thus twofold*: both object of exploitation and subject of self-valorization. *However, its self-negation as object of exploitation is not simply self-affirmation as subject of self-valorization: it is rather the negation of the relation itself... The refusal of work is refusal of the relation"* (p. 218). The refusal of work, the refusal of the relation between objectivity and subjectivity imposed by capital, is the fundamental expression of the non-dialectical antagonism that blocks a new synthesis and establishes the autonomy of the collective socialized worker. This is what Negri means when he asserts: *"The labor of the party is thus the exact opposite of that which constitutes the modification of the material constitution on behalf of capital"* (p. 219). The party must express this autonomy in a non-representative way, by highlighting again the paradox of organization that Negri had earlier tried to capture in the concept of "mass vanguards." He must insist on the one hand that *"[t]here can be no class recomposition without centralization* [in a form of party, because] [s]o long as there is a State, the political centralization of the proletariat will be absolutely necessary" (p. 222), and on the other that such centralization cannot be allowed to re-establish a hierarchy of command like that of the official labor movement. The working class must meet the new material constitution of the state with a paradoxical mutation in its own material constitution – and political composition – if it is to defeat its adversary.

Negri's inquiry into the changing forms of proletarian organization culminates in the pamphlet *Domination and Sabotage*, written and published in 1977, at the height of the inventiveness – and confusion – displayed by the Italian radical movements. The area of Autonomia was riven by disagreements over the priority of various forms of struggle, and new models of militancy were emerging that were only distantly related to the old factory model, such as the Metropolitan Indians (see Torealta 1980). The pamphlet marks the climax of Negri's period of direct militancy in at least three ways: first, it presents the most original conception of the party that he was to develop during this period; second, it lays out starkly both the similarities and the differences between the strategy he promoted and that of the clandestine terrorist groups (the Red Brigades and others) against which he had argued for years, thus constituting his most energetic attempt to influence the political direction of the movements; and third, its rhetorically ambiguous polemic against the terrorists drew the attention of the Italian state's police apparatus and resulted in Negri's arrest, which cut him off from the later development of the movements. Consequently it is important to examine *Domination and Sabotage* closely.

Negri begins by asserting, still in Leninist language, that "[d]estabilization of the regime cannot be seen as distinct from the project of destructuring the system. Insurrection cannot be separated from the project of extinguishing the state" (p. 232). This means that, in his view, it is counter-productive – indeed counter-revolutionary – to separate vanguard acts of violent assault on the commercial and state apparatus (destabilization), which were the hallmark of Red Brigades terror, from mass actions of subversion and reappropriation of wealth (destructuring), which defined the new social movements. Such separation would result in an unco-ordinated and self-defeating struggle, which would ultimately decompose the class' new political composition once again – regicidal violence against state and corporate administration would be little more than a means of provoking greater repression, if it were not articulated with the power and timing of the mass movements, while the proletarian alternatives to capital's form of value would never be able to emerge from ghettoization without organizing themselves for a confrontation with the hierarchical structure of command. It would be equally irresponsible to claim that, because the law of value has gone into crisis, the proletariat no longer needs to concern itself with the institutions and operations of capital and thus can turn all its attention to its own sub-cultural or counter-cultural satisfaction. On the contrary, "*the crisis of this law does not at all mean that the law does not operate; rather, its form is modified,* transforming it from a law of political economy into a form of state command" (p. 233). The crisis in the law of value makes the state more dangerous to the proletariat because the market mediations that were once interposed between them have now collapsed, and the adversaries must face and combat each other directly. For this confrontation to result in proletarian victory, the diverse new proletariat that was coming together from the remnants of the factory workers' movement, the feminist movement, the student move-ments, the unemployed and other groups would need to be inte-grated into a political unity capable of coordinated action, in response to the coordinated action of the state. That unity must find material expression or constitution in a form capable of responding point by point to the provocations of the state; but it must not reproduce the hierarchical, representational form of the state, as the terrorist advocates of destabilization suggest.

The success of the proletariat in establishing its separation from the logic of capital leaves capital with no option but to re-impose its command by force; but that command is formally empty, now that the mediations of exchange have failed. Command becomes indifferent because *"the mechanisms of capital's reproduction and the mechanisms of reproduction of the working class are no longer operating synchronously"* (p. 247), and thus capital's previous "rationality" no longer finds an echo in the separate world of proletarian subjectiv-ity. Working-class consumption ceases to realize capitalist value in the form of profit, so the two terms no longer mesh as dialectical dancing partners, and the timing of their respective modes of sur-vival no longer complement each other. For Negri, the crisis-state has given way to "the *State-based-on-Income-as-Revenue, the Income-State* – a state of political income. The one absolute value against which all other hierarchical values must measure themselves is political power" (p. 248). More specifically, this means that,

> at this point, *the wage is no longer...an independent variable.* It is com-pletely subordinated to the entire dynamic of power, to the entire framework of the political autonomy of the state...[so] the center of the workers' and proletarian struggle consists in *the recognition of the general aspect of the wage as a cost of reproduction of the unity of the proletariat,* of its self-valorization. (P. 249)

Both the factory wage and the social wage have become merely indices of the power struggle between capital and labor, and, if labor wishes to prevail, it must be as unified and violent as capital is. No longer can Negri assert the priority or centrality of the factory struggle, as he had over the preceding years; for

> any position which is restricted purely to the necessary struggle in the factory, and which is not connected to the proletarian majority, is a position that is bound to lose. *The factory struggle must live within*

the proletarian majority. The privileged place of the wage in the continuity
of proletarian struggles must today be extended to the struggle over public
spending. (P. 251)

The struggle must be unified and equal in all arenas, and those
elements of the factory proletariat that have won a privileged place
for themselves in capital's new hierarchy by abandoning their links
to the diffuse proletariat must be brought back into the fold.

In the course of the preceding argument Negri moves from the
subjective viewpoint of the radical worker, who recognizes his
"otherness" from capital and its institutional structure, to an objective description of the terrain of wage struggle and of the mystifications that the official labor movement deploys to confuse that
terrain. He opens the second half of the pamphlet by returning to
the subjective viewpoint for a more intensive evocation of subversive activity, and in the process he sets himself up for difficulties
both inside and outside the workers' movement. He writes:

> Nothing reveals the immense historical positivity of workers' self-
> valorization more completely than sabotage, this continual activity
> of the sniper, the saboteur, the absentee, the deviant, the criminal
> that I find myself living. I immediately feel the warmth of the
> workers' and proletarian community again every time I don the ski
> mask. (P. 259)

Negri would later describe this passage as "singularly bad writing"
resulting from the use of "risky metaphors" drawn from the inflammatory imagery of international terrorism (Negri 1980: Part 2,
Section V, my translation), but he refused to disavow his specific
aim here, which was to assert the centrality of sabotage against
capital in the process of consolidating workers' self-valorization.
This "bad writing" would come back to haunt him for years, first
in rebuttals from comrades in the radical movements and later in
questions from journalists and in charges from prosecutors outside
the movements. Such consequences came later, however, so we
should follow out Negri's argument so that we are better able to
assess the polemical uses to which his "bad writing" would be put.

The centrality of sabotage in the proletarian arsenal is a consequence of its function of decreasing the value of fixed capital and
concomitantly increasing the value of living labor in the processes
of production and reproduction. The use value of living labor

cannot be captured in its capitalist role as reflection of exchange value, as use value for the valorization of capital through circulation and consumption. "The determinate objective of the process is to increase the use value of labor, against its capitalist subsumption, against its commodification, against its reduction to a use value of capital" (Negri 2005: 261). However, having abandoned both capitalist exchange value and its mirror image, the proletariat must find a new measure of its own capacity for insubordination, autonomous production and self-valorization if it is to unify itself. It must find a common yardstick for the irreducibly diverse contents of the socialized workers' class composition. "We are in search of a *positive measure of non-work*, a measure of our liberation from that disgusting slavery from which the bosses have always profited, and which the official socialist movement has always imposed on us like some sort of title of nobility" (p. 263). Even the Marxist classics are useless here, because they accepted capital's system of measure in order to overturn it. The first indication of where to look for a measure of non-work comes from the corollary of the workerist hypothesis regarding the creativity of proletarian subversion – which Negri had earlier labeled "invention-power," by analogy with Marx's definition of labor-power. "*We define invention-power as a capacity of the class to nourish the process of proletarian self-valorization in the most complete antagonistic independence; the capacity to found this innovative independence on the basis of abstract intellectual energy as a specific productive force...*" (p. 268).[16] The most widespread and innovative form of invention-power that Negri sees operating among the many elements of the new class composition is, once again, the refusal of work.

The question is: Given that "[t]*he refusal of work is first and foremost sabotage, strikes, direct action*" (p. 270), how can it serve as a measure of self-valorization? Negri suggests two ways:

> In the first place, then, the progress of the process of self-valorization is measured, negatively, by the progressive reduction of individual and overall labor-time, that is, the quantity of proletarian life that is sold to capital. In the second place, the progress of the process of self-valorization is measured positively by the multiplication of socially useful labor dedicated to the free reproduction of proletarian society. (P. 272)

Because the refusal of work means a refusal of capitalist work discipline and of the modes of valorization that accompany it, it is consistent with the deployment of labor-power and invention-power in the service of proletarian interests – it is not just value subtracted from capital, but different value added to the proletariat. Another way to put it would be to describe the refusal of work as *"a measure of the increasing revolutionary intensity of the process of self-valorization.* At this point, finally, we should come to consider the measure not as a function of exploitation...but rather as a measure of freedom" (p. 273). It is a sublime measure in the Kantian sense, based as it is on the radical incommensurability between capitalist value and worker value, bourgeois freedom and revolutionary freedom; but what better measure could one imagine for such qualitative differences than the measure of intensity? At the same time, its sublimity makes it the only possible means of translation among the distinct modes of self-valorization that operate in the different areas of the radical movements. "It is the dynamic *nexus* that, on the basis of the practice of the refusal of work and its theoretical/practical extensions, is posited *between the workers' vanguard in direct production and the proletarian vanguard in indirect production*" (ibid.), and thus it defines the possibility of proletarian unification.

The refusal of work may be the measure of self-valorization, and as such it would be necessary for unification; but it is not sufficient. Specifically, it does not constitute a coherent form of organization that can stand up to the coherent totality of capital, the state. For this reason the question of the party must re-emerge, although all its traditional foundations – mediation, delegation, representation, mass, vanguard – have been dissolved. Indeed, the loss of foundation is the very reason for the party's re-emergence in that, for Negri and others, *"[t]he problem of the party today is the present reality of a real contradiction*...I think that the specificity of the 'party' contradiction lies in its *non-resolvability,* and that the party consists precisely of the persistence of the contradiction" (pp. 275–6). In such circumstances the party must be paradox itself. If the party cannot claim autonomy for its political action because of the dissolution of civil society, if the class will not delegate power to a party that stands above its members, if the conflict between capital and labor brooks no more mediation, then what possible function can the party have? With great care, Negri concludes that the party must be subordinate to the class as a whole, for which it performs a purely military function of offense and defense. That is, *"the party is a function of proletarian force, conceived as a guarantor of the process of self-valorization. The party is the army that defends the frontiers* of proletarian independence. And naturally it must not, cannot get mixed up in the internal management of self-valorization" (p. 276). The party must be constructed for the purpose of standing up to capital's state, and for no other. "Today, the party exists as an ensemble of inextricable functions – defense and attack, *counter-power*" (p. 277). Negri had already defined counter-power as the negative and negating image of state power, which the proletariat must deploy in order to conclude its struggle with the state. In *Domination and Sabotage* he goes further, defining the operation of specifically proletarian power beyond the necessary and transitory moment of confrontation with the capitalist state.

> In other words, *power is to be dissolved into a network of powers, and the independence of the class is to be constructed via the autonomy of individual revolutionary movements.* Only a diffuse network of powers can organize revolutionary democracy; only a diffuse network of powers can enable the opening of a dialectic of recomposition which reduces the party to a revolutionary army, to an unwavering executor of the proletarian will. (P. 279)

Even historian Steve Wright, who is on the whole deeply skeptical of Negri's work, considers this notion to be one of "the more innovative approaches" to the problem of organization that emerged from Autonomia (Wright 2005: 101). This Foucauldian conception of the socialized workers' diverse new class composition, seen as a "diffuse network of powers," anticipates the notion of the multitude, which Negri would begin to articulate a few years later.

Nevertheless, the central function of the party is not to map the network or to oversee the operation of the workers' democracy, but simply to channel proletarian violence against the capitalist state in the most productive way. As Negri has already established with respect to workers' power,

> [proletarian] violence is *not capable of homology* with capitalist violence, because the rationality that rules it is other, proletarian, absolutely different...This violence is *contrary* to capitalist violence; it aims at the destruction of capital's system and regime; it is founded on class self-valorization; it is *not equal* in intensity to capitalist violence – it is *stronger*, more efficacious than capitalist violence. (Negri 2005: 283)

This assertion, combined with the infamous ski-mask passage already cited, contributed the most to the popular journalistic image of Negri as – to paraphrase the socialist philosopher Norberto Bobbio – a prophet of redemption through violence (see Bobbio 1995: 190–1). It is crucial to recognize, however, that his conception of antagonistic violence arises from Negri's dissatisfaction with the partial violence of Hegelian dialectical negation, which always preserves its opponent, and that his conception remains subordinated to, and constrained by, the needs of the unified class subject.

> *Violence is one element of the rationality of the processes of self-valorization.* Nothing else. The party, with the vanguard functions of violence that must be assigned to it, and the contradiction that this embodies – all this is to be subordinated *not dialectically, but violently,* to workers' and proletarian power, to the direct organization of the processes of self-valorization. (Negri 2005: 283)

As early as in his *Crisis of the Planner-State*, Negri opposed the proto-terrorists' breaking of the link between class composition and organization because it would lead to a strategic result that mirrored the violent command of the state as a collective capitalist. Negri denounced this mystification and its consequences as a subjectivist impasse for the workers' movement, which "cuts itself off from that embodied, dialectical class subjectivity that pervades the tendency in Marx, as a historical individuality concretely and specifically constituted within this phase of capitalist development," and which "results in political impotence, and hence in the response of terrorism as the only possible form of struggle" (p. 15). In "Workers' Party against Work" Negri insisted that armed struggle is originally a defensive struggle against the armed violence of capital, which lays claim, through its state apparatus, to a monopoly on the legitimate use of violence. However, proletarian armed struggle goes beyond this reactive position to launch an offensive against the points of capitalist power and command. Such an offensive is only viable when it is based firmly in the new class composition; if it separates itself, for example by adopting the clandestine regicidal strategy that the Red Brigades had begun to articulate at the time, it not only mirrors the fragile command model of capital but also threatens the work of the class as a whole. The problem with terrorism is not violence per se, but disconnected, inorganic violence. "In terrorism, what we need to combat is the programmatic will that refuses to incarnate the moments of class power and is unable to grasp an *organic relation* between the subjectivity of workers' power and the subjectivism of the use of violence" (p. 91).

This argument against clandestine terrorism is consistent with Negri's attitude throughout the seventies, and his reasoning and conclusions are clear despite the sometimes difficult rhetoric through which he expresses them. So why would these same texts, in some cases these same passages, be cited in the warrants issued for his arrest on charges of armed insurrection against the powers of the state in 1979 (see Comitato 7 aprile 1979: 262–4)? Part of the answer lies in his practical proposals for how the mass vanguard party will do its job of articulating the wage struggles of the factory workers with the appropriative activities of the diffuse proletariat outside the factories. In "Workers' Party against Work" he had proposed: "The organizational unit that must extend itself molecularly is *the red base*, the liberated territory on which appropriation becomes a mass practice" (Negri 2005: 103). The red base would be a capture of non-factory social territory for proletarian self-organization, a space seized from capital for the purpose of articulating the poles of struggle and socializing their interaction. The later movement, of taking over derelict spaces in Italian cities to turn them into social centers, is an example of this practice. To establish and preserve such spaces, Negri proposes the organization of proletarian patrols to link the factories and the bases. In a slip that would have serious consequences later, Negri describes these patrols as "*the red brigades of the workers' and proletarian offensive*" (p. 109), apparently intending the lower-case phrase to indicate an attempt to co-opt the emerging clandestine groups' appeal for his own, organic conception of working-class violence.[17] Needless to say, such niceties were lost on the Italian prosecutors who later arrested him.

Although it can be difficult to follow the vicissitudes of Negri's thinking on the topics of the party and violence, the most important conclusion to draw at this point in the process is the fundamental incompatibility of this definition with the ahistorically Leninist vanguardism of the Red Brigades and of other Italian terrorist groups, which Negri would soon be accused of masterminding. Although Negri had endorsed a limited revival and historicization of the Leninist debate over the party form in the early seventies, by the late seventies his rejection of Leninist vanguardism had crystallized into a thorough and clear critique of that strategy. Lenin could still teach important lessons about the relation between class composition and political organization, or about the correct assessment of the tendency; but the specific conclusions he drew regarding organization and tendency in the 1910s were obsolete and could only hinder the proletariat's aims in the 1970s. As Michael Hardt shows, Negri's experience indicates that

> what we should adopt from Lenin is a project of reading the real and present composition of the working class and interpreting its subjectivity, its needs for organized expression. The most innovative aspect of Lenin's thought is its mass methodology, its theory of mass intelligence, its ability to dissolve theory into the practice of the masses and crystallize it again in a central insight. (Hardt 2005: 21)

That is, what is living in Lenin's thought is its anticipation of workerism, and it is precisely this anticipation that helped Negri to find a more fruitful source of organizational concepts in Marx's *Grundrisse* (p. 28).

Negri beyond Marx?

If *Domination and Sabotage* is the culmination of Negri's thinking regarding the revolutionary possibilities of political organization during the seventies, then *Marx beyond Marx: Lessons on the Grundrisse* (Negri 1984), first published in 1979, is the culmination of the philosophical and methodological reflections that began with "Labor in the Constitution" fifteen years earlier. Just as Negri's analysis of Lenin credited the latter with anticipating the insights of workerism, so Negri's reading of Marx finds theoretical precedent for, and confirmation of, many of his own most controversial political proposals. The book emerged from a 1978 seminar that Negri gave at the École normale supérieure in Paris at the invitation of Louis Althusser. Despite some similarities between their methods, Negri had long been explicitly critical of the radical anti-subjectivism or anti-humanism of Althusser's approach (and implicitly opposed to Althusser's involvement with the French Communist Party). As we saw in the section "Two Modernities" in chapter 1, Althusser based his critique of conventional Marxism on his identification of an "epistemological break" between early Marx the humanist, who criticized the alienation and exploitation of the working class on the basis of an abstract definition of human essence that was indistinguishable from the Hegelian conception of the subject underpinning liberalism, and the later, scientific Marx, who subordinated all conceptions of human subjectivity to the structural forces that emerged from class struggle. For Althusser, subjectivity was the very medium of ideology, and so struggle against capital was not a subjective project but rather a "process without a subject," which had to break with the humanist tradition of European Marxism. In 1973 Negri had agreed with Althusser that "[t]he *epistemological break is the birth of organization,* which turns the scientific point of view on existing reality into a set of technical tools for a process of destruction of the present state of things" (Negri 2005: 54); but he offered a clarification of this transition's proper meaning:

> The so-called "epistemological break" usually traced in Marx by structuralist Marxists consists in extending the understanding of the revolutionary subject. It marks a passage from the humanistic defini-tion of the revolutionary subject as abstract genera [*sic*] to its deter-mination as material, determinate negation that influences and modifies its own existence as it develops...Far from ending up in a "process without a subject," the evolution of Marx's thought instead closely follows the organizational reality of the revolutionary subject. The true result of the critique of political economy is always neces-sarily this subjective anchoring. (P. 114 n. 6)

In other words Negri accepts Althusser's critique of the ahistorical assumption of a universal proletarian subjective essence, but, instead of erasing the subject from the process altogether, he calls for an empirical study of the changing composition of the class subject under changing historical conditions of labor and socializa-tion. Althusser had long been interested in Italian communism (see Macciocchi 1973), and in Negri he undoubtedly recognized a kindred spirit as well as an adept adversary: a political theorist and militant who was also a highly original historian of bourgeois phi-losophy (as well as a fellow Spinozan, though this was not widely known at the time).

Marx beyond Marx constitutes Negri's most systematic articula-tion to date of his theory of radical subjectivity and, as a result of its rapid translation into French and English, perhaps the most internationally influential version of the workerist hypothesis to emerge from the Italian movement. From the beginning of the text, Negri enlists Marx in his own project by demonstrating how closely Marx's historical context when writing the *Grundrisse* (Marx 1973a) resembled the Italian context of the seventies. In so doing Negri implicitly insists on the continuity between organizational writing and theoretical writing, both Marx's and his own. For Marx in the

1850s as well as for the contemporary Italian movements, "[t]he imminence of catastrophe is only catastrophic for capital in so far as it is the *possibility of the party*, the possibility to establish the party. The description of the imminent crisis is, at the same time, a polemic against 'true socialism,' against all the mystifications and travesties of communism" (Negri 1984: 2). One of the most significant symptoms of socialist mystification – manifested by Althusser himself, as well as by the party for which he was sometimes allowed to speak – was the fetishization of Marx's method and mode of exposition in *Capital* and the denigration of his earlier works, especially the collection of notes and drafts published as the *Grundrisse* (see Althusser and Balibar 1970).

The problem with *Capital* lies precisely in its mode of exposition, which is objective – it pays little attention to the issue of subjectivity and, when it does, the subjectivity it interrogates is usually that of capital. From the opening investigation of the emergence of commodities to the general theory of surplus value, *Capital* focuses on the objective functioning of capitalist production and exchange to the extent that it can almost be considered a user's manual for capitalists. "*Capital* is...this text which served to reduce critique to economic theory, to annihilate subjectivity in objectivity, to subject the subversive capacity of the proletariat to the reorganizing and repressive intelligence of capitalist power" (Negri 1984: 19). In short, "[t]he objectification of categories in *Capital* blocks action by revolutionary subjectivity," while "the *Grundrisse* is a text dedicated to revolutionary subjectivity" (p. 8). Indeed, the *Grundrisse*'s focus on subjectivity gives it the character of an open work in Umberto Eco's sense, one that demands the participation of its performers and/or audience in the constitution of its meaning: "The originality, the happiness, the freshness of the *Grundrisse* rest entirely with its incredible openness. The paradoxical *non-conclusive character* of the science is derived necessarily from the fact that it contains a subjective determination" (p. 9). This characteristic of the text makes possible the imperative embodied in Negri's title: we must use Marx to go beyond Marx. He offers this as his reading hypothesis early on:

> Marx beyond Marx? The *Grundrisse* beyond *Capital*? Maybe...The theory of surplus value breaks down the antagonism [between classes] into a microphysics of power. The theory of class composition restates the problem of power in a perspective where recomposition is not that of a unity, but that of a multiplicity of needs, and of liberty. (P. 14)

Foucault's influence, already discernible in *Domination and Sabotage*, is registered here in the breakdown of the dialectical opposition between labor and capital into an antagonistic and plural microphysics of power that can only be captured by a careful workerist analysis of class composition. To go "beyond Marx," then, also means to encounter French poststructuralism.

In contrast to his host's arguments, which denounced the *Grundrisse* as the source of "all the dubious quotations needed by idealist interpretations of Marxist theory"(Althusser 1971: 103),[18] Negri peremptorily asserts: "The *Grundrisse* represents the summit of Marx's revolutionary thought" (Negri 1984: 18). While Negri accepts elements of Althusser's formulation of struggle as a mass project that is irreducible to the ideological form of essentialized subjectivity, he cautions his audience to avoid the excesses to which that formulation gives rise and the solace that that formulation can give to capital.

> In avoiding humanism, some would also seek to avoid the theoretical areas of subjectivity. They are wrong. The path of materialism passes precisely through subjectivity. The path of subjectivity is the one that gives materiality to communism. The working class is subjectivity, separated subjectivity, which animates development, crisis, transition and communism. (P. 154)

As noted, Negri accepts the critique of any essentialist conception of humanism but remains committed to a constructivist account of human collective subjectivity, for which he offers no consistent name until he and Hardt define their "humanism after the death of man" in *Empire*.

The organization of *Marx beyond Marx* effectively recapitulates the development of Negri's political writings from 1971 onward. He begins his examination of the *Grundrisse* as he began *Crisis of the Planner-State*, with an analysis of money instead of an analysis of the commodity (like the one that opens *Capital*). The conception of money that emerges at the end of the first chapter of *Capital* is the result of an objectifying process in which different products of labor, and thereby different labor processes and the workers who perform them, are reduced to general equivalence through exchange. The exchange process logically concludes in the objectification of value in money, the commodity of commodities – an objectification that rebounds on the subjects who produced it. To begin with money as equivalent, on the other hand, means to reactivate the subjectivity contained within it. In other words, "if money is an equivalent, if it has the nature of an equivalent, it is above all *the equivalence of a social inequality*... Money hides a content which is eminently a content of inequality, a content of exploitation" (Negri 1984: 26). Negri specifies that "money is not only one of the forms in which capital is metamorphosed, but also is the general form of its command and of the development of that command, the eminent form in which the continuity of value exercises its reign and, with it, the continuity of command" (p. 62). The work of Marxist criticism is to bring the social (and hence subjective) inequality of capitalist command to light, to prevent the antagonism contained in the commodity and money from reaching a mystifying objective synthesis.

> Antagonism can only exist if the capitalist relation does not resolve itself in a synthesis. [Therefore] the analysis must decide to take into account the actors who interpret the different roles of this play: the relation of value will always and only be the fiction which extends over the socio-political overdetermination of class conflict. (P. 24)

The workerist task is, as always, to invert the objectifying processes of capitalist valorization into the subjective struggles that drive them; but it is also a task of escaping the closure of the Hegelian, and even Marxist, dialectics that capital employs.

Again in terms that anticipate his alliance with poststructuralism, Negri resolves to treat "[t]he *category of production...as a category of difference*, as a totality of subjects, of differences, of antagonism" (p. 44) rather than as an objective synthesis. Two differences in particular are fundamental to his interpretation of Marx's account of capitalist production: use value versus exchange value and necessary labor versus surplus labor. Labor produces capital, but only in the form of an antagonistic exchange with capital, a wage relationship that converts use value into exchange value – in other words it converts labor-power into money. This implies a further difference – or opposition – that is contained within the first. "The opposition takes two *forms*: first, that of *exchange value against use value*, but – given that the only use value of workers is the abstract and undifferentiated capacity to work – the opposition is also *objectified labor against subjective labor*" (p. 68). Money, exchange value, is nothing but objectified (or dead) labor that is used to command subjective (or living) labor, so that, "on the one hand, *exchange value is autonomised in money and in capital,* and on the other, *use value is autonomised as the working class"* (p. 72). Money constitutes the subjective agency of capital, and the bulk of *Capital* is dedicated to analyzing that particular subjectivity. As Negri says:

> Certainly Marx developed a theory of profit, which is to say a theory of the subjectivity of capital, while – in spite of his intentions – he did not develop a theory of the subjectivity of the working class – in the figure of the wage, for instance. But this *asymmetry* of the *literary development* of Marx's work should not keep us from recognizing the *structural balance*; and from developing his proposed presuppositions, seeing in the social working day, in its division between social surplus labor and socially necessary labor, the basis for the deadly struggle that is put up by the two classes. We must see in these two spaces the formation of *opposed subjectivities*, opposed wills and intellects, opposed processes of valorization: in short, an antagonistic dynamism... (P. 93)

Much of Negri's argument in *Marx beyond Marx* (and indeed much of his organizational writing during the seventies) constitutes a conjectural attempt to write the "book on the wage" that Marx never wrote, although "his whole work constantly returns to this theme" (p. 134).[19] Negri thereby applies the method of the tendency, derived from Marx, to Marx's own thought.

The wage must be understood as the result of intersubjective struggle. The dialectical transformation of the use value of labor into the exchange value of money-capital takes place during the working day, which, as we noted in the previous section, is an asymmetrical, differential category that is divided into the period of necessary labor and the period of surplus labor. The proportion between necessary and surplus labor is the object of continuous antagonistic struggle between workers and capitalists, first over the length of the working day and later over the form and intensity of labor during the working day.

> The theory of surplus value is in consequence immediately the theory of exploitation...Everything is in fact predisposed in such a way that the quantitative definition of surplus value, the division of the working day in two parts (*necessary labor* and *surplus labor*) do not appear as elements purely of doctrine but *as weapons in workers' struggle.* (P. 74)

The antagonism between necessary and surplus labor "is at once the key to the dynamism of the process and the insoluble limit of capitalist production and of the social order that corresponds to it" (p. 82) – it drives the capitalist production process and at the same time constantly threatens to destroy that process. But how?

The struggle over the proportion of necessary and surplus labor is the cornerstone of working-class composition. Negri sees this struggle as

> the heart of a first definition of the dynamic of the working class, where its essence as creator of value is engaged in a continual struggle which has as a result on the one hand the development of capital and on the other the intensification of the class composition, the enlargement of its needs and of its pleasures, the elevation of the value of labor necessary for its reproduction. (P. 73)

As he had long been arguing, capital's need to impose higher productivity on the working class in order to increase the amount of surplus value required both the class and capital itself to become generally socialized. Social capital, as Tronti had argued, expanded to encompass the entire society within the logic of the factory. Negri agreed: "It is through this passage that all social conditions are subsumed by capital, that is, they become part of its 'organic composition'" (p. 114). In the course of debates over the party form within Potere operaio and Autonomia, Negri had used Marx's concept of real subsumption in order to extend this analysis and clarify its implications. In parallel fashion, the working class, too, had been socialized, but the result of this socialization was not simply increased productivity. "The more work becomes abstract and socialized... the more the sphere of needs grows. Work creates its own needs and forces capital to satisfy them" (p. 133). The more socialized the working class, the more productive it is, and the more productive it is, the more it demands of capital – the attempt to increase the production of surplus value paradoxically results in its reclamation by workers. As Cesare Casarino has recently observed, Negri's claim here is dangerously close to an apology for consumerism, which is "one of the most effective solutions for the problems posed by the constant widening of the sphere of [workers' needs and] pleasures... Consumerism is the apparatus of capture used by capital to reclaim the broadening sphere of nonwork..." (Casarino and Negri 2008: 242). In order to retain its critical value, Negri's concept of proletarian self-valorization through the expansion of necessary labor must instead produce pleasure out of pleasure, not out of commodity consumption, which continues to valorize capital even as it meets proletarian needs (p. 243).

From the abstraction and socialization of labor emerges an alternative cycle of value and valorization, which acts independently of capital's consumerist cycle. This cycle of working-class self-valorization reverses the objectification process of capital at the level of exchange, turning objectified exchange values back into subjective use values designed to serve workers' needs, and thereby preventing the dead labor of exchange from accumulating into monetary instruments of command. "Necessary labor touches products and transforms them, through its own consumption, into use values. Only necessary labor has this capacity to oppose its own resistance to capitalist valorization, a resistance that is its own conservation and reproduction" (Negri 1984: 135). The cycle of self-valorization, in which the proletarian self-reduction of prices is a key moment, operates outside the large-scale circulation process that valorizes and increases capital, but within the circuits of working-class reproduction.

> Small-scale circulation is the space within which the sphere of needs related to necessary labor develops. Thus it takes form and constitutes itself dynamically, consolidates itself in the composition of labor power, in the composition of the working class. It reproduces itself and grows, finally defining itself as the potential of struggle. (P. 136)

For Negri, the culmination of this process of proletarian socialization and self-valorization is the recognition, on the part of the working class, that the only possible – though not inevitable – result of its radical antagonism toward socialized capital is a logic of separation. In such a situation, the wage no longer socially mediates the working class's integration into production but merely functions as a form of immediate command to enforce that integration.

> The first result produced by the logic of separation is to displace the relationship necessary labor/surplus labor to situate it at the level of the capacity of capital to subsume society, and to *transform the relation between two complete, opposed subjectivities* that are hostile to the point of destroying each other reciprocally. This is *impossible* for capital, which lives on exploitation. It is *possible* for the proletariat, whose power [*potenza*] becomes more and more immense as capital tries to destroy its identity. (P. 145)

As Negri constantly reminds us, the logic of dialectical antithesis and sublation implies the strict symmetry, opposition and mutual dependence of the two terms, and it results in an objective synthesis – one that reduces the working class to a subordinated object in order to empower capital as a dominant subject. Capital will always need the working class to produce surplus value, but the working class does not need capital to compel it to perform necessary labor. As sociologist Alberto Toscano puts it:

> What we have here is neither an organic dialectic nor a Manichean theory of pure antagonism. Rather we are introduced to the idea that capital is concerned with a *dialectical use of antagonism*, whose ultimate if utopian horizon is the withering away of the working class and the untrammeled self-valorization of capital; whilst the working class and its political vanguard aim at an *antagonistic use of antagonism*, which refuses precisely the capitalization of antagonism... (Toscano 2009: 115–16)

For Negri, capital is the source and beneficiary of all dialectics, and this is why he struggles to displace the dialectics of *Capital* from the authoritative position that they occupy in reformist socialism. The logic of antagonism, on the other hand, leads to the working class' separation or withdrawal – in his work on Empire, Negri calls this phenomenon "exodus" – from capital as a consequence of its recognition of the radical asymmetry between them. Although its subjectivity – that is, its composition – is *"modified by its relation with capital"* (Negri 1984: 123), the working class is ultimately autonomous and independent of capital, and therefore capable of destroying it.

The autonomy that Negri claims for working-class subjectivity has been criticized both by hostile readers and by Negri's allies. However, many of these criticisms rest on misunderstandings of Negri's constructivist conception of subjectivity. One of Negri's earliest critical supporters in the US, the deconstructive Marxist critic Michael Ryan, accuses him of operating "within the liberal ideology of a decontextualized subjectivity; his theory of the realization of communism as self-expression remains beholden to a notion of self-identity that is metaphysical from the perspective of the post-structuralist critique of the subject" such as Jacques Derrida's (Ryan 1989: 57). This is a curious charge to make in light of Negri's constant attention to the historical variations in class composition that underpin his claims regarding the tendency of revolutionary subjectivity. In *Marx beyond Marx*, to which Ryan refers but which he barely cites, Negri regularly reminds his readers that

"the subject here has nothing to do with the aforementioned sub-
stantialist and humanistic presuppositions: rather it is the product
of class struggle, it is the result of the relation between the worker's
extreme alienation and revolutionary insurgence" (Negri 1984:
112). The key distinction lies in Negri's understanding of alienation, not as an existential loss of some originary subjective essence
à la Lukács, but rather as the precarious and temporary blockage
of the innovative subjective power that he calls "invention-power,"
a power that is emerging according to the logic of the tendency. For
Negri, subjectivity is an ongoing historical project with neither a
transcendent teleology nor an essence. Rather,

> *subjectivity appears as a specific and organic element of the material class
> composition*: the subjectivity which expresses itself here is an element
> certainly revolutionary, but which is situated completely within the
> contradictory structure of the relations of production. The subject is
> able to develop itself, to liberate itself from the relations of produc-
> tion in so far as it liberates them and dominates them. The self-
> valorization of the proletarian subject, contrarily to capitalist
> valorization, takes the form of *auto-determination* in its development.
> (P. 162)

In light of this, Ryan's abstract description of Negri's model of class
composition as "a purely interiorist and essentialist model of subjectivity and materiality" (Ryan 1989: 58) seems little more than an
instance of what Derrida himself decries as a dogmatic summary.[20]

Against Althusser's consignment of subjectivity to the level of
ideology and against Ryan's inability to conceive subjectivity
outside the essentialism of the Cartesian tradition, Negri insists
that "[c]ommunism has the form of subjectivity, communism is a constituting praxis. There is no part of capital that is not destroyed by the
impetuous development of the new subject" (Negri 1984: 163).
"Constitution" is a term that Negri will use increasingly during the
eighties and nineties to define the emerging subject's process of
autonomous self-construction, and it must be grasped in relation
to his earlier work on constitutional law, labor and subjectivity,
from "Labor in the Constitution" to "Toward a Critique of the
Material Constitution."

> The universal individual of the class begins to appear here as an
> activity which valorizes him/herself through use value, then mas-
> sifies and raises the value of necessary labor to very rigid levels.
> His/her power carries in itself the end of all capitalist laws of equiv-

alence, of all possibility of rationally mystifying exploitation...The universal individual *can no longer appear* as the fruit of a humanist nostalgia: *he/she is the product of a materialist process* and we must connect to the materialist character of this analysis, every leap of quality, every qualitative deepening of the subject. (Pp. 180–1)

In constituting itself as communist subjectivity, the class subject defies, exceeds and then destroys the constitutional framework, both formal and material, within which capital sought to constrain it to permanent labor. Negri will later explicate this process in terms of the struggle between the constituent power of the working-class subject and the constituted power of capital, or – in Machiavelli's terms – between virtue and fortune; but the logic is the same.

What kind of political practice would such a self-constituting class subject carry out? Clearly not the takeover of the capitalist state and its fully subsumed social order, as former workerists like Tronti and Cacciari demanded and as the PCI hoped to achieve through its Historic Compromise. No; everything that Negri has proposed so far "leads to the theory of the social individual and of communism as the negation of the capital relation. *Not* as an inversion of capitalist command, *but* as an inversion of the relation between necessary labor and surplus labor, as the negation and reappropriation of surplus labor" (p. 149). That is, the aim of communist strategy and tactics cannot be simply to replace the capitalist management of exploitation with a worker-managed self-exploitation; such an achievement, as Negri had already argued in "Labor in the Constitution," would amount to the apotheosis of socialized capitalism and not to its abolition. Instead the aim of communist struggle must be the negation of surplus labor, which means the negation of work as both capitalism and reformist social-ism conceive it. Under genuine communism,

> [w]ork is no longer work, it is work which is liberated from work. The content of communism thus consists in a reversal which suppresses at the same time the object reversed. Communism is only reversal of work in so far as *this reversal is suppression: of work*. Liberation of the productive forces: certainly. But as a dynamic of a process which leads to abolition, to negation in the most total form. *Turning from the liberation-from-work toward the going-beyond-of-work forms the center, the heart of the definition of communism*. (P. 160)

Like capitalism, socialist reformism cannot abolish work because both depend on the continued subordination of necessary labor to surplus labor that defines work, and thus both depend on the continued objectification of the working class. On the contrary, "[t]he *refusal of work* constitutes the subject – in that it projects into the world, in that it *constitutes a mode of production*... Each step toward communism is a moment of extension and of expansion of the whole wealth of differences" that the proletarian subject expresses beyond its labor-power (p. 167).

By the end of his explication of the *Grundrisse* Negri has earned the right to be taken seriously as participant in the highest levels of theoretical debate within European Marxism, though whether he has earned the right to the stronger claim he makes in the book's final pages is open to dispute:

> We can thus advance today "beyond Marx" on this path that Marx posed from the first few cobblestones. But once the leap is done, the image of the realization of communism, its dynamic, has such a strong connotation that we must really, despite our own incredulity, repeat to ourselves: yes, we have gone beyond Marx. (P. 187)

This last claim has been received in antithetical ways. Jim Fleming, the editor of the English-language edition of *Marx beyond Marx*, described the book as "one of the most crucial documents in European Marxism since... well, since maybe ever" (in Negri 1984: vii). Harry Cleaver, one of its translators and also a prominent Marxist economist, insisted rather hyperbolically that, "[i]f Marx did not mean what Negri says he did, so much the worse for Marx" (in Negri 1984: xx). Other critics have been less laudatory, chief among them the socialist political philosopher Alex Callinicos, who first began to interrogate Negri's work after the publication of *Empire*. Most of Callinicos' critiques of Negri are focused on more recent writings and we will refer to them in later chapters; but in the essay "Antonio Negri and the Temptation of Ontology" (Callinicos 2007) he traces his disagreement with Negri back to Negri's work in the seventies, and particularly to *Marx beyond Marx*.

Much of Callinicos' argument against Negri's interpretation of the *Grundrisse* is concerned with restating the objectivist viewpoint that grants *Capital* greater credibility as a result of its greater intellectual maturity and logical consistency; but he also emphasizes the young Marx's confusion regarding the relative significance of the competition among *individual capitals* in relation to the struggle between *collective capital and labor* in the determination of profit (Callinicos 2007: 177–81). Throughout his analysis in *Marx beyond*

Marx and elsewhere, Negri, too, effectively ignores intercapitalist competition – perhaps as a consequence of the high level of collusion among large Italian employers and the Italian state during the sixties and seventies – and attributes the decline in the rate of profit almost exclusively to worker resistance, which, as we have seen, he views as radically independent of capital. Callinicos follows out the implications of that view by examining Negri's argument that successful workers' struggles have rendered the wage itself an "independent variable," which can only be determined politically – that is, as a result of relations of subjective force between classes and not as a result of objective market trends (Negri 1984: 131–2). This contradicts Marx's model in *Capital*, but it also appears to contradict Negri's claim, in *Domination and Sabotage*, that the wage was becoming a dependent variable as social capital used it to divide the working class into a privileged "labor aristocracy" in the large factories and an impoverished set of isolated workers scattered throughout the social factory. In Callinicos' view, this discrepancy is not just a technicality of textual exegesis, because it results in Negri's own effort to demonize the Italian "labor aristocracy," in a gesture that was symmetrical with the PCI's effort to demonize the extra-parliamentary left (see Negri 2005: 251). Thus both positions, the reformist and the workerist, exacerbated divisions that contributed decisively to the Italian workers' defeat, which concluded the seventies and defined the eighties and nineties (Callinicos 2007: 188–9). In going beyond Marx, Negri had left the real workers' movement behind as surely as the collaborators in the PCI had.

Negri's role in the endgame of the labor struggle of the seventies was negative, in Callinicos' estimation; but what about his proposals for the future direction of that struggle? In assessing the accuracy of *Marx beyond Marx* in anticipating the development of capitalism and class struggle during the eighties and nineties, Callinicos highlights two consequences that, for him, demonstrate the inadequacy of Negri's theory: "The intensification of international economic competition and the consequent disarticulation of national capitalisms have involved also a number of serious defeats for the organized working class from the late 1970s onwards" (p. 184). That is, the increasing importance of global market forces actually raised the level of competition among individual capitals, driving them to the new, harsher methods of worker control that constitute the toolbox of neo-liberalism, and one result of this (which Negri's later work indeed acknowledges) was the resounding, long-term defeat of the supposedly "independent" working class in many countries, including Italy.

Such defeats were still to come when Negri was writing the concluding paragraphs of *Marx beyond Marx*:

> The relation of capital is a relation of force which tends toward the separate and independent existence of its enemy: the process of workers' self-valorization, the dynamic of communism. *Antagonism is no longer a form of the dialectic, it is its negation ... It refuses the dialectic* even as a simple horizon. *It refuses all binary formulae.* The antagonistic process tends here to hegemony, *it tends to destroy and to suppress its adversary. Deny the dialectic*: that eternal formula of Judeo-Christian thought, that circumlocution for saying – in the Western world – rationality. In Marx we have read the most advanced project of its destruction, we have seen enormous steps forward in this direction. (Negri 1984:188–9)

Such forward steps were the last that Negri and his comrades would take for some time: a month before *Marx beyond Marx* was published, he was charged with fomenting armed insurrection against the powers of the Italian state and imprisoned, along with many of his colleagues from Padua's Institute of Political Science and hundreds of other militants, under draconian anti-terrorism legislation that ultimately succeeded in criminalizing and demolishing much of the Italian radical movements. His next steps forward would have to wait until after his unexpected release from prison and his flight into exile in France, where his developing interest in the Nietzschean poststructuralism of Michel Foucault and Gilles Deleuze would flower into a new version of (post-) workerist political theory. That effort would ultimately expand the concepts of class composition, tendency and real subsumption to a global scale, but only after a long detour through the history of philosophy, literature and religion.

4

From Solitude to Multitude

Negri was arrested on April 7, 1979, along with many of his colleagues from the University of Padua's Institute of Political Science, and charged with the kidnapping and assassination of former Italian Prime Minister Aldo Moro (one of the architects of the Historic Compromise, which Negri had so often denounced) as well as with "armed insurrection against the powers of the state." He was immediately placed in preventive detention at a maximum-security prison near Rome. His trial began on February 24, 1983, almost four years after his arrest, on charges that had mutated repeatedly in the interim.[1] Thousands of his fellow militants would be similarly incarcerated and tried collectively. The abrupt transition from the camaraderie of the vast Italian counter-culture to the isolation of prison challenged Negri's working methods and confidence as nothing had before. For nearly 20 years his intellectual work, even when it appeared in the individualistic form of academic scholarship, had been conceived and carried out collectively; but prison radically restricted the possibility of collective work, as well as access to the theoretical and cultural expressions of the political movements on which he had drawn. He addresses this forcible transition in his preface to the English-language edition of *Marx beyond Marx*, published in 1984. That book, he writes, was assembled from

> notebooks for lessons that I taught in the spring of 1978 at the École normale in Paris. It seems to me as though a century has passed

since then. Looking back at the book, I like it. But it is as though
another person had written it, not I. A free person, while I've been
in jail for centuries. (Negri 1984: xiv–xv)

The distance between the École normale, the most distinguished
educational institution in France, and Rebibbia Prison offers a met-
aphorical measure of the disjunction he has undergone. He goes
on to stage a brief dialogue between his free and his imprisoned
selves that concludes with the following confession: "Those who
feel they remain alone naturally hope. Hope of having said the
truth, and that the truth is revolutionary" (p. xvii).

The tone of the dialogue is not entirely elegiac. In fact, the Free
Man's last lines already point the way forward that Negri will take
out of the impasse of isolation. He says: "To be communist today
means *to live as* a communist." The Prisoner replies: "This, I think,
is possible even in prison. But not outside, at least until you free
us all." And the Free Man concludes: "You're right. *Marx beyond
Marx* says this too. But don't pretend to total impatience when you
know very well that theory allows you to cope" (pp. xvi–xvii).
Theory is exactly what Negri will use to cope with defeat and isolation, and the first fruits of that theoretical project will emerge from
his engagement with three figures who used their defeat and isolation to forge radical new conceptions of humanity, the world, labor
and value: the philosopher Baruch Spinoza, expelled from the
Amsterdam Jewish community for heresy; the physically handi-
capped poet and philologist Giacomo Leopardi, trapped by illness
in a remote and backward province of Italy; and the long-suffering
Job of the Old Testament, whose faith God tests by depriving him
of family and friends. Inspired by these precursors, Negri will not
merely preserve but expand his revolutionary vocation in an affirmative direction. His solitude, like theirs, will inspire innovation
and lead him to the concepts of constituent power and the multitude. Spinoza, Leopardi and Job allow him to build the bridge that
will carry him out of the residual Hegelianism of his militant period
and into the Nietzschean conceptual universe of Gilles Deleuze,
Félix Guattari and Michel Foucault. In short, the Negri of Empire
and biopolitics, the Negri who has earned the acclaim of a new
generation of militants, starts here. In what follows we will bring
some of the key reference points of that transition to light, and in
the process demonstrate how Negri "became what he is" – in a
Nietzschean sense.[2]

The Anomaly of Immanence

Negri has repeatedly acknowledged that his experience of imprisonment imposed a fundamental re-orientation on his thought by
isolating him from the social and political movements to which he
had dedicated more than a decade of his life and by depriving him
of most of the intellectual tools necessary to continue the militant
analysis of the present, which had preoccupied him during that
period. His only alternative was to turn back to his original scholarly training in the history of philosophy, but with a significant
difference. In the preface to *The Savage Anomaly*, the first book he
wrote in prison, he notes:

> It is incontestable that an important stimulus to studying the origins
> of Modern thought and the Modern history of the State lies in the
> recognition that the analysis of the genetic crisis can be useful for
> clarifying the terms of the dissolution of the capitalist and bourgeois
> State. However, even though this project did form the core of some
> of my earlier studies (on Descartes, for example), today it holds less
> interest for me. What interests me, in fact, is not so much the origins
> of the bourgeois State and its crisis but, rather, the theoretical alter-
> natives and the suggestive possibilities offered by the revolution in
> process. (Negri 1991: xx–xxi)

We might paraphrase this shift, in terms that Negri sometimes uses,
as a transition from the *pars destruens* – the destructive step of the
dissolution of the capitalist state – to the *pars construens* – the constructive step of constitutive ontology.[3] *The Savage Anomaly*, published in 1981, is the earliest and most visible manifestation of this
re-orientation.

*The Savage Anomaly: The Power of Spinoza's Metaphysics and Poli-
tics (L'anomalia selvaggia: Saggio su potere e potenza in Baruch Spinoza)*
is the counterpart, or inversion, of *Political Descartes*; these two
works bookend Negri's most intense period of political militancy.
Just as he had argued of Descartes, Negri insists that "Spinoza's
true politics is his metaphysics," but, unlike the metaphysics of
Descartes, who virtually never wrote directly on politics, "Spinoza's metaphysics is articulated in his political discourse" (Negri
1991: 217). While Descartes' philosophy, his "reasonable ideology,"
ultimately triumphed along with the bourgeoisie whose politics
and subjectivity it expressed, Spinoza's thought resisted the free

market and the absolutist state. This resistance constitutes its
anomaly, which depends upon the political and economic anomaly
of Spinoza's homeland in the seventeenth century. At the same time
as it was developing a vibrant mercantile economy, the tolerant
Dutch Republic, led by the De Witt brothers, resisted the imposition of monarchical absolutism longer than any other European
country, and that resistance defined the historical and social context
of Spinoza's philosophy. The Republic was a haven for religious
dissenters and for minorities who were actively persecuted elsewhere (including the recently relocated Iberian Jewish community,
from which Spinoza was expelled, and the English Puritans, who
would found the New England colonies in North America; see
Negri 1991: Ch. 1). As Negri characterizes it:

> Here there is still the freshness of humanism, intact. The freshness
> of the great humanism and the great Renaissance. There is still the
> sense of freedom and the love for freedom, in the fullest meaning of
> the term, precisely in the humanistic sense: constructing and reform-
> ing. (P. 6)

Spinoza's project, like Descartes', takes its point of departure from
the crisis of Renaissance humanism; but, unlike Descartes, Spinoza
does not betray the radical discourse of constructive modern
"virtue" in favor of the accumulative "fortune" of emergent
capitalism.

Nevertheless, Negri must contend with the long tradition of
philosophical historiography that interprets Spinoza as an individualist and a defender of the bourgeois conception of economic
freedom embodied in the market. In response to this tradition,
Negri argues that, just as there are two Descartes – the early humanist and the late bourgeois – there are also two Spinozas – an early
and a late one: "The first expresses the highest consciousness that
the scientific revolution and the civilization of the Renaissance
have produced; the second produces a philosophy of time-to-
come...The first is the author of the capitalist order, the second is
perhaps the author of a future constitution" (p. 4; translation modified). The first gives rise to the liberal ideology of Spinozism, while
the second serves as the critical link between Machiavelli and
Marx: "He is the attempt to determine the continuity of the revolutionary project of humanism" (p. 142). Spinoza's career is thus
the chiasmic inversion of Descartes'. In textual terms, the first
Spinoza is the author of the early works and the first two books of

the *Ethics*, while the second emerges from the metaphysical and political crisis that interrupts the *Ethics* in 1665 to compose the political works (the *Theological–Political Treatise* and the incomplete *Political Treatise*) as well as the last three books of the *Ethics*. Other Spinoza scholars, including some of Negri's supporters, have been skeptical of this tidy bio-bibliographical division. François Matheron points out that Spinoza continues to rely on the fundamental propositions from Books I and II of the *Ethics* when he composes the final three books (Matheron 1982: 23–5), and Manfred Walther criticizes Negri's periodization as an "interpreter's preconception" that is contradicted by Negri's own discussion of survivals from the first foundation in the later books (Walther 1990: 292). Pierre Macherey insists that "the two ethics that he situates as alternatives in relation to one another are... only two complementary formulations of one and the same affirmation, which has specifically eliminated every possibility of contradiction or opposition from his discourse" (Macherey 2007: 24). In response to these critiques, Negri was compelled to clarify that, "far from opposing one another frontally, these two lines tend to nourish one another reciprocally"; but he and many other scholars remain "convinced that two different structures of thought coexist in... the *Ethics*, and... that they can be referred to a probable caesura in the development of Spinoza's thought" (Negri 2004a: 101).

As Warren Montag notes, Negri's account is "the first recent attempt to move beyond textual analysis to a consideration of the historical and material circumstances of Spinoza's philosophical writing" (Montag 1998: 14). For all its originality, however, this account explicitly builds upon the work of earlier Spinoza scholars, most importantly Gilles Deleuze. In his preface Negri acknowledges the "innovative force" with which "Deleuze shows us a full and sunlit horizon of philosophy in Spinoza: He gives us the reconquering of materialism as the space of modal plurality and the concrete liberation of desire as a constructive power" (Negri 1991: xx), themes that Negri's own analysis will extend. Later he specifies that "[t]he great merit of Deleuze's approach is the fact that he grasps the dimension of the singularity and the surface of Spinoza's thought, bringing the system all the way to the point that we have called 'the paradox of the world' [as intensive power]...[W]ithout Deleuze's work, my work would have been impossible" (p. 267 n. 4). This represents Negri's first direct engagement with a contemporary who would become increasingly important not only to his own work in the history of philosophy, but also to his political reconceptualization of the present. Deleuze expressed reciprocal esteem for Negri's work in the preface he contributed to the French translation of *The Savage Anomaly*, in which he lauded it as a "great book that renews our understanding of Spinozism in many ways" and identified its focus on Spinoza's anti-juridical conception of power and its distinction between the early and late Spinozas as the element that made Negri "authentically and profoundly Spinozist" (Deleuze 1982: 9, 12; my translation).

Negri describes the early Spinoza's system as the "first foundation" (Negri 1991: Ch. 3); despite being less radical than the later system, it was radical enough to inspire widespread opprobrium. Early Spinoza defines God not as an anthropomorphic entity capable of intervening providentially into the world from a transcendent position outside it, but as the common substance underlying all reality: "*Deus, sive natura* [God, or nature]." This univocal or immanent conception of God denies all transcendence, and thus deprives God of the sovereign Power [in Latin *potestas, potere* in Italian] of command even as it equates God with the efficient causal power [in Latin *potentia, potenza* in Italian] of nature. Another way to think of this notion of Power is as an abstract possibility that includes, but is not limited to, what exists – while power is only what actually exists and happens. Spinoza's conception reduces the former to the latter, anticipating Nietzsche's argument that power always goes to the limit of what it can do.

> The absolute essence, predicated univocally, refers as much to the divine essence (the existence of God) as it does to all the things that descend from its essence. We are at a fundamental point, at a point in which the idea of power – as univocal order, as the dissolution of every idea of mediation and abstraction (which, instead, is the idea of Power) – leaps to center stage with enormous force. (P. 62)

The distinction between *potestas* and *potentia* that Negri locates in Spinoza will (along with Machiavelli's distinction between fortune and virtue and Marx's distinction between capital as dead labor and the living labor of the proletariat) form the basis for Negri's own subsequent distinction between constituted and constituent power, which we will examine below (pp. 149–64). (Although it has become widely influential, the *potestas/potentia* distinction is still controversial in Spinoza studies; Edwin Curley, translator of Spinoza's *Collected Works* into English, has argued thus: "It is unclear that a systematic examination of Spinoza's usage would confirm even a prima facie distinction between *potentia* and *potestas*" (Curley in Spinoza 1985: 651)).

Spinoza's immanent divine substance or power expresses itself in an infinite number of attributes, of which only two – thought and extension – are accessible to humans. Those attributes are subject to modification, limitation and variation, which constitute finite modes of the divine substance and which give rise to every entity that exists in the world and in the mind. These are themselves understood to be strictly parallel: whatever affects the body also affects the mind, and vice versa.

Up to this point Spinoza's early thought is internally consistent; but, as he moves from fundamental ontology to human practice, inconsistencies emerge. If, from a metaphysical viewpoint, all the apparently transcendent Power is really just immanent power, why are most human societies structured according to a transcendent model of Power, as hierarchy and command? How can something non-existent, a mere illusion, determine the form of the existing human world? In the first foundation, this problem is sublimated by means of an implicit reliance on Neoplatonic idealism. The categories and structures of human practice emanate formally from the divine substance, but they contain less reality than that substance, just as, for Plato, the sensible world is an unreal reflection of the ideal or intelligible world of forms. Human practice is an epiphenomenon, an after-effect that is incapable of being a cause or a source of knowledge. The problem with this solution is that it re-introduces hierarchical dualism – essence versus appearance, substance versus society – into a rigorously monistic system, and hence it requires some logic of mediation to resolve the opposition that emerges between the two terms. It verges upon a dialectical system. Consequently Negri associates the transcendence of *potestas*/Power not only with theological anthropomorphism, but also with the class hierarchy necessary for both absolutism and capitalism: the transcendence of Power over power in human society is, in Marxist terms, the command of the relations of production – essentially the private ownership of the means of production – over the productive force of human labor (Negri 1991: 137–40, 223–9). This is the aspect of the early Spinoza's thought that has been appropriated to legitimate capitalism:

We refer to this as an ideological function...for a fundamental reason: because this duplication of the intellect with respect to the world determines an image of the exaltation of the substance and

the degradation of the world that functions precisely toward the
stabilization of a relationship of Power (*potestas*), toward the determination of a system of command that is separated from the free
and open flux of the self-organization of reality...The categories of
being seem to mimic that special commodity: money. (Pp. 75–6)

Money is the instrument of mediation and command between
classes, between the owners of the means of production and those
whose labor actually produces, and it is the historical and political
mark of metaphysical dualism and dialectics, as Negri's earlier
work in political economy had argued.

Out of this contradiction emerges the "second foundation" of
Spinoza's metaphysics; but this foundation also emerges out of an
engagement with politics:

The ethics could not be constituted in a project, in the metaphysics
of the mode and reality, if it were not inserted into history, into politics, into the phenomenology of single and collective life: if it were
not to derive new nourishment from that engagement...From this
perspective, why would anyone be astonished by the fact that, in
the middle of the elaboration of the *Ethics*, Spinoza quits everything
and begins his political work (and biblical and theological criticism
is directly political work in these times)? (P. 84)

Spinoza stops working on the *Ethics* in order to write the *Theological–Political Treatise*, an analysis of Scripture and Hebrew history
that is dedicated to the critique of the superstitions and theological
prejudices on which political absolutism relies and to the defense
of the freedom of thought. In that *Treatise* he develops a sophisticated account of human imagination as the faculty that gives
human practice its essential reality. Although imagination can be
used ignorantly and passively, to generate and perpetuate superstitions that enslave the mind and the body, as Spinoza's scriptural
and historical analysis shows, it can also be used actively, to find
new ways of intervening into the reality of nature and society and
of transforming them. The imagination is the essence of politics;
and, likewise, Negri insists:

Politics is the metaphysics of the imagination, the metaphysics of
the human constitution of reality, the world. The truth lives in the
world of the imagination; it is possible to have adequate ideas that
are not exhaustive of reality but open to and constitutive of reality,
which are intensively true; consciousness is constitutive; being is not

only something found (not only a possession) but also activity, power; there is not only Nature, there is also second nature, nature of the proximate cause, constructed being. (P. 97)

This demonstration, central to the second foundation, restores to human practice its immanent metaphysical power and at the same time offers a new proof of the illusory nature of hierarchical Power. "Spinoza's philosophy evolves toward a conception of ontological constitution that, touching on the materiality of the world of things, eliminates that ambiguous metaphysical substratum that the ema-nationist residues...retain" (p. 59). Human nature is a second nature that we have made and continue to remake, and history is the trajectory of that indefinite process of (re)construction. In establishing this powerful conception of an anti-essentialist subjective agency, Spinoza's philosophy re-establishes its links with the constructivist humanism of the Renaissance. This new foundation permits Spinoza to complete the *Ethics* in a different key.

According to Negri, "[i]n Spinoza's theoretico-practical experience the *Ethics* is a philosophical *Bildungsroman*," just as the *Discourse on Method* was Descartes' *Bildungsroman* (p. 48). The stages of its composition reflect the changes of direction in Spinoza's thinking. Books III and IV of the *Ethics*, written after the interruption of the *Theological–Political Treatise*, focus on the construction of the human subject and its agency through an analysis of the relation between *conatus*, the drive to preserve and expand one's existence, and the affects. Negri argues that Spinoza's *conatus*, which is an individualistic concept in the first foundation, becomes a collective or communal concept in the second foundation, in that the subject of *conatus* can only become truly active in thought and practice within the framework of sociality or community. The threatening pressures of the state of nature (of which Spinoza conceives in a Hobbesian manner) must be reduced and transformed through collective labor in order for the joyful affects associated with increases in mental and bodily power to predominate over the sad affects produced by the loss of power.

This antagonism [of the state of nature], then, is itself constitutive. The autonomy of the subject is tempered, must be tempered, in the interhuman relationship...This passage is fundamental: The collective dimension dislocates the antagonistic process of being. The *multitudo* is no longer a negative condition but the positive premise of the self-constitution of right. (P. 194)

Negri focuses for the first time on *multitudo* ("multitude"), a term that he draws from Spinoza's *Political Treatise*, in *The Savage Anomaly*, where the word names the multiplicity of human singularities whose collective power produces the world of second nature. The concept will ultimately carry him a long way, as we will see.[4]

The concept of the multitude provides the thread that leads through Spinoza's entire political discourse, from the *Theological–Political Treatise* and the later books of the *Ethics* to the *Political Treatise* (see Negri 2004a: 39–42). Negri argues that Spinoza stands radically opposed to natural right and social contract theory, the dominant political philosophies of emerging capitalism in the seventeenth century.

> Spinoza's specific formulation evades and rejects what seem to be the fundamental characteristics of natural-right philosophies: the absolute conception of the individual foundation and the absolute conception of the contractual passage. And opposed to these absolute fundamentals, Spinozian thought proposes a physics of society: in other words, a mechanics of individual pressures and a dynamics of associative relationships, which characteristically are never closed... (Negri 1991: 109)

In other words, through the multitude Spinoza emphasizes the immanent and collective nature of subject formation, as opposed to the transcendent individualism of natural right and contractarian thought, and consequently he refuses to endorse the irreversibility of the contractual delegation of the subjects' power to the sovereign. Against Descartes, Hobbes and the majority of seventeenth-century political thinkers, Spinoza defines absolute government not in terms of transcendent Power, as absolutism, but in terms of immanent power, as democracy. "But this only means one thing: that the [contractual] passage has not enacted... a transfer of rights but only a displacement of powers. It is not the destruction of antagonisms but only their more complex organization" (p. 111). That is, the subjects who come together to form a society always retain their power to re-open the constitutive process and transform the social order – and themselves – when it suits them. Their antagonisms, the singular aspects of their differing subject positions and forms, are not dissolved into, or resolved within, the institutions of abstract sovereignty and legal rights, but merely captured temporarily by them.

Therefore, it is not absolutism that constitutes political society but the self-organization of the power of the individualities, the active resistance that is rationally transformed into a counter-Power, the counter-Power that is collectively developed in active consensus, the consensual praxis that is articulated in a real constitution. Natural antagonism constructs the concrete historicity of society, following the constitutive power of the collective imagination and its material density. (P. 112)

In democracy, which maximizes the possibility of joyful encounters that expand the mind's and the body's power of acting, the immanent powers of the multitude constitute a fluid and open social order based on active consensus, not the closed system of passive representation and command required by monarchic absolutism and by the bourgeois market.

The clarity and force of Spinoza's demonstration of democracy's absoluteness highlight the anomaly of his thought not only in the seventeenth-century context, but even today. Indeed Spinoza gives Negri a further argument for the polemic against the official labor movement that had preoccupied him so often over the course of the seventies. His disagreement with Tronti and Cacciari regarding the political autonomy that the Italian Communist Party (PCI) claimed in order to justify its participation in the Historic Compromise finds a powerful confirmation in Spinoza's resistance to the contractarian delegation of power and in his ontological justification of the continuous constituent antagonism.

The destruction of any autonomy of the political from the social and the affirmation of the hegemony and the autonomy of the collective needs of the masses: Here lies the extraordinary modernity of Spinoza's political constitution of reality. (P. 202)

The radical workers' movement, then, is an avatar of the insubordinate multitude. Through Negri's reading Spinoza, like Marx and Lenin, becomes a proto-workerist who provides conceptual tools for re-imagining and refounding working-class political organization, and Negri's scholarly historical study reveals itself to be a direct political intervention in the present. In this way, as Deleuze had already insisted (Deleuze 1988: 122–30), Spinoza remains very much our contemporary (see also Negri 2004a: 1–8, 113–17).

Despite the abstruseness of its subject matter, *The Savage Anomaly* has become one of Negri's most widely read works,[5] and in response to both its critics and its supporters Negri has often revisited Spinoza's writings to clarify or extend his reading. The most significant of these later meditations is his attempt to "complete" the chapter on democracy that Spinoza left unfinished at his death (much as he attempted, in *Marx beyond Marx*, to apply the "method of the tendency" to its originator and to write the book on the wage that Marx himself never wrote). Negri does this in two essays, namely *"Reliqua desiderantur*: A Conjecture for a Definition of the Concept of Democracy in the Final Spinoza" and "Democracy and Eternity in Spinoza," published in 1985 and 1994 respectively and included in his book *Subversive Spinoza*. Unlike Deleuze, who assimilates Spinoza's notion of consensus to the seventeenth-century concept of the social contract,[6] Negri insists upon the exclusion of contractarian theory from Spinoza's *Political Treatise*. Far from being equivalent to civil consensus, as Deleuze suggests, for Negri the social contract is "an explicit sociological fiction that legitimizes the effectiveness of the transfer of Power [from civil society to the state] and thus founds the juridical concept of the State" (Negri 2004a: 31). The fiction of the contract authorizes an irreversible alienation of natural right from social subjects to the state; and, because right, for Spinoza (and for Deleuze and Negri), is not a legal or juridical concept but rather a concept of power,[7] this alienation is also one in which powers – what singular minds and bodies can do – are regimented and normalized into the transcendent Power and abstract legality of the state.

On Negri's reading, Spinoza's concept of democracy rules out such irreversible transfer in advance: "The natural right of individuals, a universal given [as singular power], thus constitutes itself into public law by traversing the social antagonism [between individuals], not by denying it in some transcendental manner, but rather by constructing collective displacements" (p. 16). Subjects do not irreversibly confer their powers upon the sovereign State, but preserve them within a framework of consensus that unifies without representation: "Democracy...means, then, that there is no alienation of power – neither in relation to its exercise, nor in relation to its formation or the specificity of executive action" (p. 38). This negative definition, in terms of non-alienation, can also be expressed positively: democracy is "the liberation of all social energies in a general *conatus* of the organization of the freedom of all" (p. 37). From this point of view, "[l]egitimation is inalienably rooted in collectivity; only the collectively expressed *potentia*, only the creativity of the *multitudo* determines legitimacy" (p. 17). This means that, even when a state or institution has been constituted, it is not inoculated against the constitutive process of the multitude that gave rise to it. It is constantly and at every point (and not just at a few points and at strictly defined intervals) under threat of withdrawal of the civil consensus that constructed it.[8]

For Spinoza and Negri, this immanence and permanence of the collective constitutive process is what makes democracy the only genuinely absolute government. "Absolute" in this case does not refer to absolutism, which is the figure of the fixed and unalterable transcendence of the despot and the state, but rather to the unlimitedness of a continuous process of re-creation or re-invention – the imaginative transformation of any constitution, formal or material, into a second or third or nth constitution:

> democracy... determined *sub specie aeternitas*... [is] a metamorphosis that does not stop, that has no end – it increasingly affirms the power of the *"absolutum"* collective body, at the very moment in which it denies the presence of fear, terror, death... Therefore the *imperium democraticum*, because it is *omnino absolutum*, because it lives on eternity, is not limited to any [positive political] Constitution... but rather constantly transcends them all dynamically since it is ever more capable of perfection. (P. 111)

If it is not limited to any specific form of constitution (which would re-introduce a version of the irreversible contractarian transfer of right and power), then, rather than being one particular form of government among others, "the Spinozian definition of democracy is the definition of 'non-government'... [It] is not a form of government but rather a social activity of transformation" (ibid.). Spinozian absolute democracy is not any historically given actual form, but rather the asymptotic limit of the constitutive process. Thus it "can in no way be defined as a constitutional democracy, that is, as a form of government based on the division and balance of Powers and on their reciprocal dialectic" (p. 36), such as exists in contemporary democratic states. Democracy *sub specie aeternitas* is closer to what Marx called "permanent revolution" (see Marx 1973b: 323, 330). This asymptotic conception of absolute democracy has puzzled some of Negri's readers. While broadly sympathetic to his reading of Spinoza, Étienne Balibar is less sanguine about the consistency of this concept in practice: "From the moment that Spinoza – wishing to link theory to practice – begins to reflect on institutions, democracy is no more than the *limit* of the perfecting of aristocracy...Every state is 'absolute' to the extent that its structure realizes the democratic tendency. But democracy itself can never be defined except as a *perfect aristocracy*: an intrinsically contradictory concept" of highly ambiguous value and use (Balibar 1994: 24–5).

This objection has not dissuaded Negri from pursuing the further implications of the concept in his later work, in which the becoming-absolute of democracy only takes place through the becoming-multitude of the political subject. What would this project of becoming-multitude entail, philosophically and practically? Negri offers us several theoretical clues. First, the multitude as a collectivity is inclusive and open to the addition of the new powers/rights of new singularities: "The *multitudo*...is the foundation of democracy insofar as it allows individuals to introduce into society as a whole their own values of freedom. Each singularity is a foundation" (Negri 2004a: 44). This introduction of values strengthens the multitude and its constitutive process: "[democracy as] absolute is constitution, a reality formed by a constitutive tension, a reality whose complexity and openness increase as the power that constitutes it increases" (p. 34). Such increase in complexity and power can only happen as a result of the non-alienated and non-representational consensus that constitutes the multitude. The representational alienation of the contract or fixed constitution can only become weaker and less complex (in the quality of its power, not in its abstract quantity) by expanding so as to include other singularities, and thus it resists such expansion. One axis of absolute democratic practice is oriented in this direction, toward an ever greater inclusion of singularities, both within and beyond the borders of constituted states.

Second, the consensus of the multitude is not a static agreement or a quantified majority, but an energetic vector that results from the paradoxical co-existence of two linked but incommensurable movements: "one movement presses with great force toward absoluteness in the strict sense, toward the unity and indivisibility of government...But the other movement of power is plural; it is the reflection on (and the recovery of) the powers of the *multitudo*" in all the diversity of its component singularities (p. 38). More precisely (and paradoxically),

> the *multitudo* is...a juridical subject, a necessary attribute of the social, a hypothesis of political unity and constructiveness...But at the same time the *multitudo* remains an elusive set of singularities[,]

an infinity [whose] power is a continuous movement – an infinite movement that constitutes a totality but is identified in it only as the actuality of a passage; it is not closed but open; it produces and reproduces. (P. 40)

The multitude is not an object of majoritarian state administration but an open process of production and reproduction of its own elements, a discontinuous and unending negotiation that generates always temporary and precarious constitutional frameworks and institutional instruments. This unending process of minoritarian negotiation constitutes the "becoming-eternal" of absolute democracy (p. 111).

From the viewpoint of economic and political stability, such an unending process appears as an abyss of anarchy that constantly threatens to open up beneath or around states and their unifying market; but Negri insists that philosophers and militants should instead "consider the non-conclusiveness of the relationship between [the multiple singularities of] social praxis and the [unified] juridical subject of Power as a metaphysical condition of absoluteness [and] the *absolutum* [as] the presence of the political process in its entirety" (p. 50) – that is, consider absolute democracy as a challenge and an opportunity to undertake a delirious Jeffersonianism: no longer merely "Every generation its own constitution," but a constantly mutating constitutive process – something like Deleuze's "ideal game," in which "there are no pre-existing rules" and "each move invents its own rules" (that game that is "the reality of thought itself": Deleuze 1990b: 59–60).

The engagement with Spinoza is second only to the engagement with Marx in its importance for Negri's development. This is because, first of all, Spinoza gave Negri the initial tools for a reconstruction – we might say a second foundation – of his own theoretical and militant agenda. In other words Spinoza's theory, and the other theories to which it led, allowed Negri to cope with defeat and isolation and to go beyond them. His revived optimism can be recognized in many passages from *The Savage Anomaly* and from *Subversive Spinoza* – passages like the following: "The prison of the world is destroyed, its bars and its mechanisms of closure are broken open. The world is a flat present, predisposed to and capable of grasping the tension of the ethical being, as a full project tending toward the future" (Negri 1991: 167). Indeed, at the very start of the project he announced its double intention: to "construct 'beyond' the tradition of bourgeois thought" and to construct "a

'beyond' for the equally weary and arthritic tradition of revolutionary thought itself" (pp. xix–xx) – an intention intimately linked to
his own situation as a political prisoner: "I would like...to think
that the solitude of this damned cell has proved as prolific as the
Spinozian solitude of the optical laboratory" (p. xxiii). Spinoza
allowed Negri to begin transforming his own solitude into a radical
concept of the multitude – a process that he would extend for three
decades.

Second, Spinoza allowed him to escape from the shadow of
Hegel and from the dialectics that haunted his political work of the
seventies. For Negri, Spinoza's philosophy is

> a postbourgeois philosophy. [Pierre] Macherey calls it a postdialecti-
> cal philosophy. And so it is, because the dialectic is the form in which
> bourgeois ideology is always presented to us in all of its variants –
> even in those of the purely negative dialectic of crisis and war. The
> materialistic transfiguration that Spinoza accomplishes on the revo-
> lutionary contents of humanism pushes his philosophy beyond any
> dialectical form...(P. 20)

How does Spinoza accomplish this? By denying "the relationship
constitution–mediation, that is to say, the basis of the concept of
bourgeoisie itself. The Spinozian alternative does not have to do
with the definition of the bourgeoisie but with the essence of the
revolution – the radical character of the liberation of the world"
(p. 158). Only a dualist or dialectical system requires mediation to
shore up its illusions of transcendence and fixed sovereignty, and,
by rigorously eliminating all dualism, Spinoza has eliminated
mediation and thereby foreclosed Hegelianism – as well as the
objectivist dialectical Marxism of *Capital*. Like Marx's *Grundrisse*,
which privileges non-dialectical antagonism over contradiction,
Spinoza's "*Ethics* is a methodological work, not because its prolix
geometrical method is a paradigm for research but, rather, because
it is an open work, a definition of a first sketch of the human task
of appropriating and constructing the world" (p. 213). Like Marx,
Spinoza provides Negri with a method oriented toward future
innovation, a method of the tendency, and at the same time submits
productively to that method himself. Beyond Marx we find a new
Marx, and beyond Spinoza we find a new Spinoza.

Lastly, Spinoza is a key figure for Negri because he provides
the terms for an intellectual alliance both with Althusser's circle
(chiefly Macherey and Balibar, both of whom have written exten-

sively on Spinoza) and with that of Deleuze (including Guattari and Foucault, who did not).[9] Following Negri's release from prison in 1983 (when he won a seat in the Italian parliament) and his subsequent flight to France, these new connections would lead not only to direct collaborations – for example with Guattari on *Les nouveaux espaces de liberté* (*New Lines of Alliance, New Spaces of Liberty*: Guattari and Negri 1985) – and to the founding of the journal *Futur antérieur* in 1990, but also to a broader adoption of the Nietzschean elements active in the thought of both circles, especially Foucault's concept of biopower. We will examine this aspect of Negri's self-transformation next.

Poetics as Ontology

The work on Spinoza is unquestionably crucial; but, to grasp the full extent of Negri's re-orientation, readers must engage the other works that bear the imprint of his prison experience, especially the 1987 *Lenta ginestra: Saggio sull'ontologia di Giacomo Leopardi* (*Gentle Broom: An Essay on Giacomo Leopardi's Ontology*) (Negri 2001) and the 1990 *Labor of Job* (Negri 2009b) – works of essentially literary or poetic analysis, which lay the groundwork for what we might call the "linguistic turn" his thought has taken as part of its *pars construens*. These works, conceived in prison but completed in exile, constitute the next stage of Negri's self-transformation. As he himself admits, "[i]t is Job who enabled me to explore that terrain of French theory of freedom on whose basis *Insurgencies* and then *Empire* would advance. It is Job who led me to a close friendship with Foucault, and then with Guattari and Deleuze, which would encourage me to attempt a synthesis" of French theory and Italian practice (Negri 2009b: xxiii). Negri's work on Spinoza has been widely analyzed, but his "linguistic turn" has attracted little attention, despite the fact that it forms the basis for his influential work on immaterial labor and network resistance.[10]

The most striking aspect of Negri's re-orientation that is bound up with his "linguistic turn" is the shift in his attitude toward the tradition of French Nietzscheanism, especially toward the work of Deleuze, Guattari and Foucault. In his pre-prison writings references to these thinkers are few and tend to be ambivalent, as in the account of Foucault in his 1977 essay "Sul metodo della critica della politica" ("On the Method of the Critique of Politics," now in Negri 1982: 70–84) or in *Domination and Sabotage* (Negri 2005: 239), whereas after his relocation to Paris Negri begins to place Deleuze's logic of immanence and Foucault's conceptions of biopower and biopolitics at the center of his own project. This rapprochement can be understood as an *ad hominem* consequence of the fact that it was the philosophical circle around Deleuze, especially Félix Guattari, that most fully embraced and supported Negri before his imprisonment and during his Parisian exile: this attitude resulted from shared political convictions as well as from the convergence between Negri's interpretation of Spinoza and Deleuze's own (see Negri and Dufourmantelle 2004: 42–50). To understand the shift *ad rem* is more complicated, however, given Negri's prior ambivalence toward Foucault's (and even more toward Massimo Cacciari's)[11] Nietzschean methods – and also the apparent absence of Nietzsche from his own earlier philosophical frame of reference. Indeed, Negri has only ever written one essay on Nietzsche: "Marxistes: une approche paradoxale" ("Marxists: A Paradoxical Approach"), published in 1992, is a brief account of Marxist responses to Nietzsche from Lukács onward. Such a brief – and belated – textual engagement with Nietzsche cannot fully account for the shift in Negri's philosophical perspective.

Yet, in the course of a careful analysis of that single essay on Nietzsche, Judith Revel shows that Negri "found in Nietzsche a reformulation of the link between subjectivity and production from the viewpoint of creation, a violent polemic against a dialectical understanding of history, and a radical critique of real socialism in all its varieties" (Revel 2007: 91–2). Central to this approach is the practice of reading Nietzsche "no longer from within a modernity for which he would serve as the signifier of a profound crisis, decadence or alternately even the horizon of redemption, but instead in an *anti-modern* manner," which entails the affirmation of "the necessity of overcoming modernity, or…the idea that a different model of modernity was possible" (p. 91).[12] In terms of Nietzsche's concepts, this approach focuses not on the eternal return or on the overman, but rather on "the will to power as the subjective power of creation and inauguration and the construction of a model of historicity that functions as a critique of scientific positivism and of the Hegelian dialectic at the same time" (p. 91). She goes on to explain clearly how, "[o]n the basis of this double lineage – a 'French-style' historicism of which Foucault will become the most striking figure, and a Spinozism of power that owes so much to Deleuze – we can understand Negri's Nietzscheanism" (p. 104).

A question remains, though: what is the immediate source of these Nietzschean elements in Negri's writings? They don't arise from direct engagements with Nietzsche; even Negri's post-prison writings contain only occasional and peripheral references to Nietzsche, often framed by Heidegger's reading (which is radically different from the French readings). They don't seem to arise from explicit reconsiderations of the Nietzschean elements in Deleuze and Foucault either; by the time Negri begins to write about his new allies, the re-orientation has already taken place. Yet Revel is undoubtedly right to describe Negri as a "French Nietzschean," and we will argue that the source of the Nietzschean elements that she identifies – (1) an "untimely" critique of dialectical and scientistic history; (2) an implacable antagonism toward the abstract administration of life; and (3) a conception of subjectivation and ontology as imaginative creation or *poiesis* – lies precisely in his interpretation of the philologist, essayist and poet Giacomo Leopardi. As Revel notes in passing, the "anti-modern" interpretation of Nietzsche "was first inferred by Mazzino Montinari [the Italian co-editor, with Giorgio Colli, of the definitive edition of Nietzsche's works], in the wake of the approach that [Cesare] Luporini and [Sebastiano] Timpanaro had applied to the works of Giacomo Leopardi, which could be considered in many ways as anticipating those of Nietzsche" (Revel 2007: 91). Thus we are claiming that Leopardi serves Negri as an anticipatory stand-in for Nietzsche, one who connects Negri's work to the thoroughly non-Hegelian works of Foucault and Deleuze. In addition, Leopardi compels Negri to confront for the first time the constitutive role that language plays in the production of subjectivity and community. Leopardi thereby provided Negri with many of the same theoretical tools that Nietzsche gave to Deleuze and Foucault, and consequently he made possible Negri's new line of alliance and his "linguistic turn" despite his minimal direct engagement with Nietzsche.[13]

In spite of his canonical stature in the history of Italian poetry, where he is lauded as the peer of Dante and Petrarch, Leopardi is not widely known in the Anglophone world; so it is not surprising that Negri's study of Leopardi has been ignored by Anglophone critics. Some background may therefore be in order. Leopardi was born into an aristocratic family, in the provincial town of Recanati, in 1798 and, after struggling most of his life to escape that suffocating environment, he died in Naples in 1837. Aside from brief periods of study with tutors, he was almost entirely self-taught in the fields of his greatest achievement, namely classical philology, the history of philosophy and poetry. Indeed, so intense was his solitary study that it permanently impaired his physical health and contributed to his early death. His poetic output was small – 36 poems, primarily in the lyric mode, which occupy fewer than 50 pages in his collected works – but it is extended and enriched by his prose writings, most importantly his *Moral Essays* and his massive, posthumously published notebooks, the *Zibaldone*. His prose writings in particular reveal his assiduous study of the anti-idealist philosophies that contributed essential elements to his own materialist metaphysics: Locke's critique of innate ideas, Condillac's sensism, the Enlightenment materialism of La Mettrie and d'Holbach – and others.[14]

Like his study of Spinoza, Negri's account of Leopardi's development stresses its discontinuities. Whereas in Spinoza he identified a later, immanent and productive "second foundation" that displaced the first, Neoplatonic and emanationist foundation of the *Ethics*, in Leopardi he identifies five stages of nonlinear development:

> In the first period Leopardi confronts the dialectical culture of the beginning of the nineteenth century; in the second he shifts his focus toward a radical sensualist theory, with points of extreme pessimism; in the third and fourth periods Leopardi attempts, with various different motivations, to develop an approach to history and strives to reconstruct an ethical perspective; in the fifth period, he theorizes human community and the urgency of liberation. (Negri 2004a: 77 n. 23)

Leopardi's last great poem, "La ginestra, o il fiore del deserto" ("The Broom, or the Flower of the Desert"], recapitulates this process of development, and in so doing it serves as the culmination of Negri's account of the poet's poetic, political and philosophical project. We will refer to "The Broom" in laying out the broad outlines of what we are calling Leopardi's anticipatory Nietzscheanism.

Nietzsche himself was well aware of his predecessor's achievements and described Leopardi as "perhaps the greatest stylist of the century" (Nietzsche 1911: § 63) and as "the modern ideal of a philologist" (§ 10). This tribute is particularly significant, because it arises in the context of Nietzsche's meditation on their shared profession, classical philology, whose methods led them to remarkably similar conclusions regarding history, society and existence.

For example, Nietzsche's conception of the "untimely" has been widely influential, but readers often forget that he first presented it precisely as the critical power of classical philology: "I do not know what meaning classical studies could have for our time if they were not untimely – that is to say, acting counter to our time and thereby acting on our time and, let us hope, for the benefit of a time to come" (Nietzsche 1983: 60). In the second *Untimely Meditation*, from which that quotation is drawn, Nietzschean untimeliness takes the form of a virulent critique of the positivistic, teleological "science" of history, denounced as the desubjectified accumulation of indifferent data that fossilizes life in the present and denies it a future. Contrasting this science to the ancient Greeks' subordination of history to life, Nietzsche traces the problem back to Hegelian philosophy of history – the inevitable coming to consciousness of spirit in its dialectical passage through matter and time, which culminates in the non-culture of the nineteenth century:

> The belief that one is a latecomer of the ages is, in any case, paralyzing and depressing; but it must appear dreadful and devastating when such a belief one day by a bold inversion raises this latecomer to godhood as the true meaning and goal of all previous events... [F]or Hegel the climax and terminus of the world-process coincided with his own existence in Berlin. (Nietzsche 1983: 104)[15]

A generation before Nietzsche, almost contemporaneous with Hegel, Leopardi was already thinking in an "untimely" fashion, on the basis of his own youthful studies in classical philology. As Negri sees it, Leopardi responds to the "catastrophe of memory" that is the confused aftermath of the Enlightenment, of the French Revolution and of the Napoleonic restoration in an anti-Hegelian – and anti-modern – way. Negri insists:

> The dialectic shatters the confusion of historical time, intervening into the catastrophe of memory and, with Hegel, re-ordering everything... the difference is resolved into a sublime, reasonable overdetermination of the totality of development. The historical delay allows Hegel to conceive philosophy as the "owl of Minerva" that explores, re-organizes and sanctifies historical effectiveness. The confusion and error of memory become the logic of history. (Negri 2001: 31, my translation)

The synthesizing teleology of Hegel's dialectical history transforms the unpredictable whiplash of revolution and reaction into an

epiphenomenon of linear development, turning history into a ruse
of reason and reducing the constituent power of the revolutionary
movement to the constituted power of the state. While Leopardi,
like Hegel, displaces the historical catastrophe, moving it onto the
metaphysical plane, for him "this translation of the event leaves the
problem open and indicates, within the time of the dialectic, not a
logical solution but an ethical opening"(ibid.) toward the future.
This opening is the immanent and material space in which subjective agency is constructed, as we will see shortly. Leopardi's commitment to poetic creation and ethical practice over logical closure
leads him to attack the teleological progressivism that his era was
just beginning to learn from Hegel. In "The Broom" he ironically
presents the unstable landscape around Vesuvius as a depiction of

> the impressive destiny
> and fated progress of the human race.
> Here see yourself reflected,
> Proud century and stupid,
> You who have left the way
> Where man's renascent thought had made its mark
> And signaled you to follow, you who take
> Some pride in moving backwards
> And even call it progress. (Ll. 50–8)[16]

The desolate environs of the volcano provide a figure for the historical regression that Leopardi sees driving the Hegelian narrative
of Absolute Spirit coming to self-consciousness. Leopardi's allusion
to Renaissance humanism here, like the untimely openness of his
concept of history, connects his project to Spinoza's.

One of the main objects of Leopardi's untimely critique of progressive history is what Negri will later call, following Foucault,
biopower. Biopower names the institutional management of life
that develops in the course of the nineteenth century through the
sciences of public health, education and administration, disciplines
that become key weapons in the arsenals of the liberal democratic
reformists and of the monarchist reactionaries alike. Leopardi
denounces what he calls the "statistical" approach of these sciences
as a project for producing docile, interchangeable social and political subjects for the European nation states, which were still being
consolidated, by both democrats and monarchists, during his lifetime. For Leopardi, this project exemplifies the subordination of
critical reason to the institutional unreason of the despotic state,

which Negri calls a "false illusion" that must be fought in the name of the "true illusion" of the revolutionary community (we will return to this point below). Linked to his denunciation of statistics is Leopardi's attack on mass-market journalism as a tool for molding public opinion, which resembles Spinoza's critique of superstition in the *Theological–Political Treatise* and anticipates Benedict Anderson's identification of the modern nation form with the rise of "print capitalism" (see Anderson 1983: Ch. 3). Leopardi's contempt for both aspects of this project of modernity leads him to parody the culmination of Italian progressivist ideology, the *Risorgimento* – the unification of the Italian nation that was underway during his lifetime – in his mock-epic "The War of the Mice and the Crabs" (see Negri 2001: 182–202). This contempt for the structural unreason of the progressivist/nationalist project appears in "The Broom" as a bitter address to the administrators of human life:

> You dream of liberty, but also wish
> To enslave that thought by which
> Alone we rose a little
> Above barbarity, by which alone
> We grow in civil living, and which only
> Betters the people's lot. (Ll. 72–7)

In Leopardi's untimely critique of statistics and mass administration we can hear echoes of Nietzsche's later critique, in *Beyond Good and Evil*, of socialism and democracy as continuations of the ascetic ideal and as "heir[s] of the Christian movement" against life. Moreover, the anarchists, for Nietzsche,

> seem opposites of the peacefully industrious democrats and ideologists of revolution, and even more so of the doltish philosophasters and brotherhood enthusiasts who call themselves socialists and want a "free society"; but in fact they are at one with the lot in their thorough and instinctive hostility to every other form of society except that of the *autonomous* herd…(Nietzsche 1968: 306)

Although Nietzsche does not focus on statistics and journalism, as Leopardi does, he identifies a similar threat in mass or "herd" democracy: the threat of de-differentiation, the reduction of difference for purposes of command and control. Nietzsche calls the statisticians of life "levelers" (p. 244) whose work "will on average lead to the leveling and mediocritization of man – to a useful, industrious, handy, multi-purpose herd animal" (p. 366). This process transforms the singular elements of the multitude into a generic unity, "the people" – *Volk* (a process that Michael Hardt and Negri will further analyze in *Empire*; see chapter 5, pp. 182–3). Nietzsche's critique of the "disease" of German nationalism, and of nationalism in general, is well known (see for example Nietzsche 1968: 377), but Leopardi's parallel critique anticipated it by a half-century.

Finally, we come to the anti-dialectical alternative to progressive or teleological history and to the statistical administration of life that Negri finds in Leopardi's "metaphysics of constitution" (Negri 2001: 217, my translation). The explication of that metaphysics or ontology, which occupies the whole of *Lenta Ginestra*, is too complex to follow in detail here, but Negri summarizes it as a prelude to his close reading of "The Broom" at the end of the volume. His analysis identifies three key steps that have clear Nietzschean resonances. The first step is

> a complete and radical revision of the concept of nature. [In Leopardi] it appears not as a unitary essence but rather immediately as a split, as one of the masks of the vicissitudes of being[,] and it is implicated in the catastrophe that constitutes its essence...This concept of nature is set before us as a context of alternative values that must be distinguished. Nature is something split, therefore it is the terrain of a choice to which we are pressed or rather constrained by the possibility of destruction and death that it implies. (Pp. 216–17, my translation)

Leopardi sees nature not as an undifferentiated unity opposed to human civilization, nor as the subordinated counterpart of a triumphant dialectical reason, but rather as an active nothingness, a faceless, non-subjective, quasi-Hobbesian antagonism toward all of its productions (including the human subject), "the ruin of all rational consistency" (p. 206, my translation), which bears comparison to Nietzsche's conception of the "original Titanic divine order of terror," "the terror and horror of [non-individuated] existence" delineated in *The Birth of Tragedy* (Nietzsche 1968: 42). In "The Broom," this conception of nature is figured as "Vesuvius the destroyer" (l. 3), whose lava flows obliterated Pompeii but later provided fields where the broom grows – though only until the next eruption. The volcano's slope starkly displays "How humankind is held / In nature's loving hand": nature is both life and death, strength and weakness, creation and destruction, and the immanent difference between those aspects offers the possibility of a choice, a selection or affirmation within and against nature that produces the human subject – which is figured as, but also contrasted with, the gentle broom itself, "denizen of the desert" (l. 7) – caught in the struggle of life against death. This conception of a differentiating and differentiated nature entails many of the same consequences as Nietzsche's ontological conception of will to power,[17] and also lays the foundation for a link with Spinoza's immanentist account of human nature as a constructed and malleable second nature.

From this split in nature a second step follows, which concerns the subject in its relation to nature, the subject that stands up to it or struggles against it. The poetic imagination constitutes the subject, empowering it to resist nature's terror.

> In the constitutive passage that we are now beginning to verify between the critical event – that is, the recognition of a gap in knowledge faced with the nothingness in which the spirit threatens to founder – and an ethical act, a constructive gap opens up, an attempt not merely to escape nothingness but rather, on the basis of this separation, an attempt to constitute the schema of the ontological imagination emerges. (Negri 2001: 217, my translation)

Negri sees Leopardi's ontology as being opposed not only to the Hegelian teleology of Absolute Spirit, but also to the source of its apotheosis of reason, namely Kant's Transcendental Analytic, which subordinates the imagination, regarded as a purely instrumental faculty, to legislative reason. Against this, Leopardi presents the imagination as an ontological activity that responds to the antagonism of nature by creating active illusions for its own survival.[18] Negri explicates the power of poetry in this ontology:

> If we return to Kantian terminology, this means that the Transcendental Aesthetic, far from seeking the analytic or demanding that it complete the possible deduction of the subject, instead opposes the analytic, recognizes it as a hostile function, as a mystifying trap from which it must free itself or preferably avoid altogether. In the critical making [fare] of poetry, the Transcendental Aesthetic reveals the essence of the subject, its opening to the world, to the imagination, to the true illusion and against the analytic prison of the logically true. (P. 208, my translation)[19]

These poetic illusions, "illusions which we have forgotten are illusions," correspond closely to the genealogy of truth that Nietzsche outlines in "On Truth and Lies in a Nonmoral Sense" (Nietzsche 1979: 84); they constitute a Spinozan second nature, a transformed or re-constituted world within which the subject can survive and thrive. This is Leopardi's way of assenting, in advance, to Nietzsche's claim that "it is only as an *aesthetic phenomenon* that existence and the world are eternally *justified*" (Nietzsche 1968: 52), if we understand "justified" to mean "made livable for particular forms of life."

But distinctions arise and choices between affirmation and negation must be made within second nature as well, ethical choices between "true and false illusions," which correspond to the Nietzschean choices between "good," life-affirming illusions and "bad," pathological ones (and to the Spinozan choices between joyful and sad encounters and the passions to which they give rise). This is the third and final step of Leopardi's constitutive ontology. Negri clarifies:

> The nature-subject antagonism is dynamic and open as a result of a double rupture: first on the side of nature, by a series of radical alternatives that oppose the values of positive and negative, life and death, youth and age; then on the side of the subject moving between nothingness and the being of consciousness, seeking life and opposing death. It seeks to understand the relation that ties it to nature across the complexity of exclusions, alternatives and ethical choices that compose this relation. (Negri 2001: 217, my translation)

Such ethical choices figure in "The Broom" as the contrast between humankind's arrogant theological–political belief that humanity itself is "the lord and end of all" (l. 189) for whose sake "the authors of the universe came down, / ...and held a conversation" (ll. 192–3) and the humble and immanent lesson of the broom, whose head

> was never bowed before
> In craven supplication and in vain
> To the oppressor [= nature]; never held erect
> Either, in crazy pride towards the stars. (Ll. 307–10)

This contrast in the poem also marks the persistence of Leopardi's critique of the Judeo-Christian God as an anthropomorphic projection of human subjectivity onto nature, which prefigures Nietzsche's declaration of the "death of God" (see Nietzsche 1974: §§ 109 and 125) and converges with Spinoza's critique of religious superstition as well.

The ultimate expression of the ethical demand to choose "true illusions" consists in the impulse toward community as a new collective subject; and this is the point at which Leopardi's thought most significantly diverges from Nietzsche's, at least as the latter is most often understood. As Negri sees it, "[t]he ethical community is born, positively, in the separation," the fissure or gap in nature that only the constitutive imagination can fill:

> the necessity of the "common war" [against nature as catastrophe] posits the conditions of solidarity and, through it, freedom...The community, therefore, is opposed to nature to the point that it is born from the conflict itself. The community is the collective subject that constructs itself within the horizon of the war. (Negri 2001: 220–2, my translation)

This conception of community appears in Leopardi's work for the first time in "The Broom"; like Spinoza, he turns his attention to the issue of political community only at the end of his life and in ambiguous terms, which have been interpreted in traditional nationalist ways by many of his readers. The identification of nature as the inescapable and undefeatable common enemy is, however, clear:

> He is a noble being
> Who lifts – he is so bold –
> His mortal eyes against
> The common doom, and with an honest tongue,
> Admits the evils of our destiny,
> Our feeble lowly state;...
> But fixes guilt where it belongs, on Mother
> Nature: mother because she bears us all,
> Stepmother, though, by virtue of her will.
> She is his enemy. (Ll. 111–17, 123–6)

On Negri's reading, because of the disproportion of power between nature and humankind (registered explicitly in the poem's meditation on infinity in lines 167–83), the only effective resistance to such an enemy lies in community:

> since he [= the noble being] thinks,
> What is the simple truth,
> Mankind has been united, organized,
> Against her from the first,

> He sees all men as allies of each other,
> And he accepts them all
> With true affection, giving
> The prompt assistance he expects from them
> In all the varying danger and the troubles
> Their common war gives rise to. (Ll. 126–35)

The broom, too, reflects this recognition of the power of community to promote the powers of its component singularities – at the start of the poem, the flowers are "spread...in solitary tufts" (l. 5), but by the end they grow into "sweetly scented thickets" (l. 298).

This ethical affirmation of community is predicated not on pure or practical reason, but on the aesthetics – or rather the poetics, which is to say the *poiesis* or imaginative "making" [*fare*] – of empowering "true illusions." Such practical empowerment is the only possible immanent meaning of truth for Leopardi, as it is for Nietzsche. As Negri says: "The true can only be constituted in making. It only exists as subordinate to making" (Negri 2001: 208, my translation). The ontological making, construction or *poiesis* at stake here goes far beyond the literary genre of poetry, but it does include poetic language as a privileged instance. At the close of his study, Negri sums up its results as follows:

> In a materialist universe, truth is a name and the universal is a con-vention, but poetry, on the contrary, is a concretization, a process of construction. Poetry is the conclusion of a making within the con-crete and within immediacy. Thus every truth has a poetic aspect from the moment it becomes real...Ethical practice is situated between poetry and the true. It is a "making" set in motion by freedom that determines the constitution of the true. (P. 227, my translation)

Accordingly, poetry not only constitutes the true but also gives history an immanent meaning and direction:

> To confer a sense on history, poetry must appear as an act of the practical constitution of being, not as a handmaid of the true but as productive of the true in the practical and material sense. In this way it constitutes a significant ontological activity...It is the voice of an analytical making whose comprehensive material and constitutive force extends from sense to feeling, from experience to history. (Negri 2001: 203–4, my translation)

Therefore poetry is the aesthetic justification of existence and the world that Nietzsche demanded of Greek tragedy, as well as the necessary counter-power – both to the dialectical reduction of history to linear progress and to the biopolitical administration of life.

This Nietzschean insistence on the productive priority of *poiesis* and poetry over reason and truth represents a final rebuke of Hegel, who proclaimed in his *Lectures on Aesthetics* that poetry, "the universal art of the mind which has become free in its own nature," must end "by transcending itself, inasmuch as it abandons the medium of a harmonious embodiment of mind in sensuous form, and passes from the poetry of imagination into the prose of thought" (Hegel 1993: 96).[20] For the dialectical tradition of modernity, poetry can only serve as a temporary relay for spirit, an imaginative detour that must close once philosophical reason (and the state that embodies it) reaches maturity. For the anti-moderns Leopardi, Nietzsche and Negri, however, poetry is the constituent power of imagination that, constantly though discontinuously, produces true illusions, and as such it can only be suppressed temporarily, through the institutionalization of reason, whether pure or instrumental.

For Negri, Leopardi's example points forward directly to Ludwig Wittgenstein and to the "linguistic turn" that his work gave to philosophy and social science in the twentieth century:

> [I]n the Wittgenstein of the *Investigations*, subjectivity as limit subtends expression and thereby the relation between the experience of reality and the insertion into the linguistic community...[T]he subject seeks the linguistic world because it is only in the community that she can give a definition of herself. This definition is always incomplete and the process is indefinite, yet we arrive no less at the ontological consolidation of the linguistic community, and with it the perfecting of the subject's capacity for expression. (Negri 2004b: 360)

This means that

> Wittgenstein's discourse reveals to us a new world of production, one made of signs and woven by the community. The community alone produces, but by means of signs; in other words, signs are productive insofar as they are the expression of the community. Moreover, signs sketch the contours of reality and emancipate meaning: the relationship between community and production of signs is thus real, ontological. (P. 361)

From here it is only a short step – by way of Marx's notion of living labor – to the tendency toward immaterial labor and network resistance, which defines Hardt and Negri's conception of the subject as self-made through communication and that of the multitude as "counter-empire." It is no accident that the chapter with that title in *Empire*, the "Intermezzo" around which the book's entire argument pivots, is filled with poetic and literary references (Hardt and Negri 2000: 205–18). Poetry, linguistic *poiesis*, is counter-power, constituent power, ontological action or activism, and ultimately radical democracy. We might conclude by citing Negri's account of Leopardi one last time: "When it conflicts with the world, in the tragedy of life, poetry can create new being. The ontological power of poetry becomes historically effective, and thus illusion can become truth" (Negri 2004a: 75).

Negri's linguistic and poetic turn takes, next, what might seem an unexpected direction with his study of the Old Testament Book of Job, *The Labor of Job* (Negri 2009b). However, this biblical meditation shares with Negri's work on Wittgenstein a focus on pain as the constitutive experience for the founding of a new community (pp. 89–93). Like his engagements with Spinoza and Leopardi, this project, too, emerged from an experience that was both collective and personal.

> I had been held in a high-security prison for some time, solely on political grounds, and I had no idea of how to get out…Once I had overcome the illusion that one could defend oneself from an absolute Power, the problem became that of not becoming immersed in the pain and misery of prison. It was the question of how to develop an adequate understanding of repression so as to resist it and to find a way to interpret political defeat as a critique of Power. (P. xvii)

The similarities he finds between his own experience and Job's are fundamental to his interpretation. Negri insists that "the relationship between the two subjects [Job and God]…is a trial. *A juridical, formal trial*…But the trial is not a simple, coherent one, because *God is both one of the parties and the judge*. The trial is therefore a fraud" – as was Negri's own trial, on abstract charges of inspiring a revolution that never quite materialized (pp. 26–7). More than this, at the time the trial opens, "Job is already serving a terrible sentence. This sentence has preceded the trial" – just as Negri's own imprisonment preceded his trial by almost four years (p. 31).

As the theologian Roland Boer notes, Negri's study of Job is best understood as an example of homiletics,

the art of connecting a text like the Bible with the realities of everyday life, moving from the intricacies of textual analysis to the application to life. Negri's homiletics is radical on two counts, one
political, resting on Marx, and the other textual, reading Job as a
preeminent document for our time. (Boer in Negri 2009b: 109)

Thus Job is presented not only as a precursor of Negri's individual
experience of suffering in prison, but also as a precursor of the collective transformation that the world of labor is undergoing at the
end of the twentieth century. In order to make these connections
with contemporary life accessible, Negri approaches the Book of
Job from a literary perspective, attempting to read its historically
distinct levels and sections both piecemeal and as a whole. Recall
that the Book of Job begins with a wager between God and Satan
over Job's piety: God allows Satan to strip Job of all his possessions
– including his children and his health – in order to test whether
Job's faith is steadfast. Job is punished without having sinned.
Negri reads this dramatic situation as a figure for the breakdown
of the standards of measure that ruled the purportedly rational
system of moral exchange: good works and solid faith no longer
guarantee reward, and the guiltless are punished worse than the
guilty. In other words justice, the assignment of consequences
according to acts, breaks down. This situation corresponds to the
breakdown in the measure of economic value as labor time that
Negri had diagnosed during the seventies, in the rise of the socialized worker and in the corresponding mutation of capitalist
command into Tronti's social factory: "Value, labor, and justice
cannot be apportioned according to a common measure" (Negri
2009b: 36). Labor time no longer measures the value produced, and
thus wages can no longer reward production. The law of value,
operating through the market, no longer produces a just distribu-
tion, if it ever did.

Job's friends Eliphaz, Bildad and Zophar attempt to convince
him that, despite the appearance of injustice in his unwarranted
punishment, God is still good and His behavior still defines justice.
They justify God formally and deductively, insisting that measure
still exists (though it may be unknowable to humans), and hence
justice still exists, too. Like capital itself, they attempt to re-impose
measure, by force if necessary. Job stubbornly denies this attempt,
not only to his friends but ultimately to God himself. By punishing
the sinless Job, God has lost his claim to universal authority and
justice; he has become nothing more than an adversary, a despotic
Power. He sinks to the level of his servant (p. 25), or even below

it. "If in this unfinished relationship there is a creative subject, then it is Job. *His power opposes the Power of God*" (p. 29). Job passes through his pain and thereby comes to recognize his power, as Negri himself must do: "It is necessary *to go beyond the justification of pain and comprehend the practical transfiguration of pain.* There is no value – there is only the possibility of creating it. There is no judge – there is only the possibility of practicing justice" (p. 68). Job, the figure of living labor, becomes a precursor or figure of the Messiah, understood as a *"new human universality"* (p. 73), or, better, as an almost Spinozian "second nature: a machine that produces and accumulates energy and applies it to *materia prima* so as to transform it" (p. 102). The clearest proof of Job's immanent power lies in his success in compelling God to show Himself, to let Job see Him. What does this mean for Job, and thus for human beings?

> I have seen God, thus God is torn from the absolute transcendence that constitutes the idea of him. God justifies himself, thus God is dead. He saw God, hence Job can speak of him, and he – Job himself – can in turn participate in divinity, in the function of redemption that man constructs within life – the instrument of the death of God that is human constitution and the creation of the world. (Pp. 96–7)

The world is formed and re-formed in the common struggle against evil, which Negri understands in Spinozian, Leopardian or Nietzschean terms as pain and suffering, as what deprives us of the powers of our bodies and minds.

> *Pain is a key that opens the door to the community.* All the great collective subjects are formed by pain – those, at least, that struggle against the expropriation of the time of life by Power; those who have rediscovered time in the form of power, as the refusal of exploited labor and of the orders that are established upon that exploitation. *Pain is the democratic foundation* of political society, whereas fear is its dictatorial, authoritarian foundation. (P. 90)

Despite its origins in antiquity, Job's vision of this human emancipation from fear and participation in divinity is profoundly contemporary in its emphasis on the struggle between domination and liberation and on the pain that accompanies the passage to the new world of labor.

To conclude this discussion of Job, we must insist on the paradoxically but fundamentally atheist character of Negri's biblical reading. As he said to Anne Dufourmantelle,

I've never had anything against religion – I'm simply against transcendence...But certain aspects of religion, and above all certain
religious experiences, truly have the capacity to construct, not only
in a mystic way but also in an ascetic way...Asceticism is a constituent state, a transformation of the senses and the imagination, of the
body and reason. In order to live well and to construct the common,
asceticism is always necessary. (Negri and Dufourmantelle 2004:
158)

Asceticism, the immanence of sensual and imaginative practice, is
the link between Spinoza, Leopardi and Job, and it must be understood as their subjective intensification, their reduction to nothing
more than their bodies and minds, which grants all three figures
the power to construct a new world within the old. This is why
Negri denies that Job, in confessing the littleness of his power in
the face of God's Power, ever repents; and this is also why Negri
himself has never repented.

Job does not repudiate, nor does he retract – because he accepts his
own dramatic destiny as something from which he was produced,
and from which he was then freed after falling into the abyss of evil
and pain. His confession is not one of repentance, for it does not
reveal constituted experiences, but it constructs an absolute, it
"sees." Confession is redemption, that is, a process of transformation
that is, at the same time, a process of the constitution of a new reality.
(Negri 2009b: 106)

Such redemption is not a transcendent or conventionally religious
result, despite appearances, because the constitution of which the
Book of Job speaks is "not only the rule of metaphysics but also
that of poetry" (ibid.).

Constituent Power

In the preface to *The Savage Anomaly* Negri wrote: "Prison, with its
daily rhythm, with the transfers and the defense, does not leave
any time; prison dissolves time: This is the principal form of punishment in a capitalist society" (Negri 1991: xxiii; see also Hardt
1997). Prison also reduces space to the empty indifference of the
cell and the yard, a bare disciplinary space of surveillance that, as
Foucault had shown in *Discipline and Punish*, underlies all the institutional spaces of capitalist exploitation and epistemic subjection.

The goal of Negri's effort to constitute a second foundation for his thinking and his militancy was therefore to reclaim a time and space of resistance and revolution from the domination of capital and its dialectics. His reading of Spinoza had led him to the distinction between transcendent Power and immanent power, the first being allied with a homogeneous and repetitive form of time and the second with a differential and innovative form of time. In the 1981 essay "The Constitution of Time," written immediately after *The Savage Anomaly*, during his first two years of imprisonment, Negri elaborates upon this distinction by means of a materialist history of time:

> the history of the idea of time...starts from a maximum subordination of time to space [and leads] to a maximum subordination of space to time; from a maximum *spatialization of time* to a maximum *dynamization of space*. It is not therefore possible to confuse ancients and moderns. The philosophy of the Renaissance constitutes, even in the case of the history of the idea of time, the decisive watershed. (Negri 2003a: 101)

As in his other works, here the Renaissance marks the simultaneous insurgence and repression of a new form of human temporal practice, whose promise of liberation through innovative self-reconstruction is foreclosed in repetitive accumulation. The dynamization of space, its domination by time, emerges from the new possibilities of human self-construction that, for Negri, define the power of Renaissance humanism; but it is quickly absorbed into the emerging strategy of capital, since capital works ceaselessly to reduce production time – as well as the time that it spends, unvalorized, in circulation – to zero, in order to maximize its Power. As it develops, capital increasingly strives to impose a single, uniform, measurable and reversible time upon the increasingly differentiated spaces of production, which ultimately means upon the whole of society. Labor resists this imposition of temporal uniformity by laying claims to plural and irreversible times of socialization and reproduction in the struggle over the working day and, more broadly, over the time of life. As Cesare Casarino notes, Negri articulates "a concept of time as essentially *productive*, as constitutionally *collective*, and as potentially *constitutive* of new, antagonistic, and revolutionary subjectivities" (Casarino and Negri 2008: 225). In this struggle over time, as in Job's struggle with God, common measure ultimately fails: "When the entire time of life has become the time of production, who measures whom?" (Negri 2003a: 29).

This struggle of times or temporalities reaches its zenith in the contemporary period with the real subsumption of labor within capital.

> The transition to real subsumption, in so far as it affirms the collective as sole temporal and real substrate of action, not only does not reduce it to the formal indifference of equilibrium, but reproduces, reproposes, refounds the antagonism of subjects. So collective time and the temporal *Umwelt* [surrounding world] tend to present themselves to us immediately within *two horizons*: that of the closed time of legitimation and of equilibrium, the zero tendency of the absolute circularity of the social; and that of multiple, antagonistic, productive, constitutive, open time. (P. 42; translation modified)

To the Spinozian distinction between Power and power, then, corresponds the distinction or *"asymmetry of the time of command and of the times of liberation from exploitation"* (pp. 44–5). Like Machiavelli's virtue and fortune, which we will examine below, the two antagonistic times are defined by the irreducibility and inescapability of their difference. "In real subsumption *time divides itself in reality*: on the one side time of living labour, on the other time of dead labour. Both are internal and external, both are rooted to the dimension of the collective, although they are materially and historically different and antagonistic" (p. 62). We could just as easily say time of innovation or self-valorization, constitutive time (p. 91) versus time of accumulation or command, the "hard time" of capital (p. 82).

The subjectivity of the proletariat is made of constitutive time, but it is constrained within, and reduced to, command time. Only collective action is able to expand constitutive time as well as to defend it from capital:

> [T]ime is collective and productive essence. Collective essence means that[,] *without* collectivity, the only time known by the class and the plurality of individuals that compose it, both internally and externally, is that of capital. Time with tendency to zero. Antagonistic essence means that time is here defined as transformation of refusal into co-operation, of co-operation into production, of production into liberation. (P. 80)

The struggle over time reveals the resistant, negative quality of constitutive time to be the only temporality that is open to affirmation and innovation, to a future that can escape from the measure

of the past – just as Nietzsche's untimeliness does. Virtue or immanent power is also a *"prefigurative power,"* in that "[t]he time of class
struggle in itself contains the future and it continually attempts to
shape it" (p. 97). This prefigurative power is another variation on
the workerist hypothesis and on the method of the tendency.

As Negri acknowledges, these initial reflections on constitutive
time, like his party hypotheses during the seventies, were blocked
by dialectical residues of which he was aware but which he could
not then eliminate.

> My concern evidently was to remove any possibility of a dialectical
> recuperation of the antagonism...But the result became hysterical
> and led to the blockage of the investigation: indeed, how would it
> have been possible concretely to open once again the radical differ-
> ence of the subjective and constitutive temporality once it was
> defined in a sort of symmetry with the analytic temporality of
> capital? (P. 131)

Although this flawed dualistic model of antagonistic times confirms and extends his analysis of the distinction between Power/
potestas and power/*potentia* in Spinoza, its primary importance lies
in the fact that it ultimately led him to write an audacious revisionary history of the revolutionary impulse, *Il potere costituente*, originally published in 1992 (literally *Constituent Power*, translated into
English as *Insurgencies: Constituent Power and the Modern State*:
Negri 1999). As philosopher Charles T. Wolfe has noted: "For the
mature statement of a theory of 'political time,' or time as the constitutive trait of the political, one has to turn to the massive work
on 'constituting power'" (Wolfe 2007: 212).

In that book, which finally allowed him to settle accounts with
Leninism, Negri undertakes a systematic re-reading of the most
significant conceptual and practical innovations to emerge from the
four great revolutions that both attacked and perfected the modern
Western state form: the English Civil War; the American Revolution; the French Revolution; and the Bolshevik Revolution. In each
case study he follows out the discontinuous antagonism between
constituent power and constituted power by focusing on the writings of the major contemporary theorists of each event, both radical
and reactionary: James Harrington in the Civil War; Thomas Jefferson, the Federalist writers and John C. Calhoun in the American
Revolution and its subsequent constitutionalization; Jean-Jacques
Rousseau, Emmanuel-Joseph Sieyès and Edmund Burke in the

French Revolution (as well as Marx's retrospective analyses of it); and Marx and Lenin in the lead-up to and eruption of the October Revolution. But this thorough comparative approach to the subject of political revolution is not what sets Negri's work apart from that of other historians of political philosophy like Hannah Arendt, whose book *On Revolution* (1963) he criticizes and rewrites.[21] His originality lies instead in the debt that he demonstrates the modern revolutionary moments owe to the thought of the Renaissance humanist Niccolò Machiavelli. Louis Althusser once argued that "Machiavelli is alone because he has *remained isolated*; he has remained isolated because, although there has been ceaseless fighting over his thought, *no one has thought in his thought*" (Althusser 1999: 123). In *Insurgencies* Negri takes up this challenge and tries not only to think in Machiavelli's thought, but also to demonstrate how fruitfully other revolutionaries have already done so.

Constituted power corresponds to Spinoza's Power: it is defined by the formal, written constitution, structured according to dialectical logic and located in the fixed institutions of political mediation and hierarchical sovereignty. Constituent power, on the other hand, corresponds to Spinoza's power, the fluid and creative activity of immanent collective desire and insurrection that exceeds and dissolves the formal constitution, evades dialectical logic and is most clearly visible in the revolutionary ruptures that overthrow sovereigns and destroy political mediation. Since traditional political science is concerned almost exclusively with constituted power – the division and balance of the branches of government, the forms of representation, the mechanisms of governance – Negri must operate another workerist inversion in order to open up the question of constituent power in its full radicalness. Against the tradition that posits constituent power as the evanescent exception, the momentary interruption in the normative continuity of constituted power, he insists not only upon the ontological priority of constituent power over constituted power, but also on the persistence of constituent power during every period of apparently stabilized constitution.

> It does not come after the political, as in a tormented sociological pause or in a suspension of institutional reality...No, constituent power comes first, it is the very definition of the political, and where it is repressed and excluded, the political is reduced to pure mechanical nature, to being an enemy, and a despotic Power" (Negri 1999: 335; translation modified)[22]

Just as the workerist hypothesis asserted not only the historical and structural priority of labor over capital, but also the continuing agency of the working subject, so too does Negri's conception of constituent power: "To acknowledge constituent power as a constitutional and juridical principle, we must see it not simply as producing constitutional norms and structuring constituted powers but primarily as a subject that regulates democratic politics" (p. 1). This subject is not the individualist, transcendental subject of the essentialist humanism of modernity, but rather the variable collective subject of the constructivist humanism of the Renaissance – in a word, the multitude. "Constituent power stands as a revolutionary extension of the human capacity to construct history, as a fundamental act of innovation..." (p. 24).

Constituent and constituted power express different temporalities as well – essentially the same antagonistic temporalities that Negri theorized in "The Constitution of Time." Constituted power marks time as strict repetition of the past, an empty time to be filled by the accumulation of things, commodities or capital – that is, dead labor. Constituent power, conversely, breaks with static temporal repetition to create real novelty. "In the concept of constituent power is thus implicit the idea that the past no longer explains the present, and that only the future will be able to do so" (p. 11). This is where Negri locates Machiavelli's profound contribution to the revolutionary tradition: in his "definition of 'virtue' and 'fortune' as different apparatuses for grasping time, as producers of subjectivity on a certain temporal rhythm. The political is configured as a grammar of time" (p. 42). Machiavelli does not use the term "revolution" to label the insurgence of virtue (constituent power, the productivity or constructiveness of human labor) that disrupts the stability of fortune (constituted Power, the accumulation of wealth and command); this fact leads Arendt to marginalize him within the revolutionary tradition (Arendt 1963: 36–9). He uses the classical term *mutatio* for this clash, but he gives it an entirely new meaning. In Negri's interpretation, Machiavelli posits that

> the constituent principle and power are in fact absolute, but any actualization opposes them, wants to deny their absoluteness. If the absolute overflows or is dislocated, it finds itself confronted by the rigidity and irrationality of the constituted. This is the problem of constituent power, and this is the problem of the new prince. Every time virtue is realized, it discovers that it is working to accumulate something that, once it becomes powerful, is opposed to it. Virtue

against fortune: the opposition is still simple, elementary – but the violence it carries is enormous. (Negri 1999: 61)

Machiavelli's *mutatio* is not the predictable cycle of fixed governmental forms theorized by Plato and Aristotle and much later synthesized in Polybius' proto-liberal doctrine of a mixed constitution – a form that balanced the fixed ones by combining monarchical, oligarchic and democratic elements, as in the Roman Republic; it is rather a break in the cycle, a moment in which the future – or the time-to-come – can differ from the past. Far from being the cynical advocate of transcendent princely power into which traditional political science (mis)translated him, Machiavelli is actually the originator of a radically immanent concept of democracy. The triumph of virtue depends on the people in arms, fighting to express their own collective antagonistic power, and only they can set up, preserve or tear down a prince's rule. While *The Prince* can be (mis)read as a manual for the maintenance of monarchical Power, Machiavelli's *Discourses* are, conversely, "nothing but the demonstration that the only content of the constituent form is the people, that the only constitution of the Prince is democracy"; they are "an apology of the people, of the constitution of freedom, and finally an explicit declaration of the absoluteness of democracy as government" (pp. 66, 68). As such, they anticipate Spinoza's conception of democracy. But, no matter how original and accurate they are, Machiavelli's demonstration and apology cannot preserve the disorganized collective subject of constituent power from enclosure within an absolutist constitutional structure – a proto-Cartesian "reasonable ideology" (p. 89) – at the end of the Renaissance: "even when all the conditions exist for the ideal to become the real, and virtue to become history, even in this case the synthesis does not realize itself...Constituent power never materializes except in instances: vortex, insurrection, prince" (p. 89). When the subject is not adequate, "this revolution is not yet possible" (p. 96); Machiavelli's project must remain a utopia, and in that impossible form it is taken up in radically different ways by Descartes and Spinoza, as we have seen.

The succession of more recognizably revolutionary events develops the constituent subject further and transforms Machiavelli's utopia into what Negri calls a "disutopia": not an Orwellian dystopia, but rather "the sense of an overflowing constitutive activity, as intense as a Utopia but without its illusion, and fully material" (p. 14). If utopia is an idealist pipedream, disutopia is a practical materialist project. In the context of the English Civil War, Harrington takes up Machiavelli's insight and for the first time grounds virtue or constituent power in a theory of property and representative procedure. Like Spinoza, Harrington is often misinterpreted as a proto-capitalist, an apologist of the market – whereas, for Negri,

> Harrington is a revolutionary; but he is not a forerunner of capitalism. He is a modern man who conceives the revolution as an alternative to rising capitalism...For him the concept of property is never generic but, rather, is the concept of a property that organizes itself in a collective regime, of a property that is fundamentally egalitarian and socialistic. (Pp. 11–14)

In his "utopian" text *Oceana* (which, according to Negri, is "not very Utopian, because it is not a project outside of time, but a realistic analysis of the political and social trends ongoing in England at his time, and of their consequences," p. 112), Harrington proposes a reform of agrarian law designed to guarantee that a majority of landed property remains in the hands of the multitude and a reform of the system of political representation designed to limit individuals to short terms of office (pp. 115–18). In a predominantly agricultural society, these reforms would sharply restrict the accumulation of capital and command (Machiavelli's fortune) and preserve the virtuous power of the actual producers of value, the people in arms. "An absolute democracy and a radical republic are described here, on the basis of only one principle: that of popular power, therefore of the impossibility of transferring the basis of sovereignty to any other place but the people" (p. 123). Harrington's practical utopia is soon overtaken by the development of mercantile and industrial capital, however, which subordinates and renders inoperative the agrarian power he sought to protect. His model is, paradoxically, an attempt to *conserve* constituent power, and as such it collapses in the face of the expansive dynamic of nascent capital. Nevertheless, "constituent power can live beyond its own temporal defeat," as a "latency that traverses a world where the violence and the unnaturalness of unjust social relations have triumphed...thus a world that will be destroyed by the rebirth of the constituent power of the multitude" (p. 135).

The American revolutionaries, who may have invented the phrase "constituent power" (p. 146), take up the property aspect of Harrington's model, however, and they situate it in the expansive space of the New World, which promises to increase the power of the multitude exponentially.

Constituent power at this point is destined to constitute a "second nature" proper – in the American case, a nation that spreads between two oceans, an immense territory to construct. American constituent power poses freedom as frontier, as its frontier – and the historical frontier of the American states as an obstacle to continually over- come, to give more and more freedom to its citizens. (P. 154)

This expansiveness, an effective and appropriate response to the new expansiveness of capital, is simultaneously the most radical constituent innovation of the American Revolution and the founda- tion of the constitutional imperialism of Manifest Destiny and of the Monroe and Truman doctrines. Jefferson's Declaration of Inde- pendence rhetorically enacts this American mutation of constituent power in its insistence not only on rights to life, liberty and the pursuit of happiness, but also on the "right to expression of con- stituent power" (p. 149), which is defined as follows:

[W]henever any form of government becomes destructive of these ends, it is the right of the people to alter or to abolish it, and to institute new government, laying its foundation upon such princi- ples, and organizing its powers in such form, as to them shall seem most likely to effect their safety and happiness. (Jefferson, cited in Negri 1999: 149)

This passage explicitly posits a right to insurrection or revolution that the passage to the US Constitution will absorb and suppress: such a transition will redefine the expansion of power and freedom as the imperialist export and imposition of a unified constitutional order. The Federalists (mainly Alexander Hamilton and James Madison) re-introduce the institutional logic of constituted power, with all its familiar elements – delegation of right, division and balance of governmental powers, hierarchy of command, and so on – which the constitution will subsequently formalize. Once this is accomplished, "the people, as mass of individuals, as multitude in the new space, which the democratic and revolutionary power had defined, here are erased, reinvented as political society, as element of a second nature prefigured and produced by the repub- lican government" (Negri 1999: 162–3).

The re-insertion of the multitude into the constitutional order has concrete effects: the elaborate institutional architecture of the US Constitution has "absorbed not only constituent power, but also the subject of constituent power... [A]fter erasing in the con- stitution the subjects that were at its origin, it gives back to society pure and simple constitutional products, juridical individuals"

(p. 167). Antagonistic collective subjects are redefined as individual property-owners, confirming the constitution's capitulation to capitalist ideology. The division and balance of powers restores the Polybian schema of mixed constitution (the executive branch representing monarchy, the judicial representing oligarchy and the legislative representing democracy) and, in so doing, it expropriates the constituent power that Jefferson had acknowledged in the Declaration. The power of the multitude to "alter, abolish and institute government" is replaced by the judicial Power to interpret the constitution and thereby oversee the performance of the executive and legislative branches. The constitutional machine defeats constituent power by including the procedures for its reform within itself, thereby suppressing the right to revolutionary change. "Its space is broken; universality is taken away from it; in the multitude a bitter destiny of loneliness and strict individuality is assigned to the subject" (p. 189).

Paradoxically, the most powerful – yet ultimately unsuccessful – challenge to this defeat comes from the reactionary John C. Calhoun, the leading ideologist of slave government in the period prior to the US Civil War. In his attempt to preserve the veto power of the minority bloc that he called the "concurrent majority," Calhoun articulated a last-ditch defense of American constituent power:

> When, through constituent power, we organize a situation of sovereignty, says Calhoun the "reactionary," we are not renouncing constituent power. Constituent power is not alienable from constituted power. The constitution is a pact: but a pact among constituent interests is always a compromise of position that can become hostile once again. It is in the nature of the constituent compromise to unite opposites, not to annihilate them ... [C]onstituent power, inalienable as it is, appears to be at this point a negative power, the power of delimitation of agreement, the power of resistance. (P. 184)

Calhoun's conception attempts to restore the constituent right to insurrection as a right to resist the tyranny of the numerical majority. It reaffirms the intrinsic power of antagonism within the body of the multitude, though with much less emphasis on the plurality and singularity of that antagonism. Ironically, among American political thinkers only Calhoun's pro-slavery position acknowledged constituent power as "permanent revolution" (p. 186).

The American Revolution was followed almost immediately by the French Revolution – which, in Negri's earlier work on Descartes, Kant and Hegel, constitutes the crux of the modern state's developmental process (see chapter 2). Its importance, like that of the American Revolution, is double in that it represents both a radically republican rupture and a successful bourgeois constitutional project. This paradox is embodied in the work of Rousseau, who provided concepts that legitimated both aspects. His conception of the general will, established through the delegation of power in the social contract, formalized the logic of constituted Power and led ultimately to the Hegelian apotheosis of the popular state; but on the other hand "Rousseau is assumed by the masses because his concept of constituent power, if isolated from his theory, practically allowed (in fact, demanded) to take a stance against any constitutional line that made of social inequality an essential element in the organization of the State" (p. 202). In this the French revolutionaries went beyond the Americans: they initially insisted on total social and political equality, and on that basis they took constituent violence much further than the more timid Founding Fathers did. But, as in the transition from the Declaration of Independence to the constitution in the American case, here Negri follows the gradual foreclosure of constituent power through the successive versions of the Declaration of the Rights of Man.

> In each declaration the fundamental problem is thus that of the production of the constituent subject... In each of the declarations the principles of freedom, security, and property are affirmed in a homogeneous manner; and yet in each declaration the general will is the new formalism into which constituent power is translated, expropriated of its mass radicality and exposed as mere foundation of individual rights. (Pp. 204–5)

The great revolutionary advocate of the Third Estate, Emmanuel Sieyès, follows essentially the same course: "after having emptied Rousseau's concept of general will of any possibility of democratic grounding... he transforms this representation into juridical absolute, into the exclusive seat – if it is not yet the exclusive source – of sovereignty" (p. 218). The radical demand for absolute social and economic equality contained in the early versions of both these polemics is first qualified by, and finally imprisoned within, a constitutional defense of private property that reduces equality to the juridical abstraction – or fiction – of equality before the law. The revolution is thereby terminated in the sanctification of bourgeois property and its representation in the state.

The historical significance of the French Revolution can be seen most clearly in the lessons that the conservative Edmund Burke and the communist Marx derived from it. Burke's great reactionary invention is his ideological appropriation of political reform as a project of constituted power that can subsume and overdetermine the constituent power of the Revolution. "For the first time the discourse of reform is opposed to that of revolution. And this happens in entirely new terms: that is, the power of reform is grafted onto the same dimension of constituent power..." (p. 238). Unlike Harrington's radical conception of agrarian and representative reform intended to preserve and strengthen the multitude's constituent power, Burke's notion of reform encloses the temporal rupture of constituent power within the continuity of the institutions of property and delegation of sovereignty, guaranteeing that virtue will not threaten fortune but will instead increase it. In other words, antagonistic living labor will become the motor for capitalist development. In this way Burke founds the dialectics of modern liberalism, which will reach its philosophical apotheosis in Hegel and its embodiment in the national constitutions of labor that define mature capitalism.

For Marx, on the other hand,

> The French revolutionary archetype consists of the fact that it poses the theme of the mediation between the social and the political, it fixes the concept of constituent power, and it introduces us to the problematic of the "party" (that is, of the subject that lives and operates the passage from the social to the political). (P. 222)

Marx acknowledges the success of Burke's resolution to the rupture – as Negri puts it, "the French Revolution must not be considered as the revolution of labor, but as the 'bourgeois' revolution of labor...meant to block the liberation of the social forces exploited in the slavery of the division of labor" (p. 224) – but he looks beyond it, to the new relation of forces it reveals and to the future revolutions it portends.

> In Marx, the constitution of labor – which, from the French Revolution on, in the nineteenth century constitutions becomes the central element of the definition of the modern State – opens thus to an immanent and continuous alternative, characterized by the ever new opening of constituent power. This temporality is solicited in two senses: extensively, that is, in the sense of the permanence of the revolutionary and constituent process; and intensively, in the

sense of a process that, through accelerations, moments of crisis and offensives, makes the contents of constituent power itself develop in theoretical–practical directions, in the direction of the consolidation of collective consciousness and of its conditions of freedom, more and more universal. It is the time of the masses that makes constituent power. (Pp. 226–7)

Constituent power is not only Harrington's latency that follows every republican defeat, but also the "old mole" of Marx's *Eighteenth Brumaire of Louis Bonaparte*: the subterranean continuity of revolutionary subjectivity and subversion that is constantly at work, though only intermittently visible on the surface of the state and of the market. The mole undermines the division of labor and the division between social and political equality – the originary form of the "autonomy of the political" – that derives from it.

If, as Negri claims, the French Revolution first "gives shape to the new political subjects of class struggle: the bourgeoisie and the proletariat" (p. 198), then the Soviet Revolution takes those subjects as its point of departure. Lenin builds on Marx's analysis of the French Revolution and its aftermath, recognizing significant similarities between the political situations of eighteenth-century France and twentieth-century Russia. In both contexts the conditions for a bourgeois revolution and for a proletarian one co-exist uneasily, so "Lenin's position on the revolution in Russia, and consequently on the revolutionary organization of social democracy, takes shape in the continual confrontation of these two terms" (p. 270). The function of the soviets themselves – those local organizations of mass worker resistance – provides a clear example of this ambiguity:

They appropriate the [reformist] slogans of social democracy for an eight-hour workday and a constituent assembly and fight their democratic battle with [revolutionary] proletarian tools. The ambiguity of the relationship – which the worker's spontaneity always carries with it – between the immediate aims of democratic reform and radical revolutionary refusal is thus represented in the Soviets in a typical manner, the direct product of the workers' spontaneity. (P. 273)

Lenin's challenge is to use the soviets, which emerged independently of his Bolshevik movement and prior to the events of 1916, as instruments of insurrection and frameworks of organized struggle only so long as they remain effective as revolutionary manifestations of constituent power. As soon as they begin to settle into a stable, constituted role, as institutions of democratic delegation, they become counter-revolutionary. The task of the vanguard party, in this situation, is to give the soviets autonomy when they function constituently, and to give them command when they begin to fossilize into formal constitution. In the course of the revolution the soviets shift function repeatedly, from revolutionary to reformist roles, and their shifts require parallel shifts in party activity. The victory of Lenin's forces depends on the party–soviets relationship, yet that victory already foreshadows the part that both of them play in the termination of the revolution, its constitutionalization:

> Even though, in fact, the soviet begins to function as "organ of proletarian dictatorship," nonetheless it is the party that actually exercises power, in the form and only in the form of the soviet. The soviet tends thus to be reduced to a democratic instrument of the "organization of consent," and as such it is once again interchangeable with other instruments of advanced democracy. Therefore, far from being configured as a moment of the process of the abolition of the State, the soviet ends up being, in the best of instances, "organ of the administration of the State." (Pp. 290–1)

From there, Negri acknowledges, it is only a short step to Stalinism, in which "[a]ny singularity of the Marxist and Leninist constituent potential is subjected to an administrative decomposition and to an executive recomposition, whose definitive sign is the absoluteness of constituted power" (p. 298). The practical measure of this is the extent to which the soviet "is institutionalized as participation in the organization of production, as support of the ideology of labor, as instrument of planning" (p. 300). Even in the Soviet Revolution, constituent power is finally trapped within the constituted structure of the state and deployed as the motive force of accumulation.

Once again, as always since Machiavelli, virtue is defeated by fortune and the revolution is terminated before it can succeed. Yet, Negri insists, "the pattern of rationality that the Renaissance revolution had proposed as plot of the political is affirmed...: the rational expression of a dense project of the emancipation of social freedom and its realization in the political" (p. 304). This project of absolute equality constitutes an open set of "alternatives to modernity" (the original Italian subtitle of Negri's book) within modernity, thus an anti-modernity or counter-modernity. If "[t]he rationality of modernity is in fact...a linear logic that corrals the multitude of subjects into a unity and controls its difference through the dialectic" (p. 328), then the opposite is true of the rationality of constituent power:

> The rationality that goes beyond modernity seizes in diversity and in the richness of equal and irreducible individualities the keystone of its very logic. Constituent power takes shape not as reduction to one of the singularities but as the place of their intertwining and their expansion. Its creative force is revealed in this unraveling of the multitude toward the richness of its infinite expressions. The new rationality will therefore represent itself in a logic of the singularities in process, in fusion, and in continual surpassing. (P. 331)

Machiavelli's subject of virtue, Spinoza's free man, Marx's old mole: whatever we call it, constituent power repeatedly emerges from the confines of modern rationality to confirm the radical subjective agency of the multitude. "[T]he subject itself continues to take shape through the world that it itself has constructed by shaping and reshaping itself. Living labor becomes constituent power within this process. And it is within this process that the multitude is brought back to power and discovers itself as subject" (p. 327). The postmodern crisis of meaning and subjectivity marks the transition to the open struggle of singularities, which, ironically, implies the return of a revolutionary practice that we might call Machiavellian in its subtlety as well as Marxist (and Jeffersonian?) in its recurrence:

> In this sense the concept of constituent power shows the normality of the revolution and offers a definition of being as movement of transformation. We need to reduce the dramatics associated with the concept of the revolution by making it, through constituent power, nothing but the desire of the continuous, relentless, and ontologically effective transformation of time. (P. 334)

The project of subordinating fortune to virtue, of producing the new in a time-to-come, of storming the Bastille and freeing its prisoners remains the challenge. Even though Negri wrote it in exile, *Insurgencies* is as clearly marked by his prison experience as *The Savage Anomaly*. Indeed he acknowledges that "this book on 'constituent power' [is] a sort of extension of the studies done in that book on the development of modern political metaphysics"

(p. 352 n. 90). It completes the earlier book's design by fleshing out the long and illustrious counter-tradition of modernity to which Spinoza gave Negri access for the first time. Longtime adversary Alex Callinicos is not alone in considering *Insurgencies* to be Negri's best book (Callinicos 2007: 169).

This is not to say that its methods and conclusions have been universally acclaimed. Perhaps the sharpest critique of *Insurgencies* has come from political philosopher Miguel Vatter, who questions the validity of Negri's fundamental opposition between constituent and constituted power even though he is largely sympathetic to Negri's aim. He sums up Negri's radical concept in a concise "formula: constituent power articulates the political as *absolute resistance*. I find this formula for the political to be essential to radical democratic theory" (Vatter 2007: 65). The problem, for Vatter, is that the irresolvable opposition Negri establishes between constituent and constituted power, like the Neoplatonist first foundation of Spinoza's metaphysics, is unable to explain the persistence and stability of constituted power. Vatter agrees that "constituent power must be thought starting from its non-synthetic relation to constituted power, and hence in terms of a resistance to legality"; but, because Negri absolutizes that non-synthetic relation into a subjective process of permanent revolution, "one is left with the most difficult and pressing task of explaining how constituted power comes to be and lasts, how it is self-standing. *Insurgencies* never accounts for this in *political terms*, but solely in *economic terms*" (p. 66). In short, Vatter considers Negri's model in *Insurgencies* to be not only an unexpected revival of vulgar Marxist economism but, more significantly, another instance of the exaggerated dualism that Spinoza scholars questioned in *The Savage Anomaly* and that Negri acknowledged as an obstacle in "The Constitution of Time."

Instead of rejecting Negri's conclusions, however, Vatter offers counter-proposals – drawn, like Negri's own model, from Machiavelli. "What must be accounted for," he insists, "is the relation between constituent and constituted powers in terms of their capacity for *mutual* resistance" (p. 67). What does this mean? He specifies:

> The political can express a process (or subject or substance) of resistance that is absolute in the sense of being absolved from every thing-like (mode-like) determination. This is Negri's "Spinozist" understanding of constituent power, where the latter is radically

delinked from any determination as constituted power. But the political can also be understood in a "Nietzschean" way, if one takes it to express the absoluteness of resistance with respect to any process- or subject-like determination. In this second sense, resistance is found everywhere, in the constituted powers of the state as much as beyond it, in the constituent powers of revolution. (Pp. 68–9)

Vatter's proposal for a Nietzschean approach to constituent power undermines the latter's direct identification with the revolutionary subject that Negri's approach emphasizes, and in consequence it renders the political impact of this approach ambiguous. By locating autonomous resistance on both sides of the antagonism, Vatter deprives Negri's workerist conception of its foundation. This becomes clear when Vatter offers a counter-reading of Machiavelli's virtue and fortune:

For Machiavelli there cannot be a radical change of situation (*virtù* as constituent power) unless the situation (*fortuna* as constituted power) is essential, radically non-accidental. It is part of the essence, of the grammar, of a situation that it can be changed...Machiavelli's theory of the match (*riscontro*) between constituent and constituted powers shows that a radical change of situation is possible only if the encounter between constituent power and situation (constituted power) is itself situational, i.e. eventual. If this constituent power acquires the character of a subject or substance, if it is absolute process as Negri holds, then no discontinuity, no rupture is truly possible, and hence also no revolution as event of innovation. Either the revolution is finite, an eventuality, rather than a permanent process, or it never comes to pass. (Pp. 71–2)

This is the real reason why, for Vatter, Machiavelli's own historical moment could not yield a revolutionary event comparable to the other case studies in Negri's book: the new prince or the civil prince could not resolve the radical antagonism between the multitude's constituent desire for absolutely no rule – Negri's absolute positive liberty – with the demand for control of the proprietor class; so all he could accomplish was the displacement of that antagonism into the establishment of a civil society based on "negative liberty, with the security of possessions that follows from it" (p. 73). The upshot is that "constituent power is employed by the civil prince on the people so as to make them serve as foundation of constituted power, by arming them and securing them at the same time, and by captivating their desire for no-rule in the form of the secure pursuit of negative liberty" (p. 74). If Machiavelli's prince prefigured Spinoza's multitude, he was also the architect of Descartes' reasonable ideology. Constituent power both terminates and is terminated at the end of the revolution; it is fortune as well as virtue, the state as well as the revolution.

Negri's friend Giorgio Agamben noted a similar difficulty in the brief remarks he dedicated to *Insurgencies* in his book *Homo Sacer: Sovereign Power and Bare Life*:

> The problem of the difference between constituent power and sovereign power is, certainly, essential. Yet the fact that constituent power neither derives from the constituted order nor limits itself to instituting it – being, rather, free praxis – still says nothing as to constituent power's alterity with respect to sovereign power...Negri cannot find any criterion, in his wide analysis of the historical phenomenology of constituent power, by which to isolate constituent power from sovereign power. (Agamben 1998: 43; translation modified)

For Agamben, the true originality of Negri's book is instead the force with which "it shows how constituent power, when conceived in all its radicality, ceases to be a strictly political concept and necessarily presents itself as a category of ontology...The problem is therefore moved from political philosophy to first philosophy (or, if one likes, politics is returned to its ontological position)" (p. 44; translation modified). As Negri's friend and collaborator Félix Guattari used to say, politics comes before being, and Negri would no doubt agree.

***

In the summer of 1997, after 14 years of political exile in France, Negri returned to Italy to serve out the prison sentence that remained after the exhaustion of his appeals. He did so voluntarily, in an effort to resolve not only his own situation but also that of the many other Italian refugees who had fled abroad to escape the repression of the seventies radical movements. Unfortunately, the bills of amnesty that he had been promised were not approved, and he was forced to languish in a cell for several more years. But his second stint in prison was quite different from his first. He had gone willingly this time, but, perhaps more importantly, he had taken with him a new conceptual foundation for his work, a new confidence in the multitude and a new openness toward the time to come. He and Michael Hardt, who had been a graduate student when Negri met him in the late eighties and who thereafter began to teach at Duke University in North Carolina, had already drafted *Empire*, although it would not appear for another three years. If Negri's intent during his first, involuntary period of incarceration was to make his cell as theoretically productive as Spinoza's optical workshop, his main project during the second, voluntary period was to sum up the range and intensity of that undeniable productivity in a materialist credo: *Kairos, Alma Venus, Multitudo*. This book, published in 2000 and subtitled "Nine lessons to myself," takes the compression that always characterized Negri's style to its highest level. It is organized as a numbered sequence of propositions that evoke both Spinoza's *Ethics* and Wittgenstein's *Philosophical Investigations*. It translates Negri's new philosophical historiography, poetics and political theory directly into the language of materialist ontology that Agamben had identified as the greatest strength of *Insurgencies*. This is the language that underpins the collaborations with Hardt.

Negri's ontology, as expressed here, is a radically nominalist one, which begins from the production of the "common name" at the "moment of rupture and opening of temporality" that classical philosophy (and medicine) calls *kairos* – the "right moment" to act. Charles T. Wolfe has emphasized that *"Materialism is a theory of action for Negri, not a theory of science or of truth"* (Wolfe 2007: 218), and the focus on *kairos* confirms this. *Kairos* is "the modality of time through which being opens itself, attracted by the void at the limit of time, and it thus decides to fill that void" (Negri 2003a: 152). Naming in this sense is the material creation of meaning and of being in a single gesture, an imaginative innovation that produces the present.

> If we wish to give to the common name the direction of the arrow of time and place it in relation to its irreversibility without losing its singularity, it is necessary then that the common name is grasped as an act or *praxis* of temporality... The common name is therefore a mode of affirmation of being; that is to say, the common name is a force of being, something that constructs new being. (P. 160)

This creative conception of the common name links it to the other productive concepts in Negri's new theoretical arsenal: virtue, power, living labor. Its temporal agency or *kairos* connects it to the constitutive time of antagonistic living labor and opposes it to the constituted time of fortune, command and capital. The latter drives inexorably into a "future" that is distinguishable from the past only in quantitative terms of accumulation.

> In the perspective we are criticizing (and which seems to us to be the most widely held), "future" is a mystified, erroneous name. On the contrary, we give the name of *"to-come"* to the horizon of experimentation of the adequation of the name and the thing, and to the imaginative perspective that – in realizing itself – presents itself as new being. The passage to the *to-come* is always a difference, a creative leap. (P. 163)

Knowledge and time are not objects of accumulation but makings, processes of innovation or *poiesis*. As Wolfe demonstrates in a careful explication of *Kairos, Alma Venus, Multitudo*: "Thinking, speaking, and acting are traceable back to a common root, *poiesis*. We are parts of Nature, but our acts of creation or fabrication, of production or transformation, are also parts of Nature. The world of the intellect is linked to the world *tout court* by the productive imagination" theorized by Spinoza, Leopardi and Nietzsche (Wolfe 2007: 205).

Kairos is also the foundation of subjectivity, or rather of the open-ended processes of subjectivation and self-reconstruction in and of time. "For subjectivity is not something that subsists: it is – on the contrary – produced by *kairos*, and ... depends on the connection of monads of *kairos*. Subjectivity is not before but after *kairos*" (Negri 2003a: 173). The plural forms of subjective singularity comprising the multitude are themselves common names, productions of new being on the edge of time. As Negri's analyses of Leopardi, Job and Wittgenstein had established: "The production of subjectivity, i.e. of needs, affects, desire, action, *techne*, is carried out through language, better still it is language in the same way that language is subjectivity" (p. 190). Subjectivity and language are parallel, intersecting modes of living labor, and so is the world.

> Production constructs the world following a trace of which temporality is the substance. Dead labour, the finished time of creation, continues to accumulate on the "before" of this process; the "after" is represented by living labour, that is, by the *kairos* of bodies that create truths through *praxis*. On the edge of being, living labour is thus the power of the world, of that which has already been (and that remains there in a constant manner), and which is now regener-

ated by that which will appear from the work of creative living labour. (P. 176)

In this conception Negri articulates a new materialism, which moves beyond the descriptive "spatialism" of the European materialist tradition to meld space and time through action.

The arguments that Negri presents in *Kairos, Alma Venus, Multitudo* are not new to his work, but they are expressed in a more universalizing and assertive language than ever before. This language highlights the Spinozian serenity of the second foundation of Negri's lifelong militant project. His affirmative tone comes closer here to Deleuze's Nietzschean rhetoric than anywhere else in his writings.

> Everything flows and everything hybridizes on the edge of time. On all sides, in the face of the void, the singularities mount assaults on the limit so as to construct in common another plenitude for life. That is what the biopolitical production of the multitude consists in: stretching itself out from fullness to emptiness so as to fill the void. (P. 232)

Only such serenity and assurance could ground the massive project of analysis and synthesis that was about to emerge in Negri's collaborations with Michael Hardt on an innovative theory of globalization. Echoing Agamben, Wolfe sums up the achievement of Negri's new materialist ontology of *kairos* and common names: "To be able to say 'what is' and thereby introduce difference into what is, is ontology; it is freedom...Here ontology instantly becomes political, since freedom amounts to the positing of difference within an already unified world, and thus a rejection of a certain kind of order" (Wolfe 2007: 208). Ontology can only be freedom if it is first resistance, and the ontological project of the creative multitude is perhaps best expressed in one of the most limpid and direct statements to be found in this book (or indeed in any of Negri's books): "There is a time, there is a common *kairos* in which one says: all together, let us decide" (Negri 2003a: 256). This time of renewed intellectual collaboration and common decision, after years of incarceration and solitude, would culminate in Negri's re-emergence as an important influence on – and participant in – political militancy, not just in Italy and France, but around the world.

5

Empire and Counter-Empire

Negri's notoriety – in the seventies as a radical theorist and organizer, in the eighties as a political prisoner and exile – was paradoxical in that he was singled out as a privileged individual – first for surveillance and persecution and later for support – from what were really collective experiences. Indeed this isolation from mass militancy, which constrained him in various ways from 1979 until 2003, constituted a fundamental problem that he had to solve in order to continue his work. The solution he found had two aspects, one of which we examined in the last chapter: the conceptual refoundation of militant theory and practice in the face of massive political defeat. The second aspect, which overlapped with the first, remains to be examined, and it offers another key to the influence that Negri's thought is exerting over the first decades of the new millennium. That aspect is the practice of formal collaboration, which allowed him to develop a much more accessible style of writing and to acquire a much broader audience.

As we saw in chapter 3, Negri's theoretical and practical engagement had always been predicated on his collective work as an organizer in the factories of the Veneto, as a teacher at the University of Padua and as a committed intellectual on the European political scene; but as a writer he had relatively little experience with collaboration before his Parisian exile. He had been a member of various editorial collectives from his student days onward; as director of Padua's Institute of Political Science he had overseen many conferences and seminars; and as a high-profile member of Potere operaio and Autonomia he had organized demonstrations and congresses. Yet virtually all the writings that emerged from those contexts were signed by him alone. Aside from short introductions to journal issues or books that he had co-edited, the first genuinely collaborative text that Negri published was *New Lines of Alliance, New Spaces of Liberty* (Guattari and Negri 1985), which he co-authored with Félix Guattari in his first year of Parisian exile. If, as we argued in the last chapter, Negri's work on Spinoza, Leopardi and constituent power enabled him to "become what he is" as a Nietzschean thinker of power, language and subjectivity, then the experience of working with Guattari on *New Lines of Alliance* enabled him to achieve a collaborative displacement of self that would ultimately bring his work its largest audience ever.

New Lines of Alliance announces its intentions in its first line: "The project: to rescue 'communism' from its own disrepute" (Guattari and Negri 1985: 26). This means rescuing communism from derogatory associations with the "real socialism" of the Soviet bloc, which was then on a rapid course of self-destruction. For Guattari and Negri, communism means instead "the assortment of social practices leading to the transformation of consciousness and reality on every level: political and social, historical and everyday, conscious and unconscious" (p. 28). Far from being the extermination of individuality, as Stalinism practiced it and as capitalist propaganda portrays it, communism is rather "the continuous reaffirmation of singularity," indeed the "process of singularization" itself (p. 31), which must manifest "the singular as multiplicity, mobility, spatio-temporal variability and creativity" (p. 43). This language, although compatible with the one Negri had evolved in the course of his work on Spinoza and Leopardi, was transposed from Guattari's work with Deleuze, and *New Lines of Alliance* should also be considered a kind of proxy collaboration between Negri and Deleuze. This initial melding of Negri's Marxist language with the delirious materialist language of Deleuze and Guattari would be refined later on, in his collaborations with Michael Hardt, who wrote an important critical work on Deleuze (see Hardt 1993).

Perhaps the book's most interesting passages, however, involve the authors' conception of the emerging global order, for which they use Guattari's phrase "integrated world capitalism" (IWC):

Integrated World Capitalism is not limited to recomposing, using new forms of unification, the flux and hierarchies of statist powers in their traditional sense. It generates supplementary statist functions which are expressed through a network of international

organizations, a planetary strategy of the mass media, rigorous
taking control of the market, of technologies, etc. (Guattari and
Negri 1985: 48–9)

A key feature of IWC is the subordination of the nation state to
production and to the market in the current phase of capitalism
(see Guattari and Alliez 1984: 239, 24–6). Although this theory is
very schematic (or "diagrammatic," as Deleuze and Guattari would
say), its use here marks the start of an important transition in
Negri's thinking. While he had occasionally discussed the role of
multinational corporations and of international monetary policy in
his political writings of the seventies, he had focused more consistently – almost obsessively – on the structural evolution of the
individual nation state, the command center of postwar capitalism.[1] In the collaboration with Guattari, Negri first begins to conceive of a model of global capitalism that is no longer governed by
fully sovereign nation states.

Like the project to rescue communism, this aspect of IWC positions the theory as a preliminary version of the concept of Empire
that Hardt and Negri would articulate a dozen years later, which
also focuses on the notion that the sovereignty of nation states is
being "supplemented" and undermined by non-state organizations of transnational governance. Elsewhere in the book Guattari
and Negri adduce additional elements that would reappear in the
collaboration with Hardt, such as the use of precarious employment as a weapon of post-Fordist economic control, the systemic
attack on the poor's social safety net, and the redefinition of war
as the internal policing of a smooth (that is, largely unbounded)
social and productive space. In order to re-ignite struggle against
this emergent stage of capitalism, Guattari and Negri call for a new,
non-Leninist strategy of alliance among radical subjects that also
foreshadows the logic of counter-globalization:

> Why ask a feminist movement to come to a doctrinal or program-
> matic accord with ecological movement groups or with a communi-
> tarian experiment by people of color or with a workers' movement,
> etc.?…On the contrary, what is essential is that each movement
> shows itself to be capable of unleashing irreversible molecular revo-
> lutions and of linking itself to either limited or unlimited molar
> struggles…(Guattari and Negri 1985: 80)

Deleuze and Guattari's language of the molecular (or small-scale)
and of the molar (or large-scale) is deployed here to articulate an

immanent notion of militant coordination, but the result is a clear foreshadowing of the non-hierarchical logic of the multitude's political project that would be proposed more than a decade later. Just as the theory of IWC begins a process of modeling a de-centered global capitalism that will come to fruition later, the logic of molecular revolutions that would enable a de-centered articulation of discordant militant movements presages the political organization of the contemporary multitude.

Collaboration with Guattari set the stage for Negri's better known and more successful collaboration with Michael Hardt a few years later. Hardt, born in Washington, DC in 1960, trained as an engineer at Swarthmore College and became involved in Central American radical politics in the mid-eighties. He met Negri while completing a doctorate in comparative literature at the University of Washington – during which he translated Negri's *Savage Anomaly* into English – and first began to work closely with him on the Parisian journal *Futur antérieur* in 1988–9.[2] Although they became friends quickly and their collaboration developed without major obstacles, it required an effort to overcome the culture and generation gap between them. As Giuseppina Mecchia puts it, "if they wanted to write a book about contemporary history, Hardt and Negri had, first of all, to invent a past, present, and future that could be common to the two of them since they wanted to write together" (Mecchia 2010: 134).[3] In 1994 their first collaborative book, *Labor of Dionysus: A Critique of the State-Form*, was published in English. A curious mix – translations of four of Negri's major essays from the sixties and seventies (which we discussed in chapter 3, pp. 66–8, 85–7) preceded by a collaborative introduction and two collaborative concluding chapters – the book was well received but did not attract an unusual amount of attention. Dedicated to Guattari, it constitutes a different kind of prolegomenon to *Empire* than *New Lines of Alliance* did. Whereas the Guattari collaboration laid out the broad outlines of a theory of globalization and resistance, *Labor of Dionysus* cleared the ground for the further elaboration of such a theory by summing up Negri's long engagement with the evolving nation state and by drawing upon that body of work in order to analyze the "postmodern state," which constitutes the building blocks of the global order of *Empire*.

The authors describe their project as an exercise in "juridical communism" (Hardt and Negri 1994: 6), and all the chapters focus on legal and juridical aspects of the state's effort to contain worker militancy within capitalist relations of production. The two collaborative chapters focus on the analysis of John Rawls' *Theory of Justice* as a model of the "thin" police state pursued by the neo-liberal Reagan and Thatcher doctrines and on the inadequacies of contemporary radical legal theory respectively. This emphasis on the juridical constitution of the contemporary state harkens back to Negri's youthful work on Hegel and the Kantian formalists and looks forward to the opening chapters of *Empire*, which introduce the duo's model of the transnational form of governance through juridical analyses. *Labor of Dionysus* reiterates the thesis of the two modernities and of the centrality of Renaissance humanism and materialism, which we have seen unfolding from Negri's earliest writings:

> Materialism should never be confused with the development of modernity; materialism persisted throughout the development of modernity as an alternative – an alternative that was continually suppressed but always sprang up again. The Renaissance discovered the freedom of labor, the *vis viva*: materialism interpreted it and capitalist modernity subjugated it. Today the refusal of waged labor and the development of intellectual productive forces repropose intact that alternative that at the dawn of modernity was crushed and expelled. (P. 21)

The book also introduces several new notions that would spark heated debate on the left when they were extended in *Empire* – most importantly cyborg labor or immaterial labor (pp. 10–13), which will be discussed below. *Labor of Dionysus* concludes, as many of Negri's books of single authorship did, on a note of intense radical fervor, which also dominates much of *Empire* and its sequels, *Multitude* (Hardt and Negri 2004) and *Commonwealth* (Hardt and Negri 2009):

> How is it possible at this point, once and for all, to abandon the conception of constituent power as necessarily negating itself in posing the constitution, and recognize a constituent power that no longer produces constitutions separate from itself, but rather is itself constitution? (Hardt and Negri 1994: 309)

This passage poses clearly the stakes of Hardt and Negri's overall project: to refound communist social and political practice by rethinking the fundamental concepts and categories of modern political philosophy.

Why did neither of Negri's earlier collaborations achieve anything like the influence that *Empire* would, despite their undeniable originality and sophistication and despite sharing with the latter work many significant characteristics? The answer to this question lies, at least in part, in the works' respective modes of exposition. Both *New Lines of Alliance* and the collaborative sections of *Labor of Dionysus* are relatively brief, and, while the former is abstractly conceptual or "diagrammatic," the latter is highly technical and specialized in its framework. Once Hardt and Negri found a way to combine these two expository approaches, their appeal to a broad audience grew as a result of the philosophical and political gestalt shift they successfully communicated to their readers. Guattari and Negri had recognized this requirement even though they could not fully meet it: "Recognizing that discourse is action, we will forge a new discourse in such a fashion as to initiate the destruction of the old way" (Guattari and Negri 1985: 28). In *Labor of Dionysus* as well, Hardt and Negri recognized that "[c]onstructing the names of reality constitutes the cognitive space within which being develops the passage from *cupiditas* (the desire to live) to cooperation" (Hardt and Negri 1994: 287). Naming, or rather theorizing, is itself material political practice. By giving productive names – Empire, multitude, and common – to the new conditions of struggle against capital, Hardt and Negri would significantly advance that struggle.

From Imperialism to Empire

In order to understand the tremendous response, both positive and negative, that *Empire* elicited, we must first understand the historical situation into which it erupted. The late 1980s and early 1990s were dominated, in the social sciences and humanities, by the problematics of postmodernism and poststructuralism. Although postmodernism and poststructuralism are broad concepts that developed in complex ways during debates across these fields, we can identify their most important components without difficulty. First, these critical schools positioned themselves as self-critiques of modernism and modernity that revealed the incoherence of modernity's metaphysical project for the re-establishment of subjective agency, cultural unity and political sovereignty after the crisis of historical traditions that led to world wars, decolonization struggles and genocides in the first half of the twentieth century. Jacques Derrida's analyses of the "closure of metaphysics" from Plato to Heidegger are probably the most influential examples of this critique. Second, these two critical approaches were defined by their attention to the proliferation of incompatible sign and code systems, the rapidly accelerating circulation of which obscured the productive basis of social life; Jean Baudrillard's provocative celebration of the eclipse of the real under the "hyper-reality" of signs and media is the best known version of this notion. Third, this plurality of sign systems undermined the traditionally understood continuity of historical development by offering a plethora of incommensurable counter-histories; the most influential account of this "incredulity towards meta-narratives" was presented by Jean-François Lyotard in *The Postmodern Condition* (Lyotard 1984) and related works, but other versions from different political perspectives abounded, most importantly Francis Fukuyama's neo-conservative announcement that the "end of history" had been reached when the cataclysmic struggles that defined history were finally resolved in favor of the West through the collapse of the Soviet bloc (Fukuyama 1992).[4] Under such conditions, collective political theorization and struggle became precarious when they remained possible at all; this is the situation to which Negri, Guattari and Hardt responded in their initial collaborations.

In his 1991 study *Postmodernism, or, The Cultural Logic of Late Capitalism*, Fredric Jameson challenged cultural critics and historians, Marxists in particular, to "think the present historically in an age that has forgotten how to think historically in the first place" (Jameson 1991: ix) by developing a historicized concept of postmodernism that would be able to "coordinat[e] new forms of practice and social and mental habits...with the new forms of economic production and organization thrown up by the modification of capitalism – the new global division of labor – in recent years" (p. xiv). To accomplish this, he proposed a method that combined urban theorist Kevin Lynch's notion of cognitive mapping – the mental map of a city's space that allows residents to navigate it – with Louis Althusser's definition of ideology as a representation of "the imaginary relationship of individuals to their real conditions of existence" (Althusser 1971: 162). Specifically, Jameson called for a sophisticated and workable account of

> the gap between the local positioning of the individual subject and the totality of class structures in which he or she is situated, a gap

between phenomenological perception and a reality that transcends all individual thinking or experience; but which ideology, as such, attempts to span or coordinate, to map, by means of conscious and unconscious representations. The conception of cognitive mapping proposed here therefore involves an extrapolation... to the totality of class relations on a global (or should I say multinational) scale. (Jameson 1991: 415–16)

In short, Jameson called for a cognitive map of what we now call globalization. Over the following decade, and especially following the 9/11 events and the wars that followed (which definitively refuted Fukuyama, if not Lyotard), a number of models were proposed that, intentionally or not, attempted to answer Jameson's challenge. Most of them, whether conservative or progressive in their political orientation, offered maps that were repetitions or revivals of previous historical formations: Samuel Huntington's "clash of civilizations," Niall Ferguson's sympathetic defense of British (and US) imperialism, Giovanni Arrighi's "systemic cycles of accumulation" dating back to the Renaissance (see Arrighi 1994 and Hardt and Negri 2000: 238–9), and so on.

The merit of Hardt and Negri's analysis in *Empire* was to offer a cognitive map of globalization that emphasizes the novelties and opportunities of the current situation in a language that synthesizes a huge array of previous critical work into a manageable number of intuitively accessible terms. In other words they convincingly historicized postmodernism as the mystified ideology of globalization, and in so doing they pointed to a way forward out of post-modernism (rather than backward, to some earlier cultural formation), both for critical analysis and for militancy.[5] And they did so in confident and aggressively affirmative terms (their detractors preferred to describe them as "messianic"), of a kind that had been missing from leftist theory for many years. We will examine their specific analysis of postmodernist, poststructuralist and post-colonial cultural theory in detail below.

Like Negri's earlier works in the history of philosophy, *Empire* offers a counter-history of modernity; and, like his earlier works in political organization, it promotes a project of escape from the reactionary, dialectical wing of modernity. The combination of these two aspects in a single, detailed and lucid work no doubt contributed to its success as a handbook for analysts of and participants in struggles over globalization. Much of the credit for the work's lucidity should go to Hardt, who was responsible for melding the equal contributions of the two authors into a formal and stylistic unity, translating Negri's Italian into the English of their books' original publication and finalizing the texts for printing. *Empire* is organized into two parallel counter-histories: one of sovereignty, or of the "formal constitution" of contemporary Power, and one of production, or of its "material constitution" (Hardt and Negri 2000: xiv). Both of them lead, through occasional digressions into the more complex implications of these counter-histories, to the identification of the defining features of the contemporary world order and of resistance to it. "Along with the global market and global circuits of production has emerged a global order, a new logic and structure of rule – in short, a new form of sovereignty. Empire is the political subject that effectively regulates these global exchanges, the sovereign power that governs the world" (p. xi).

At first glance this might be read as another restatement of the classical theory of imperialism propounded by Lenin and Rosa Luxemburg; yet to think that would be a mistake, for, as Hardt and Negri assert, "[b]y 'Empire' ... we understand something altogether different from 'imperialism'" (p. xii). Unlike earlier imperialisms (such as the British Empire), the new Empire is not one among many parallel political constructions, centered on a particular nation state and controlling numerous subordinated colonial territories at its periphery; it is rather a single global entity with no territorial boundaries, no clear-cut geographical polarities and no center or periphery, and just as it encompasses the totality of global space, so it aspires to encompass all time by suspending temporal boundaries, and indeed history itself. It rules over subjects and objects that its own functioning produces and seeks to control, doing so in the name of universal peace, but by means of continual warfare (pp. xiv–xv). This concept synthesizes many of the key ideas that had emerged from Negri's earlier work with concepts drawn from other important schools of analysis such as postcolonial studies, new media studies and feminism. The task of Hardt and Negri's first fully collaborative book, then, is to explicate the metaphysical, economic and political paradoxes and crises that constitute Empire.

Empire rules over an unbounded territorial space because all nation states are parts of it, but no single nation state (or group of nation states) fully controls it.

> Even the dominant countries are now dependent on the global system; the interactions of the world market have resulted in a gen-

eralized disarticulation of all economies. Increasingly, any attempt at isolation or separation will mean only a more brutal kind of domination by the global system, a reduction to powerlessness and poverty. (P. 284)

Not even the United States, which is seen by many left critics as the last imperialist super-power, is in a position of unilateral command. As Hardt and Negri regularly remind us, "the coming Empire is not American and the United States is not its center" (p. 384). But if Empire is not controlled by one or more imperialist nations, who does control it, and from where? Its dominant institutions are non-democratic intergovernmental organizations (IGOs) like the World Trade Organization, the World Bank and the International Monetary Fund,[6] which work to produce an economically smooth global field over which transnational corporations – but not most of their workers – can easily move.

The activities of corporations are no longer defined by the imposition of abstract command and the organization of simple theft and unequal exchange. Rather, they directly structure and articulate territories and populations. They tend to make nation-states merely instruments to record the flows of the commodities, monies, and populations that they set in motion. (P. 31)

These institutions and the corporations they empower, which are answerable not to the worker-citizens of the nation states but only to the investors who provide them with capital, have no fixed locus of Power, but exist instead in constant circulation: "In this smooth space of Empire, there is no *place* of power – it is both everywhere and nowhere. Empire is an *ou-topia*, or really a *non-place*" (p. 190).

This situation constitutes the fulfillment of Marx's forecast of the real subsumption of society within capital, which we discussed in chapter 3: capitalism not only has become the abstract general horizon of accumulation and socialization, but it has infiltrated all productive relationships and re-created them according to its own logic. Consequently, the capitalism of Empire no longer has an outside; and this situation constitutes its novelty, since heretofore capitalism has developed by absorbing its outside. "In the process of capitalization *the outside is internalized*. Capital must therefore not only have open exchange with non-capitalist societies or only appropriate their wealth; it must also actually transform them into capitalist societies themselves" (p. 226). This process takes place in every part of the globe, though it is by no means uniform. But, now that the world is entirely – though unevenly – dominated by capitalist logic, how can capital continue to develop? Only by shifting its operations from extension – the absorption of the geographical outside – to intensity – the more efficient exploitation of what lies inside it. It must even out the conditions of production without evening out the results of unequal accumulation. The key to this intensified internal exploitation is Michel Foucault's concept of biopower, which Hardt and Negri see as the lifeblood of Empire: "Biopower is a form of power that regulates social life from its interior, following it, interpreting it, absorbing it, and rearticulating it...Biopower thus refers to a situation in which what is directly at stake in power is the production and reproduction of life itself" (pp. 23–4). Biopower takes the fundamental elements of life – bodies, affects, minds, social relations – as its material inputs and outputs, producing (with) these elements – just as industrial capitalism produced (with) iron, steel, coal and oil. Through a variety of overlapping institutions (of education, public health, welfare and so on), the biopolitical state produces, reproduces, develops and controls the population as well as the physical infrastructure that will produce its wealth.[7] This operation of biopower gives rise to what Deleuze calls a society of control, "that society (which develops at the far edge of modernity and opens toward the post-modern) in which mechanisms of command become ever more 'democratic,' ever more immanent to the social field, distributed throughout the brains and bodies of the citizens" (p. 23; see also Deleuze 1995). The society of control, which corresponds to the smoothing of boundaries in Empire, replaces the institutional discontinuities or "striations" of the modern disciplinary society that Foucault analyzed – the asylum, the clinic, the prison, the school, the factory – with continuous network monitoring and with the constant extortion of its subjects' consent.

Since the intensive exploitation of the global Empire depends upon the maintenance of fine social and technological tolerances, anything that threatens to throw those tolerances off balance is ruthlessly suppressed – not by warfare among sovereign states, justified by imperialist ideologies of exceptional national right, but by an equally brutal international policing of the smooth space, justified by appeals to universal right and perpetual peace (Hardt and Negri 2000: 17–18). Whereas during the Cold War the capitalist and socialist worlds, constrained by the structural unreason of nuclear deterrence, fought a ferocious series of proxy wars in order to preserve their increasingly precarious structures of imperialist control, today the agents of global Empire – collections of states, IGOs and the corporations that both command and service them – fight only non-sovereign, "criminal" enemies like drug cartels or terrorist networks, and they only attack other "rogue" nation states with the approval of the international bodies themselves. Multilateralism is the watchword of Empire, as the Gulf War, the Kosovo conflict and the Iraq/Afghanistan Wars demonstrate.

To trace the origin of this new form of de-centered global governance or "governance without government" (p. 14), we must follow Hardt and Negri's account of its historical emergence as an innovation in both sovereignty and production. As in Negri's earlier works, the story begins in the crisis of Renaissance humanism, which spawns the two conflicting modernities. "Modernity itself is defined by crisis, a crisis that is born of the uninterrupted conflict between the immanent, constructive, creative forces and the transcendent power aimed at restoring order" (p. 76) – in other words, the conflict between virtue and fortune. As we discussed in chapters 1 and 4, during the Renaissance the powers of immanence in philosophy, science and the arts dissolved the transcendent stasis of medieval social and conceptual relations, opening a space of intense intellectual, social and political creativity and productivity. The subject of this constructive humanist project was the multitude, Machiavelli's "people in arms," the open set of irreducible singularities that demanded democracy and energized the new creativity. This creativity recognized no external constraints of convention or heredity, so it came into conflict with the existing institutions of rule. The latter sought to constrain the powers of immanence within the structures of hierarchical authority. The old transcendence had to be eliminated in order to create new wealth and power, but a new transcendence had to be invented so that wealth and power could continue to accumulate on a radically inequitable social basis. Summarizing Negri's academic works that we examined in chapter 2, *Empire* restages the history of European metaphysics as a history of bourgeois ideology from Descartes to Hegel (pp. 79–82) and concludes as follows:

> Politics resides at the center of metaphysics because modern European metaphysics arose in response to the challenge of the liberated singularities and the revolutionary constitution of the multitude...In politics, as in metaphysics, the dominant theme was thus to eliminate

the medieval form of transcendence, which only inhibits production and consumption, while maintaining transcendence's effects of domination in a form adequate to the modes of association and production of the new humanity. (P. 83)

The eruption of immanence and its demolition of transcendence constitute the first, radical version of modernity, and the reconstruction of transcendence in order to channel immanence into inequitable economic accumulation constitutes the second, reactionary version of modernity.

The primary metaphysical task of second modernity was the construction of a new logic of sovereignty, which acknowledged immanence but trapped it within a transcendent structure of Power as the latter's docile but productive motor. It accomplished this by means of the logic of generalized representation that corresponded to the emergence of the nation state out of the ruins of medieval Europe. Against the traditional conception of rule that focused on collective submission to the divine body of the monarch, the new model of sovereignty based itself upon well-defined geographical contiguity and population. In other words,

> the physical territory and population were conceived as the extension of the transcendent essence of the nation. *The modern concept of nation thus inherited the patrimonial body of the monarchic state and reinvented it in a new form*...This uneasy structural relationship was stabilized by the national identity: a cultural, integrating identity, founded on a biological continuity of blood relations, a spatial continuity of territory, and linguistic commonality. (P. 95)

Spatial contiguity was easy to define in theory (though it required extensive warfare and policing to maintain the national boundaries in fact), but the biological and linguistic integration of a national identity required more effort. In order to found itself, the nation form had to project backward into the past a collective subject whom it could claim to represent, and thereby it could legitimate itself once the divinity of the monarch had been debunked. Thus the concept of the people was born.[8]

Hardt and Negri contrast the multitude and the people in clear terms:

> The multitude is a multiplicity, a plane of singularities, an open set of relations, which is not homogeneous or identical with itself and

bears an indistinct, inclusive relation to those outside of it. The people, in contrast, tends toward identity and homogeneity internally while posing its difference from and excluding what remains outside of it. (P. 103)

This identity and homogeneity were not given but had to be constructed through a process consisting of two moments, both of which were tied up with the contemporaneous emergence of European imperialism. The first moment depended upon "the mechanisms of colonial racism that construct the identity of European peoples in a dialectical play of oppositions with their native Others" (ibid.). The second involved "the eclipse of internal differences through the representation of the whole population by a hegemonic group, race, or class" (p. 104). The people on whom the nation state was founded were circumscribed externally and negatively against the subhumanity of their colonial subjects, and then represented internally by a single subset of the geographical nation's actual population. The subject that assumed Power as a result of this double construction was the adult, white, male property-owner, in other words the aristocracy and bourgeoisie; and this is the subject that took charge of the institutional articulations of the sovereign state. This institutionalization, which corresponds to the historicist reduction of Kant's juridical philosophy and to Hegel's celebration of the *Volksstaat* as Negri described them in his early books (see chapter 2, pp. 58–60), was the culmination of a sequence of representational substitutions whose precariousness continues to underpin the nation form today. As Hardt and Negri note: "The entire logical chain of representation might be summarized like this: the people representing the multitude, the nation representing the people, and the state representing the nation. Each link is an attempt to hold in suspension the crisis of modernity" (Hardt and Negri 2000: 135).

From its origins in the horrific warfare of the seventeenth century, the nation state as a European political form stabilized itself through colonial conquest and internal class repression over the course of the eighteenth and nineteenth centuries. The next crucial step in the development of modern sovereignty was taken by the American revolutionaries, who went beyond the closed and exclusionary national conceptions of their European forebears to propose an open-ended model of sovereignty that would ultimately come to underpin Empire.

> The new sovereignty can arise...only from the constitutional forma-
> tion of limits and equilibria, checks and balances, which both con-
> stitutes a central power and maintains power in the hands of the
> multitude. There is no longer any necessity or any room here for the
> transcendence of power...Power can be constituted by a whole
> series of powers that regulate themselves and arrange themselves in
> networks. (Pp. 161–2)

As we will see, the network forms the basis not only of the new
constitution of sovereignty, but also of the new mode of production. In political terms, it refers to the functionalist logic of the
mixed constitution, the separation of powers that reduces – but
does not eliminate – the hierarchical concentration of command
and maximizes the space of immanence within the expanding territory of the nation state. One of the consequences of the network,
which emerges gradually through further conflict, is the overcoming of the older idea of the people. "The new democracy had to
destroy the transcendental idea of the nation with all its racial divisions and create its own people, defined not by old heritages but
by a new ethics of the construction and expansion of the community" (p. 172). That is, a new people had to be – and was – forged
from an unruly mass of immigrants without a pre-existing geographical locus, common language or cultural heritage. This is not
to deny the real contradictions that remained in the structure of the
new US formal and material constitution – most importantly, the
exclusion of indigenous people and the partial inclusion of slaves
with respect to the new national subject form – but rather to emphasize the self-correcting constitutional apparatus that was produced,
an apparatus that would ultimately prove capable of integrating
more differences, and thus more of the multitude, than the older
European model of the *Volksstaat*. As Negri had shown in *Insurgencies*, the American Constitution enclosed the revolutionary constituent power of the Declaration of Independence within its
functional architecture and thereby permitted the constitutional
order to modify or reform itself while remaining in force.[9]

The subsequent steps in the evolution of Empire's preconditions
pass through the rise of internationalism, initially in Woodrow
Wilson's doomed attempt to found a League of Nations (p. 175),
and finally in the establishment of the United Nations after the
Second World War, which "can be regarded as the culmination of
this entire constitutive process, a culmination that both reveals the
limitations of the notion of international order and points beyond

it toward a new notion of global order" (p. 4).[10] The increasing
symbolic power of international consensus mediated by the UN –
multilateralism, in short – reaches its apex in the first Gulf War,
which "presented the United States as the only power able to
manage international justice, *not as a function of its own national
motives but in the name of global right*" (p. 180). The American constitutional model, which permitted an indefinite extension of governance by positing the continual expansion of geographical
borders and a continual renegotiation of the category of the people,
forms the basis for the immanent productive operations of Empire.
Empire is "American," then, only in the limited sense that the
governing logic of its system of sovereignty is an export of the US.

As described so far, the process of the formal constitution of
Empire may appear as the inexorable unfolding of a historical
necessity, or as a conscious project of capital itself; but nothing
could be further from the truth. Hardt and Negri admit that

> [f]rom one perspective Empire stands clearly over the multitude and
> subjects it to the rule of its overarching machine, as a new Leviathan.
> At the same time, however, from the perspective of social productiv-
> ity and creativity, from what we have been calling the ontological
> perspective, the hierarchy is reversed. The multitude is the real
> productive force of our social world, whereas Empire is a mere
> apparatus of capture that lives only off the vitality of the multi-
> tude...(P. 62)

These two perspectives are not symmetrical or equivalent; this is
not a relativist or Manichean model, and certainly not a dialectical
one. On the contrary, the theory of Empire stands solidly in the
workerist line of Marxist thought and views the productive laboring subject as the source of all social, political and economic development. Thus Hardt and Negri proclaim that "the construction of
Empire and its global networks is a *response* to the various struggles
against the modern machines of power, and specifically to class
struggle driven by the multitude's desire for liberation. The multitude called Empire into being" (p. 43). Empire is dependent on the
multitude for the productive energy that drives its development,
but the multitude is not dependent on Empire. Our next task, then,
is to follow the evolution of the material constitution, the forms
and relations of production that underpin the formal constitution
of imperial sovereignty and permit Empire to draw its energy from
the multitude.

The early struggles of the multitude against the forces of transcendent monarchic rule and feudal economic obligation precipi-
tated the crisis of the static medieval world, and the irrepressible
antagonism that the multitude bore toward the newly created representative structures of national sovereignty periodically threw
almost every nation state into crisis during the modern era. Indeed,
classical imperialism is based as much on the need to control the
domestic workforce as on the need for sources of raw material and
captive markets. As Cecil Rhodes and other reactionary nationalists
realized, "the modern European nation-states use imperialism to
transfer outside their own borders the political contradictions that
arise within each single country" (p. 232). Slavery and peonage in
the colonies encouraged the domestic proletariat to identify with
their respective national bourgeoisies rather than with their fellow
workers abroad. But imperialism cannot contain the multitude
forever, because "[i]mperialism actually creates a straitjacket for
capital – or, more precisely, at a certain point the boundaries created
by imperialist practices obstruct capitalist development and the
full realization of its world market" (p. 234). The rigid boundaries
necessary to imperialist command impede the circulation of capital,
goods and labor necessary for the further expansion of the capitalist system, and therefore they must be dissolved. The American
Revolution marks the formal start of the era of decolonization; but
it is really the Haitian Revolution and the slave revolts it inspired
that define the process, which would accelerate during the first half
of the twentieth century (see pp. 116–23). The European imperialist
systems gradually collapsed in the face of native independence
movements and of the inefficiencies of imperialist administration,
and their colonial holdings became new capitalist nations (or state
socialist ones, which is not much different in Hardt and Negri's
view) that borrowed their form from their former masters. This
process, in which decolonization goes hand in hand with modernization and capitalization, reached its climax in the Vietnam War.
Prior to its defeat in Vietnam, the US had toyed with a classical
imperialism of its own – most obviously by stepping into Indo-
china to finish the job of violent pacification that the French had
abandoned – but the intensity of Vietnamese popular resistance
dissuaded the US state apparatus from such a project (pp. 178–9).
Empire became, for capital, the only alternative to ruin.

An internal movement of dissolution corresponded to the
external opposition to, and struggle against, modern imperialism.
Imperialist states successfully pacified their domestic working

classes over the course of the nineteenth and early twentieth centuries by paying an increasing share of social wealth to the workers
in return for their participation in development. "Out of this development came the trinity that would constitute the modern welfare
state: a synthesis of Taylorism in the organization of labor, Fordism
in the wage regime, and Keynesianism in the macroeconomic regulation of society" (p. 242). These features of the welfare state reached
their fullest expression in the American New Deal; but they could
be found virtually worldwide (see chapter 3, pp. 72, 82). The mechanisms of the welfare state laid the foundations for the disciplinary
biopower of Empire in that the Keynesian safety net of social services (education, healthcare, pensions and so on) and the consumerism made possible by the Fordist wage regime were created not
for humanitarian reasons but rather to control the multitude's
antagonism, to render it docile and predictably productive as the
basis of national wealth and productivity. But this docility and
predictability broke down at the same moment as the US imperialist project collapsed. Just as the Vietnamese resistance marked the
end of classical imperialism, so the resistance movements of the
1960s – from the anti-war and civil rights movements to feminism
and ecology – spelled the end of the Fordist–Keynesian compromise. "The various struggles [of the sixties] converged against one
common enemy: *the international disciplinary order*... The refusal of
the disciplinary regime and the affirmation of the sphere of non-
work became the defining features of a new set of collective practices and a new form of life" (p. 261). As Negri intuited in the
seventies, the refusal of work marked a massive rebellion against
capitalist command. In its place, "[t]he entire panoply of movements and the entire emerging counterculture highlighted the
social value of cooperation and communication" (p. 275). In short,
as we saw in chapter 3, the re-emerging multitude refused to
work in the old way, and its refusal forced capital to restructure
production into the form of Empire.[11] This is how the multitude
calls Empire into being: "*The proletariat actually invents the social
and productive forms that capital will be forced to adopt in the future*"
(p. 268).

Hardt and Negri propose 1968 as the year when everything
began to change from modernity to postmodernity, in production
as well as in government.

Whereas the process of modernization was indicated by a migration
of labor from agriculture and mining (the primary sector) to industry

(the secondary), the process of postmodernization or informatization has been demonstrated through the migration from industry to
service jobs (the tertiary)...Just as through the process of modernization all production tended to become industrialized, so too
through the process of postmodernization all production tends
toward the production of services, toward becoming informational-
ized. (Pp. 285–6)

The two authors do not claim that all production is now informa-
tized, or that services dominate the global employment of labor, as
some critics allege. Rather, they are again applying the method of
the tendency in order to identify an ongoing structural transformation that is not yet complete. Just as modern industrialization transformed even those forms of work that remained non-industrial,
such as agriculture, so postmodern informatization is transforming
even those forms of labor that remain stubbornly manual. This
process of postmodernization or informatization corresponds, in
the material constitution of Empire, to the emergence and dominance of the network model of sovereignty in the formal constitution. "In the passage to the informational economy, the assembly
line has been replaced by the *network* as the organizational model
of production, transforming the forms of cooperation and communication within each productive site and among productive sites"
(p. 295). Network production, dependent as it is upon multimedia
communications technology, arises as an apparatus of capture, in
response to the cooperative desires and practices of the counter-
cultural multitude. The network economy is dominated by service
work: financial services, personal services and so on. "Since the
production of services results in no material and durable good, we
define the labor involved in this production as *immaterial labor* –
that is, labor that produces an immaterial good, such as a service,
a cultural product, knowledge, or communication" (p. 290). Hardt
and Negri's conception of immaterial labor, first introduced in
Labor of Dionysus, includes the symbolic labor of computer pro-
gramming, marketing and media production, as well as the affective labor of care-giving, sex work and teaching. "What affective
labor produces are social networks, forms of community, biopower" (p. 293), which capital captures for profit.[12]

Immaterial labor differs from preceding forms of labor in
one important way, which brings the workerist hypothesis to the
fore:

the cooperative aspect of immaterial labor is not imposed or organized from the outside, as it was in previous forms of labor, but
rather, *cooperation is completely immanent to the laboring activity
itself*...In the expression of its own creative energies, immaterial
labor thus seems to provide the potential for a kind of spontaneous
and elementary communism. (P. 294)

Previous forms of labor, industrial labor in particular, depended
upon the entrepreneurial initiative of capitalists for its effective
cooperative organization; but immaterial labor does not. As the
extension and refinement of Negri's earlier concept of the socialized worker, the immaterial laborer can only do her work because
she is already thoroughly socialized, and that means that she does
not require external command in order to cooperate. Immaterial
labor is network labor for network production. This is the flipside
of biopower's installation of control within the individual subject:
the diffusion of self-discipline and self-organization throughout the
social structure, which makes biopolitical resistance not only possible but inevitable.[13] Postmodern capital does not have to expend
itself in organizing immaterial labor; on the contrary, it has to
expend itself making sure that immaterial labor does not organize
itself in threatening ways. Immaterial labor produces an excess of
its own organization that capital cannot fully capture for profit, and
this is what constitutes its "potential for spontaneous and elementary communism." Hardt and Negri claim that "the fundamental
condition of the existence of the *universal network*, which is the
central hypothesis of this constitutional framework, is that it be
hybrid... that the political subject be fleeting and passive, while the
producing and consuming agent is present and active" (p. 320). To
put it another way, "Empire recognizes and profits from the fact
that in cooperation bodies produce more and in community bodies
enjoy more, but it has to obstruct and control this cooperative
autonomy so as not to be destroyed by it" (p. 392). This subjective
hybridity is both a condition of expanded production and a means
of restraining that expansion.

Hardt and Negri recognize that hybridity alone is not a sufficient
condition for successful struggle against Empire, as recent models
such as poststructuralism and postcolonialism assume. These
theoretical approaches to philosophy, culture and history are
subsets of postmodernism, the conceptual expressions of economic
postmodernization. Hardt and Negri assess postmodernist and

poststructuralist theory in Part 2 of *Empire*, "Passages of Sovereignty," where they acknowledge the progressive intent of these forms of postmodern critique:

> the world of modern sovereignty is a Manichaean world, divided by a series of binary oppositions that define Self and Other, white and black, inside and outside, ruler and ruled. Postmodernist thought challenges precisely this binary logic of modernity and in this respect provides important resources for those who are struggling to challenge modern discourses...(P. 139)

The authors view postcolonial critique, the study of the socio-cultural impact of colonialism and of the transition out of it, as part of postmodernism because of its reliance upon poststructuralist analyses of subjectivity and discourse; so this form of study is subject to the same limitations as its models. Both modes of critique, postcolonial and postmodern, affirm the plurality and the hybrid combination of expressed differences – of gender, ethnicity, sexuality and culture – as antidotes to the monolithic uniformity of modernity, which produced, and was produced by, imperialism and colonialism. The problem with these modes of critique is that they mistake their object – because, as Hardt and Negri demonstrate, "Empire too is bent on doing away with those modern forms of sovereignty and on setting differences to play across boundaries. Despite the best intentions, then, the postmodernist politics of difference not only is ineffective against but can even coincide with and support the functions and practices of imperial rule" (p. 142).[14] Empire and its commodities are as hybrid as any postcolonial subject.

Postmodernism and postcolonial critique both take aim at a system of rule that no longer exists in its binary modern form, and consequently they end up collaborating unintentionally with the new system of de-centered rule that has supplanted modernity. "Postmodernism is indeed the logic by which global capital operates...Postmodern marketing recognizes the difference of each commodity and each segment of the population, fashioning its strategies accordingly. Every difference is an opportunity" (pp. 151–2). The centrality of the practices of niche marketing and diversity management to contemporary capitalism demonstrates this. At the other end of the global system, fundamentalism, too – both Islamic and Christian – constitutes a postmodern critique of modern sovereignty, and thus it is "a symptom of the passage to

Empire" (p. 147). This account reverses the conventional interpretation of these phenomena, which presents them as regressive refusals of modernity. *Empire* emphasizes instead the novelty of their conceptions and, implicitly at least, the contemporaneity of the technological and communicational structures on which they rely.

> Simplifying a great deal, one could argue that postmodernist discourses appeal primarily to the winners in the processes of globalization and fundamentalist discourses to the losers. In other words, the current global tendencies toward increased mobility, indeterminacy, and hybridity are experienced by some as a kind of liberation but by others as an exacerbation of their suffering. (P. 150)

Fundamentalism, too, is a hybrid, network phenomenon, which again demonstrates that hybridity alone is not enough to define a resistance movement of the multitude against Empire.

The material constitution of Empire is not rigidly exclusionary, as postmodernists think, but differentially inclusive, as befits its origin in the American network model explicated earlier. This does not mean that racism and other forms of discrimination do not persist within Empire, but it does mean that those forms are no longer identical with their modern versions. For Hardt and Negri, who follow Étienne Balibar's lead (see Balibar and Wallerstein 1991, and "Racism as Universalism" in Balibar 1994), imperial racism is no longer predicated on a pseudo-biological essentialism of genetically innate racial characteristics, but rather on environmental and historical differences of culture and socialization. Racialized differences still determine patterns of segregation, but in a pluralist way: "Racial differences are thus contingent in principle, but quite necessary in practice as markers of social separation. The theoretical substitution of culture for race or biology is thus transformed paradoxically into a theory of the preservation of race" (Hardt and Negri 2000: 192). Racial differences are no longer absolutized as differences of nature, but relativized as degrees of difference or deviation from the norm of the imperial subject – who remains the straight, white bourgeois subject of the European nation state. Hybrids, racial, gendered and sexual Others who would have been strictly excluded under modernity, are now included in the new concept of the people, provided that they express their hybridity and differences in docile and accommodating ways. Empire accepts and even embraces differences, but only "nonconflictual differences, the kind of differences that we might

set aside when necessary" and that can therefore be managed hierarchically (p. 199). In this way, Empire evades much of postcolonial, postmodern and poststructuralist critique by anticipating its
moves, and so critique must find other tools to dismantle the imperial order.

> Difference, hybridity, and mobility are not liberatory in themselves:
> but neither are truth, purity, and stasis. The real revolutionary prac-
> tice refers to the level of *production*. Truth will not make us free, but
> taking control of the production of truth will. Mobility and hybridity
> are not liberatory, but taking control of the production of mobility
> and stasis, purities and mixtures is. (P. 156)

The task of effective critique is to wrest the production of truth and
difference from Empire's control, and in so doing to reclaim political agency for the multitude.

Empire works to control the cooperative subjects on which its
production depends, but not in the same way in which modern
imperialism controlled its subjects. "The breakdown of the institutions, the withering of civil society, and the decline of disciplinary
society all involve a smoothing of the striation of modern social
space. Here arise the networks of the society of control" (p. 329).
The society of control, as we noted, operates within individual
subjects and their relationships, but it also overdetermines the field
at the highest level. "Imperial control operates through three global
and absolute means: the bomb, money, and ether" (p. 345).
Although its threat has declined from the heights of the Cold War,
nuclear terror remains the trump in the hands of the "monarchy"
of global mixed constitution, the US military, and it is normally
deployed symbolically (as in the justification for the Iraq War
through the threat that "weapons of mass destruction" may be in
rogue hands). Money is the means of control in the hands of the
global "aristocracy," the dominant nation states and the transnational corporations, while the media serves a quasi-"democratic"
function of legitimating governance and of producing consent (see
pp. 309–14).

Imperial control measures itself against the protean struggles of
the global multitude, which is excluded from the mixed constitution. "Having achieved the global level, capitalist development is
faced directly with the multitude, without mediation. Hence the
dialectic, or really the science of the limit and its organization,
evaporates" (p. 237). Modern dialectical sovereignty, theorized

from Descartes to Hegel and implemented by the nation state, has reached the limit of its effectiveness in the face of the multitude's intransigent and irrecuperable antagonism.

> The creative forces of the multitude that sustain Empire are also capable of autonomously constructing a counter-Empire, an alternative political organization of global flows and exchanges. The struggles to contest and subvert Empire, as well as those to construct a real alternative, will thus take place on the imperial terrain itself – indeed, such new struggles have already begun to emerge. (P. xv)

Such struggles – from the Zapatista revolt in Chiapas, the Los Angeles riots and the Palestinian Intifada to the counter-globalization demonstrations of Seattle and Genoa – draw upon a long history of counter-modernity; but they are also novel in that they are "at once economic, political, and cultural – and hence they are biopolitical struggles, struggles over the form of life. They are constituent struggles, creating new public spaces and new forms of community" (p. 56) without hierarchy or representation. Indeed, these struggles are as singular as the components of the multitude by which they are enacted, so singular in fact that the "*struggles have become all but incommunicable*" even among themselves, and they do not form a coordinated and accelerating cycle, like the one that characterized nationalist decolonization struggles (p. 54). Powerful though these struggles are, the multitude's full realization of counter-Empire requires yet another effort.

Perhaps the most impressive and original form of the multitude's struggle that Hardt and Negri identify is rarely recognized as such by critical theory or conventional politics:

> A specter haunts the world and it is the specter of migration. All the powers of the old world are allied in a merciless operation against it, but the movement is irresistible...Whereas in the disciplinary era *sabotage* was the fundamental notion of resistance, in the era of imperial control it may be *desertion*...Desertion and exodus are a powerful form of class struggle within and against imperial postmodernity. (Pp. 212–13)

Exodus, which in Hardt and Negri's definition includes the involuntary flight of refugees as well as the voluntary movement of legal and illegal immigrants and guest workers, is the form of struggle against Empire that involves the largest number of subjects, mostly from what was once known as the Third World. Their withdrawal

from their immediate social, cultural and political locales constitutes a massive intensification of the refusal of the disciplinary
regime of modern/imperialist sovereignty that characterized the
counter-cultural movements of 1968 – what Negri called "separation" in his writings of the seventies. This intensifying refusal poses
the most profound challenge to Empire's model of control and
exploitation. Despite its eroded sovereignty, the nation state is the
front line of imperial defense against exodus. The ultimate aims of
Empire are to recognize the originality of these singular struggles
and experiences of exodus and to endow them with concepts that
will allow them to communicate, while preventing them from
falling into dialectical forms of hierarchy, delegation and militariza-
tion that will ultimately compromise and recuperate them within
the imperial system. Although the authors repeatedly insist that
"no such effective blueprint will ever arise from a theoretical articulation such as ours" (p. 206), nevertheless they offer some guide-
lines for the articulation of constituent struggles as well as a shortlist
of demands that, in their view, should accompany any effort to
oppose Empire.

Hardt and Negri's project is essentially an update of Potere
operaio's and Autonomia's: to find a theoretical framework that
can accelerate the development of a political composition to match
the new technical composition of the multitude, which we have
just examined. "We need to investigate specifically how the multitude can become a *political subject* in the context of Empire" (p. 394).
It can only do so by reflecting on the conditions of its re-emergence
from the representational structure of the people and on the form
of command that it has driven capital to adopt in order to recuperate it within the dialectical mechanism of development. It is impossible for any theorist, no matter how prescient, to anticipate what
political composition will arise from the activities of the global
multitude; but Hardt and Negri are confident enough of their
overall analysis to offer three preliminary planks for the multitude's political platform. These are as follows:

1 *"global citizenship* ... [T]he political demand is that the existent
   fact of capitalist production [that is, its mobility] be recognized
   juridically and that all workers be given the full rights of citizenship ... *The general right to control its own movement is the
   multitude's ultimate demand for global citizenship"* (p. 400).
2 *"a social wage and guaranteed income for all* ... The demand for a
   social wage extends to the entire population the demand that

all activity necessary for the production of capital be recognized with an equal compensation such that a social wage is really a guaranteed income" (p. 403).

3   "the right to reappropriation... The right to reappropriation is really the multitude's right to self-control and autonomous self-production" (pp. 406–7).

These basic demands are both revolutionary in that the current procedures of Empire are tending in the opposite direction, toward a violent constriction of such rights, and reformist in that the demands are within the capacity of imperial Power to accommodate them without a thorough change in its form. Some critics have noted this slippage and accused Hardt and Negri of hedging their bets. Their only response was to reiterate: "We do not have any models to offer for this event. Only the multitude through practical experimentation will offer the models and determine when and how the possible becomes real" (p. 411).

Empire under Fire

Empire was published by Harvard University Press on March 10, 2000, while Negri languished in his second stretch of prison time, and for over a year it received a steady stream of largely positive reviews in scholarly journals from a variety of disciplines. At the same time, its theses were taken up by new militant organizations around the world, especially in Italy, where workerism's legacy had never been fully suppressed or forgotten. The Tute Bianchi ("White Overalls") group, which was originally organized in the mid-nineties to defend the occupation of derelict urban spaces for "social centers [*centri sociali*]," was among the first to adopt a militant line showing the influence of Hardt and Negri's ideas – or rather the confluence between their ideas and the residual workerist elements that persisted among the younger members of the Italian left (see Wu Ming 1 2001). Their protests against the closing of the social centers, in which they donned white padded clothing (hence their name) and moved in tight formations to minimize the effects of police violence, spawned later, more ambitious protests against global capital in Prague and Genoa during 2000 and 2001 – protests that made explicit reference to *Empire*'s concepts.[15] In an interview with the Italian newspaper *Il Manifesto*, the group's most prominent spokesman, Luca Casarini, described the group's thinking in

Hardt and Negri's terms: "We have talked of Empire, or better of an imperial logic in the government of the world. This means the erosion of national sovereignty. Not the end, but an erosion and its redefinition in a global, imperial, framework" (Casarini, quoted in Callinicos 2003: 122). Casarini later explained to a skeptical Alex Callinicos why the group drew upon *Empire*:

> To turn now to the issue of daily political activity – we found that it is very useful to talk about empire when we're talking about globalisation because those people who stand in the classic tradition of analysing American imperialism are those who believe in vanguards and the masses. They are also the same people who believe these movements, the anti-capitalist movements, are reformist movements, and so it's very useful to us to introduce new categorisations. (Casarini 2001)

The Tute Bianchi eschewed the Leninist organizational model of vanguards, preferring to immerse themselves in the uncompromised and unrepresented revolutionary singularities of the multitude; and, when the group disbanded, its members simply melted back into the multitude, to find other organizational opportunities.[16]

Empire's simultaneously cross-disciplinary and street-level success ultimately attracted the attention of the mainstream US press, which reacted in a predictably neutralizing manner. In the July 7, 2001 issue of *New York Times*, journalist Emily Eakin suggested that *Empire* was turning into the "Next Big Idea" in cultural studies scholarship, a fashionable model that would address "the need in fields like English, history and philosophy for a major new theory" to replace structuralism, poststructuralism and psychoanalysis (Eakin 2001). Two weeks later, in the pages of *Time Magazine*, journalist Michael Elliott declared *Empire* "the hot, smart book of the moment" (Elliott 2001a: 39), and at the end of the year he nominated Hardt and Negri for *Time's* list of "Next Wave Innovators" on the grounds that they had written "the most talked-about work of social theory in years" (Elliott 2001b: 68). A special issue of *Rethinking Marxism* was the first large-scale critical project organized in response to *Empire*, but before that issue appeared the 9/11 attacks on the World Trade Center and on the Pentagon took place, radically transforming the intellectual environment worldwide. Given the book's explicitly communist framework, it's no surprise that few right-wing reviews of *Empire* appeared before 9/11; but soon afterward that gap was filled with a vengeance. In the October 2001 *New Criterion*, Roger Kimball asserted: "Books like *Empire* are not innocent academic inquiries [but rather] incitements to violence and terrorism" – which shouldn't surprise anyone, since one of its authors "was an architect of the infamous Red Brigades" who was unquestionably responsible for the murder of Aldo Moro. He concludes by denouncing *Empire* as "a poisonous book whose ultimate goal is not to understand but to destroy society. Harvard University Press should be ashamed of publishing it" (Kimball 2001). A somewhat more moderate review, by Alan Wolfe, in the October 1 issue of *The New Republic*, extended the same line of argument (see Wolfe 2001), which was intended to demonstrate that the US academic left was at least sympathetic to acts of terrorism like the one that had just struck – if not actively engaged in it.[17] This charge constituted one of the earliest salvos in the right's global attack on political dissent during the period leading up to the Iraq War; but an analysis of that attack is beyond the scope of this chapter.

For more perceptive and substantive engagements with *Empire*, we must focus on the responses from the left, which were by no means homogeneous. Left critics were no more immune to post-9/11 hysteria than their right-wing counterparts; but, while the right's response to Hardt and Negri's continuing work has remained largely the same since the beginning (see for example Brian C. Anderson's review of *Commonwealth* in the *Wall Street Journal*, in which he calls the book "evil": Anderson 2009), the left's reaction has gone through several stages, which can be seen in the differing perspectives that dominate the volumes of commentary on *Empire* published between 2001 and 2007. The dominant tone of the *Rethinking Marxism* issue, assembled before 9/11 but published just after it, is one of cautious partial approval, while many of the contributors to *Debating Empire* – the volume edited by Gopal Balakrishnan in 2003, while preparations for the Iraq War accelerated – see their contemporary situation as a blatant refutation of *Empire*'s arguments.[18] Some deploy a language of terrorism to describe those arguments, just as right-wing critics did (see Bull 2003: 89). The participants in Paul Passavant and Jodi Dean's 2004 collection, *Empire's New Clothes*, take a more balanced view of *Empire*'s strengths and weaknesses, perhaps because of their greater distance from the 9/11 events (and their more skeptical assessments of the ongoing Afghanistan and Iraq Wars); and, like the criticisms of the writers in *Rethinking Marxism*, theirs presage Hardt and

Negri's further development of their ideas in *Multitude* and *Commonwealth*.[19]

The most hostile responses to the concept of Empire coming from the left, or rather the most hostile serious ones that are not simply crude *ad hominem* denunciations such as Timothy Brennan's (Brennan 2003), are easy to identify: they are the ones that reject the notion completely, generally in order to re-assert the continuing utility of the classical conception of nationalist imperialism, which Empire is supposed to have superseded. Many critics accuse Hardt and Negri of overstating the contemporary transition from state-centered imperialism to de-centered Empire, none more stridently than Ellen Meiksins Wood and Atilio Boron.[20] Boron, a defender of Latin American left nationalism, begins his polemic by insisting that

> the fundamental features of imperialism, pointed out by the classical authors at the time of the First World War, remain unchanged in their essentials[,] given that imperialism is not an ancillary feature of contemporary capitalism or a policy implemented by some states, but a new stage in the development of this mode of production whose fundamental traits have persisted to the present day. (Boron 2005: 3)

Wood does not assume the modernist mantle of the struggle against imperialism quite as boldly as Boron does, but her viewpoint is essentially the same: she denies that there are sovereign functions emerging in the global system that are not state-centered, primarily because nation states are still the main agents of capitalist coercion (Wood 2003: 65–8). Both Boron and Wood view the United States as the global economic system's center of command and profit, and their chief piece of evidence is the looming Iraq War itself. As Boron puts it: "Blinded by the inadequacies of their faulty theoretical framework...Hardt and Negri are unable to see what was evident to everybody else: the invasion unilaterally decreed by President George W. Bush caused the contradiction between their theorization and reality to become as glaring as it was unsustainable" (Boron 2005: 8–9). Like Boron, Wood takes the rhetoric of the Bush White House at face value, declaring: "The 'war on terrorism' is the model US war in the era of the new imperialism" (Wood 2003: 71) – and therefore the model of Empire must be an illusion (or, less charitably, "a manifesto for global capitalism" in itself: pp. 61–3). In the fall of 2002, Negri had already disputed this claim by presenting US unilateralist plans for Iraq as a case of "imperialist backlash," a doomed effort made by the US in order to impose a classically imperialist solution by force upon a fundamentally different – imperial – world order (Negri 2002); Hardt and Negri would take up this issue again in *Multitude* and in *Commonwealth*. The subsequent developments in the war after Bush's infamous "Mission Accomplished" photo opportunity on the aircraft carrier *Abraham Lincoln*, especially the rapid intensification of an apparently irrepressible insurgency and the failure of Iraqi petroleum extraction to pay the escalating costs of the occupation, have undercut the US government's imperialist self-representation, and also the claims of those who see it as a successfully imperialist power.

Many of Wood's and Boron's individual points regarding the ways in which the US benefits disproportionately from the transnational operations of capital – the way in which US hegemony "forc[es] the restructuring of the regimes that are its targets" (Wood 2003: 71), say, or the "elementary distinction...between the theatre of operations of the [transnational] companies and the territorial space in which their ownership and control materialize," which is often the US (Boron 2005: 15) – are indisputable; but they fail to recognize that these do not constitute a demonstration of the sovereign, independent centrality of the US state. Boron almost admits this when he notes:

> There is no doubt that there are supranational and transnational organizations, just as there is no doubt that behind them lies the American national interest. It is obvious that the American national interest does not exist in the abstract, nor is it in the interests of the American people or the nation. It is in the interests of the big corporate conglomerates which control as they please the government of the United States... (P. 72)

The "American national interest" is behind the supranational organizations, but that interest does not correspond to "the interests of the American people or the nation" (by which Boron must mean the state apparatus). Why, then, call it the "American national interest," if both the people and the state are under the control of transnational corporations? For Boron, what follows from this is simply a substitution of congruent imperialist centers; but this is a myopic assessment of the situation. Wood reveals a similar blind spot in her failure to recognize that the US itself is a regime that has been forcibly restructured by global capital – by means of massive outsourcing, de-unionization, public debt crisis and other strategies that have driven the ongoing dismantling of the welfare state and the retreat from a half-century of progressive social and ecological legislation. The scale of these transformations may so far have been smaller in relation to the US national economy than what other nation states experienced, but this is a difference of degree, not of kind.

Once the major military engagements of the 2003 US invasion of Iraq were over, other critics of *Empire* acknowledged that the Iraq War in fact demonstrates the validity of the transition from imperialism to Empire, which Wood and Boron deny has taken place. Kam Shapiro states:

> In the aftermath of the attacks on the World Trade Center, Hardt's and Negri's seemingly dystopian account of Empire has become increasingly realistic. The subsequent war on terror has precipitated a rapid elimination of vestigial barriers to transnational juridical authority and a remarkable intensification of "exceptional" police powers... (Shapiro 2004: 298)

Paul Passavant and Jodi Dean concur, noting that "the attacks on the World Trade Center as a signifier of global financial markets" and "the emergence of a transnational military coalition in response to the attacks outside of UN governance... resonate in profound ways with Hardt's and Negri's theorization of the new world order" (Passavant and Dean 2004b: 318).They go further, however, arguing as follows against Wood's and Boron's reliance on the logic of classical imperialism:

> Bush's line in the sand is not territorial in the sense of two national sovereigns involved in a boundary dispute. It is a line invoking a constant and mutual production of the civilized and the savage throughout the social circuitry. Put somewhat differently, if it is U.S. policy to attack nations that harbor terrorists, then the United States would of course have to attack itself. (P. 321)

And the US has indeed done so, curtailing civil rights and pursuing its own citizens with the same extra-judicial means and according to the same logic of generalized exception that it deploys against non-citizen "enemy combatants."

Less hostile assessments of *Empire* than Wood's and Boron's arise from the perspective of postcolonial criticism, which, as we saw, Hardt and Negri accuse of misperceiving its opponent and consequently of misplacing its struggles. Such postcolonial responses are deeply skeptical of the duo's proposal, although at the same time they acknowledge that the mode of global command is no longer the same as in the days of direct colonialism. However, *Empire*'s account of the development of imperial sovereignty out of European colonialism and American constitutionalism tends, in spite of its professed intentions, to attribute all agency to the centers of imperialism and to deprive the colonized regions of it, as Susan Koshy explains.

> What we are left to infer from this world-historical account of empire is that Third World figures and events have lacked *transformative agency* and *theoretical comprehensiveness* in engaging, resisting, evading, or colluding with Western expansionism and that, hence, the narrative of the emergence of a global order can be told without reference to non-Western temporalities or modernities... *Euro-American dominance is mistaken for sole authorship of the global order*. (Koshy 2005: 112)

Koshy argues instead for a pluralist conception of globalization, which acknowledges Euro-American practical hegemony but also attends to the important contributions of non-Western cultures and struggles to the emergence of global capitalist rule.[21] For his part, Kevin Dunn claims that Hardt and Negri's models of both national and post-national sovereignty suffer from a failure to deal with important variations that emerge in the colonized and postcolonial world. For example: "In various parts of Africa, a system of overlapping authority and multiple loyalties exists, a system in which the state must share its authority with regional, international, substate and subnational authorities to such an extent that the concept of modern sovereignty has become increasingly complicated" (Dunn 2004: 150). Thus, "[b]y paying attention to African experiences, we can see how the state, like sovereignty, has been discursively constructed and performed in new and contradictory ways (within both the colonial and the postcolonial context), thus undermining Hardt's and Negri's assumption of a universal norm of statehood" that is in the process of declining in the face of imperial globalization (p. 148).

Not all postcolonial critics are dismissive of *Empire*. Mohammed Bamyeh and Pramod K. Mishra, writing in *Rethinking Marxism*, admit the validity and utility of some of Hardt and Negri's

categories and claims, but they draw more attention to their limitations. Bamyeh focuses on the duo's claim that fundamentalisms,
especially non-Western ones, constitute a form of resistance to
modernity and are therefore alternative forms of the postmodern
contestation of Empire. For Bamyeh,

> Fundamentalism occasioned not so much the failure of modernity
> as a far more specific failure: namely, the *failure of the state*, not
> society, to become truly modern and, as a crucial corollary, *sover-
> eign*....Fundamentalism has been anything but opposed to modern
> capitalism, and has responded not so much to the incursions of
> capitalism as to the failure of the state to undertake the tasks expected
> of it by its impatient, transitory, or volatile "nation." (Bamyeh 2001:
> 205)

In short, he insists that the appeal of fundamentalism lay not in its
rejection of modernity but in its claim that "it could do modernity
better than the corrupt and impotent secular state" (ibid.). From this
follows Bamyeh's suggestion that postcolonial critique still has
something to teach globalization theorists. Mishra, too, believes
that postcolonial theory is still a valid form of contestation, not
least because of the aspects of formerly colonial cultures that are
simply left out of Hardt and Negri's analysis.

> Epistemologically, Hardt and Negri are right to privilege the nomad-
> ism, miscegenation, and migration of the multitude as a solution to
> empire, but this privileging does not present the full picture.
> The number of [Third World] people who have migrated to the First
> [W]orld remains minuscule in comparison to those who still live
> there. (Mishra 2001: 97)

And those who still live there are at least as likely to embrace the
requirements of global capital – to imagine themselves as regional
Bill Gateses – as they are to resist in any way. A theory that fore-
grounds exodus without adequately relating it to stasis cannot offer
a convincing picture of global order.

More cosmopolitan or cosmopolitical critics locate a crucial contradiction not in the gap between *Empire*'s claims and the empirical
facts of the world order it seeks to describe, but rather among the
book's own interpretive and militant categories. For example,
many critics found Hardt and Negri's only concrete organizational
proposals, the three demands with which the book concludes,
jarring in their apparent reliance on political logics they claim to

reject. For Slavoj Žižek, "[i]t is a paradox that Hardt and Negri, the poets of mobility, variety, hybridization, and so on, call for three demands formulated in the terminology of universal human rights" (Žižek 2001: 192), just like the non-governmental organizations (NGOs) that they criticize as agents of Empire. Similarly, Ernesto Laclau admits that

> what sounds strange, after a whole analysis centered on the need to strike everywhere from a position of total confrontation with the present imperial system, is that these three political aims are formulated in the language of *demands* and *rights*. Because both demands and rights have to be *recognized,* and the instance from whom that recognition is requested cannot be in a relation of total exteriority vis-à-vis the social claims. (Laclau 2004: 30)

Hardt and Negri might respond that they conceive of these rights in Spinozian terms, as demands that can only be realized, not by the transcendent agency of some state or other sovereign body, but by the immanent power of the multitude to produce and claim them. *Tantum juris, quantum potentiae* – as much right as there is power, to cite Spinoza. Nevertheless, the ambiguous rhetoric of their demands for rights can be read as a minimal claim to recognition and thus requires a structure of representation in order to be granted, which runs counter to the anti-representational logic of the multitude's radical immanence.

Indeed the chief source of confusion and disagreement over *Empire* lies in the ambiguity of the concept of the multitude, which is supposed to have created Empire and now promises to destroy it. The two elements of Hardt and Negri's discussion of the multitude that trouble readers the most, even those sympathetic to the authors' overall strategy, are the thesis of the incommunicability of contemporary struggles and the apparent indeterminacy of the multitude's actions according to Hardt and Negri's definitions. Nick Dyer-Witheford speaks for many readers of *Empire* when he states categorically:

> Negri and Hardt's "incommunicado" thesis, declaring communication between global struggles both impossible and unnecessary, should be not only abandoned but reversed. To the degree that "immaterial labor" *is* a crucial component of revolt against global capital, perhaps its *main* contribution is that of weaving networks of communications between insurgencies, not just by cyber-activism but in a wide range of autonomous and alternative media (video,

film, guerrilla radio, print) that in turn are elements in hybrid networks of pre- and postindustrial communication forms, complex
relays that transfer news and information from email exchanges to
in-person meetings and back again. (Dyer-Witheford 2001: 77)

In support of this critique, Dyer-Witheford and other analysts (Cox
2001: 161–2, Levinson 2001: 211–12, Callinicos 2003: 137, Boron
2005: 33–5 and still others) point to the reliance of the Zapatista
uprising in Chiapas, Mexico upon global solidarity networks that
organized themselves through internet communications. The rapid
communicability of the Zapatistas' changing situation helped to
preserve and extend their struggle, and other insurrectionary situations since then – most notably the World Trade Organization
(WTO) and G8 protests of Seattle and Genova, but also the Arab
Spring of 2011 – have used many of the same techniques.

The incommunicability thesis, for all the attention it has received,
is not a crucial point in Hardt and Negri's definition of the multitude. However, the issue of the determinability or decidability of
the multitude's actions – how we tell what collective acts constitute
real challenges to Empire – is crucial both to our understanding of
the concept and to the possibility of organizing resistance to Empire.
For some critics who echo Miguel Vatter's critique discussed in
chapter 4, this problem derives from "the impossibly clean division
between constituent and constituted power reappearing throughout *Empire* as well as *Insurgencies*" (Dean 2004: 284). For Wood
(2003: 75) and for Malcolm Bull, the problem goes all the way back
to Spinoza, whose theory that

> everyone...has as much right as they have the power to exercise,
> limited only by the antagonist power of others...licenses tyranny as
> much as democracy, counter-revolution as well as revolution.
> Whoever exercises sovereignty has the right to do so for as long as
> they have the power to maintain it. (Bull 2003: 86)

From this viewpoint, as Bull notes, "[c]onstituent power is therefore essentially conservative in that it reflects the existing social
order and the established interests of every group within it," and
not a revolutionary challenge to that order (p. 88). In his analysis
of *Empire*'s account of US constitutionalism, Paul Passavant, too,
concludes that, "if we recognize the mutually imbricated and constitutive relation between law and society, then the relation of strict
separation between forms of constituent and constituted power in

Hardt's and Negri's narrative cannot be maintained" (Passavant 2004: 106).

Related to these critiques of constituent power but distinct from them, John Holloway's doubts about the multitude arise from his Adornian refusal to accept its radically positive character. He argues that, in workerist theory in general (which he and others prefer to call "autonomist") and in Hardt and Negri's theory in particular,

> the working class becomes the positive subject: that is why the positive concepts of class composition and class re-composition are on the side of the working class, while the negative concept of de-composition is placed on the side of capital. In the reversal of the polarity, identity is moved from the side of capital to the side of labour, but it is not exploded or even challenged. This is wrong. Subjectivity in capitalism is in the first place *negative*, the movement against the denial of subjectivity. A truly radical reversal of the polarity involves not just transferring subjectivity from capital to the working class but also understanding that subjectivity as negative instead of positive, as the negative subjectivity of the anti-working anti-class. (Holloway 2005: 164)

From this viewpoint the original workerist hypothesis of proletarian agency is itself the problem, or at least the source of the problem. In Holloway's view, Hardt and Negri's failure to acknowledge the negative status and vocation of the subjectivity constituted within capital leaves them unable to address the need for subversive action to undo the forms of subjectivity imposed by capital. In contrast to Hardt and Negri's rejection of dialectics as the logic of capital itself, Holloway calls for a negative dialectics of global capital, the negation of negated working-class subjectivity, as a precondition for global struggle.

Other critics pose the dilemma of the multitude in more practical and empirical ways, in terms of the concrete practices that might be attributed to the multitude's contestation of imperial biopower. Brett Levinson pointedly asks:

> [I]s not the movement of a spontaneous and "bodily" multitude, without plan or communication, the very formula for the most aestheticized political models, above all popularism, even fascism? And is it not true that the American far right, opposing both (American) government and global institutions such as the United Nations – opposing, in essence, "empire" – frequently rallies as a multitude in

reaction to a "singular" event or policy, such as Waco, Texas?...
Empire's theoretical model, no doubt unintentionally, lends itself as
much to the right as to the left. This is why one cannot but hesitate
before espousing the politics of the multitude or production that
Negri and Hardt advocate: not because such a politics necessarily
fails as an intervention but because, once placed in circulation, situated into "empire," it could well yield the most despotic political
project. (Levinson 2001: 213)

Similarly, in light of new "green," "socially responsible" corporate
models like the Spanish clothing manufacturer Zara, Alberto
Moreiras notes that apparently one and the same entity can be "an
example not just of the passage to Empire in contemporary times
but also and at the same time of the passage to counter-Empire: an
example of the new global economy that becomes liminally indistinguishable from the production of an alternative global
economy...ruled by the multitude" (Moreiras 2001: 221). Slavoj
Žižek anticipated this argument in his critique of Deleuze and
Guattari's politics of accelerated deterritorialization that would
outpace the dissolving operations of capitalism – the yuppie marketing manager is already an immaterial laborer, a producer of
affective intensities, and Transformer toys make becoming-cyborg
into child's play, but neither of these activities threatens capital at
all (Žižek 2004: 261).[22]

For many of the critics, what was missing from Hardt and
Negri's diffuse definition of the multitude was attention to how it
could be organized into an effective force of resistance to global
capital. Most of these critics located the prospect of organizing the
multitude at the level of representation. Passavant and Dean
express this clearly:

> September 11 allows us to see that what democratic politics needs
> now more than ever, Hardt and Negri do not offer. Because they
> avoid the terrain of representation, the ways in which the global
> might be represented, or the question of what represents an act or
> the interests of the multitude, Hardt and Negri have not provided
> tools that resist the present hegemonic project of militarized response
> in the name of global capital... (Passavant and Dean 2004b: 319)

They agree with Hardt and Negri that the multitude manifests itself
in singular events, but those events must be brought together into
a common project in order to become something more than local
reforms that reinforce capital's grip. Passavant and Dean define

politics itself as the struggle over the representation of such events, to which "*Empire* remains unresponsive" (p. 325). Likewise, Ernesto Laclau regrets that "[w]hat is totally lacking in *Empire* is a theory of *articulation*, without which politics is unthinkable" (Laclau 2004: 26). In other words, how can we bring the constituent singularities of the multitude into concrete and stable alignment for the global project of overcoming Empire? What strategies and tactics are available and adequate to this task? Hardt and Negri not only do not say, they flatly rule out such representation and articulation.

Multitude and Commonwealth

Hardt and Negri were not surprised by the intensity of the criticism they received; on the contrary, they insist that "[o]urs is the kind of book that asks to be criticized," yet they have rarely responded directly to their critics.[23] Indeed they admit candidly that "we are not inclined to respond...by defending ourselves or our arguments" (Hard and Negri 2001: 236–7). Nevertheless, in their subsequent works they have implicitly modified the positions they staked out in *Empire*, starting with the delineation of the multitude. In a 2003 interview, Hardt recognized that the multitude

> may be relatively clear conceptually, but it is still not at all evident how to understand the multitude in social and sociological terms. This appears to us now as the most significant shortcoming of our book. After a theory of Empire, we now need to write a theory of the multitude. (Hardt 2004a: 173)

In 2004, soon after Negri's full parole from prison was granted, the duo published the first sequel to *Empire*, entitled *Multitude: War and Democracy in the Age of Empire*, which attempted to do just that. More a supplement than a fully independent work, *Multitude* assumes almost all the arguments of *Empire*, and its primary labor is to extend and refine the authors' earlier model so that it may account for the apparently changed circumstances of the US "War on Terror" and for its global consequences. To that end, they first address the imperial functions of war, and then they go on to define more fully the multitude and its project of Spinozian "absolute democracy."

Hardt and Negri remain intransigent in the face of critics who see the War on Terror, and its Afghan and Iraqi theaters, as evidence of continuing US imperialism. Reiterating the general outline of Empire, they insist, on the contrary: "The attacks on the Pentagon and the World Trade Center on September 11, 2001, did not create or fundamentally change this global situation, but perhaps they did force us to recognize its generality" (Hardt and Negri 2004: 4). The key aspect of the global situation, in their view, is the structural transformation of military power that has been forced upon the "sole superpower" and its allies by the demands of asymmetrical warfare. Since the enemy, whether it is the Taliban, Al Qaeda or Latin American "narco-terrorists," is no longer a nation state with a centralized command, a hierarchical structure and a uniformed army, but rather a de-centered network of autonomous and clandestine "cells," it cannot be defeated the way a nation state can be defeated. There is no commander-in-chief to sign an armistice agreement or to order demobilization. Network struggle is insurgency, and the only effective form of counter-insurgency is, likewise, a network form. If "[o]ne hard lesson that the leaders of the United States and its allied nation-states seemed to learn reluctantly after September 11 . . . is that the enemy they face is not a unitary sovereign nation-state but rather a *network*" (p. 54), a second hard lesson was the fact that "[i]t *takes a network to fight a network*" (p. 58). Network insurgency is a capillary form, to use Foucault's language: it settles into the intimate interstices of the occupied society, emerging only to strike and then disappear quickly. Counter-insurgency must become equally capillary, and it has a model for this ready at hand. "What is required . . . is a 'full spectrum dominance' that combines military might with social, economic, political, psychological, and ideological control. Military theorists have thus, in effect, discovered the concept of biopower" (p. 53). Since armed force cannot simply obliterate the social order, it must instead infiltrate and reorganize it at every level. In other words the imperial military must win "hearts and minds" as well as firefights, if it is to succeed.

The tactical, battlefield application of biopower is matched by its strategic deployment as perpetual surveillance, informatization and warfare.

> Postmodern warfare . . . has many of the characteristics of what economists call post-Fordist production: it is based on both mobility and flexibility; it integrates intelligence, information, and immaterial labor; it raises power up by extending militarization to the limits of outer space, across the surfaces of the earth, and to the depths of the oceans. (P. 40)

Postmodern, network warfare is imperial warfare, and as such its primary obligation is to "accomplish a constituent or regulative function: war must become both a procedural activity and an ordering, regulative activity that creates and maintains social hierarchies, a form of biopower aimed at the promotion and regulation of social life" (p. 21). The tasks of "regime change" and "nation building" fall to military forces under Empire, and they constitute the other face of the universal socialization of labor that post-Fordist production undertakes: both faces of Empire seek to impose not direct rule, but relatively autonomous self-discipline, upon their adversaries, and that entails different methods – and different measures of success – from those of imperialism. Hardt and Negri acknowledge: "A single power may attempt – and the United States has done so several times – to circumvent this necessity of the network form and the compulsion to engage the plural relations of force, but what it throws out the door always sneaks back in the window" (p. 61). The attempt to resurrect imperialism necessarily fails, reinforcing the new, biopolitical demands of Empire.

Although Hardt and Negri deny that the War on Terror refutes their theory, their account of network struggle under Empire does implicitly acknowledge the force of other critiques of their original formulation. Their unconvincing claim that struggles against Empire are incommunicable is simply dropped and replaced by the acknowledgement that communication is the key to a new global cycle of resistance. They even use their critics' preferred case study, the Zapatistas:

> Communication is central to the Zapatistas' notion of revolution, and they continually emphasize the need to create horizontal network organizations rather than vertical centralized structures... The Zapatistas... demonstrat[e] in the clearest possible terms the nature and direction of the postmodern transition of organizational forms. (P. 85)

In Hardt and Negri's defense, we should note that *Empire* was drafted between 1994 and 1997, when the commonality of global struggles was harder to see and conceptualize; only after the confrontations in Seattle and Genoa, which brought together a range of activist groups inclined toward broader communication, did something like a common set of strategies and goals become visible. Only at that point could Hardt and Negri realistically argue that, like biopolitical production and postmodern warfare,

[t]he global cycle of struggles develops in the form of a distributed
network...Each struggle remains singular and tied to its local conditions but at the same time is immersed in the common web. This
form of organization is the most fully realized political example we
have of the concept of the multitude. (P. 217; see also pp. 284–6)[24]

This example of the multitude in action is one of several clarifica-
tions of the concept that Hardt and Negri provide. They distinguish
it not only from the people that underpins the nation state but also
from the masses, the mob and the crowd – collective entities that
"are not singularities" and "so easily collapse into the indifference
of the whole" and the passivity of the represented (p. 100). To more
traditional leftists – like John Holloway, Stephen Resnick and
Richard Wolff, who decried the "exclusion of class in its surplus
labor sense" from the definition of the multitude in *Empire* (Resnick
and Wolff 2001: 68; see also Holloway 2005: 172–4) – they respond
that "[m]ultitude is a class concept" intended "to demonstrate that
a theory of economic class need not choose between unity and
plurality" – as the tradition of political philosophy has generally
assumed (Hardt and Negri 2004: 103, 105). The Marxist tradition
has aimed for the unity of class as a condition of its political organization, while the liberal tradition has inversely stressed the
empirical diversity of class strata in order to deny the need for such
organization; neither model meets present needs.

Hardt and Negri attempt to address many critics' reservations
about the multitude's immaterial labor by introducing a new
concept to define its foundation and consequences: "The difference
of immaterial labor...is that its products are themselves, in many
respects, immediately social and common...This becoming
common, which tends to reduce the qualitative divisions within
labor, is the biopolitical condition of the multitude" (p. 114). The
common will become increasingly central to their theorization of
the multitude and of its political potential, as can be seen from the
title of their fourth collaboration, *Commonwealth*. The common
offers another way to displace the opposition between unity and
plurality, as well as a means for creating alliances among irreducibly different social struggles. As we have seen, the multitude is
a collective made up of singularities; but

[s]ingularities do communicate, and they are able to do so because
of the common they share. We share bodies with two eyes, ten
fingers, ten toes; we share life on this earth; we share capitalist

regimes of production and exploitation; we share common dreams
of a better future. Our communication, collaboration, and cooperation, furthermore, not only are based on the common that exists but
also in turn produce the common. (P. 128)

The common, then, is a feedback spiral of communication, socialization and production that generalizes the logic of self-valorization that Negri theorized during the workers' struggles of the
seventies (see chapter 3, pp. 92–4).[25] Hardt and Negri trace the
emergence of the common through the decline of older subjective
forms of labor like the peasantry, whose isolation posed insur-
mountable problems to radical political organizing and justified
the adoption of representational political structures by radical
movements (pp. 115–25). Because biopolitical production incorpor-
ates everyone differentially, no form of labor is outside its purview,
not even the poor of the global South; "since the poor participate
in and help generate the linguistic community by which they are
then excluded or subordinated, the poor are not only active and
productive but also antagonistic and potentially rebellious"
(p. 132). Indeed, the total inclusiveness of imperial biopolitical
production multiplies the risk that capital takes in subordinating
the multitude and the common it produces. Nevertheless, imperial
capital must take that risk or die: "Just as we must understand the
production of value in terms of the common, so too must we try to
conceive exploitation as *the expropriation of the common*" (p. 150).
    In order to advance this conception of the common as the mul-
titude's mode of productive activity, Hardt and Negri propose a
somewhat ambiguous Deleuze-Guattarian language to describe it.
Adapting their predecessors' logic of the "body without organs,"
they contrast the organic, unitary and hierarchical "political body"
of the people with the formless and plural "flesh" of the multitude:
"A democratic multitude cannot be a political body, at least not in
the modern form. The multitude is something like singular flesh
that refuses the organic unity of the body" (p. 162). It refuses the
conventional, representational forms of polity and it generates
unprecedented new forms, which appear monstrous from the traditional viewpoint. In this sense the common is not what political
theorists posit as public interest or communitarianism; for "[t]he
common does not refer to traditional notions of either the community or the public; it is based on the *communication* among singularities and emerges through the collaborative social processes
of production" (p. 204). If the multitude manifests its common as

monstrous, singular yet collective flesh, which is "pure potential, an unformed life force" (p. 192), then the expropriation of that common by capital is also a theft of the flesh, as for example in the recent explosion of intellectual property claims upon genetic information and bio-engineered species, or in the "seed wars" over patented agricultural stocks (pp. 182–8).

To these depredations and others, the multitude has responded with a continuing cycle of singular but communicating struggles, but Hardt and Negri insist that it must do more. They explain this demand in philosophical terms, as the necessary transition between the "ontological multitude" – the multitude-in-itself, which has always been the root of subjective agency, even when constrained within the represented figure of the people or masses – and the "political multitude" – the multitude-for-itself (or, more accurately, for-"itselves"), which requires a new logic of organization to bring its subversive power to fruition. This distinction between the ontological and the political multitude also permits us to recognize how sharply Hardt and Negri's version of the multitude differs from Paolo Virno's: whereas for the former the multitude, defined as an open set of singularities, is an ontological point of departure or even a metaphysical a priori, for the latter

> [t]he crucial point is to consider these singularities as a point of arrival, not as a starting point; as the ultimate result of a *process of individuation*, not as solipsistic atoms...The individual of the multitude is the final stage of a process beyond which there is nothing else, because everything else (the passage from the One to the Many) has already taken place. (Virno 2004: 76)

According to Judith Revel, this disagreement hinges upon the issue of the internal difference or articulation of the multitude: Virno's

> identification of the Many with the multitude does not pose the problem of the articulation of singularities among themselves – which must be the characteristic element of the multitude – and it is limited to describing a process of subjectivation (or singularization) outside of any reference to the constituent process of the common. (Revel 2004: 46; my translation)

– as Hardt and Negri conceive that process in *Multitude* and later *Commonwealth*. She goes on to say:

> The solution lies not at all in opposing, as Virno does, the Many and the One (both are fully *within* modern political thought, they fully belong to it...) but on the contrary in restoring the absolute hetero-

geneity of the multitude with respect *to the Many and the One at the same time*. The multitude is a multitude of singularities as such; and it is also – immediately – the production of a common with neither foundation nor universal form. (Pp. 49–50; my translation)

Because it lies outside the modern dialectical logic of the Many and the One, the multitude must find a new form of organization to articulate its political agency.

For Virno, then, the multitude always and only exists in its political form; but not so for Hardt and Negri. The multitude, they write, is "always-already and not-yet" (Hardt and Negri 2004: 221–2). What defines the common of the multitude's organizational project is democracy.

> In the hand-to-hand combat of the multitude and Empire on the biopolitical field that pulls them together, when Empire calls on war for its legitimation, the multitude calls on democracy as its political foundation. This democracy that opposes war is an "absolute democracy." *We can also call this democratic movement a process of "exodus," insofar as it involves the multitude breaking the ties that link imperial sovereign authority to the consent of the subordinated.* (Pp. 90–1)

Absolute democracy, as we saw in chapter 4, pp. 129–31, is Spinoza's phrase for a mode of self-organization ever more capable of perfection; and in *Multitude* that means the abandonment of representational structures in favor of "the rule of everyone by everyone" (Hardt and Negri 2004: 100). As they had already done in *Empire* (and as Negri had done in *Insurgencies*), Hardt and Negri trace the practical possibility of realizing this concept back to the revolutionaries of the eighteenth century, who did not succeed in instituting it but set it up "as a goal toward which modern revolutions and struggles have tended" (pp. 240–1). Further, Hardt and Negri re-trace the development of representational models of democracy, from the Federalist debates to the Bolshevik party and to the workers' councils, to reveal the exhaustion of all these forms (pp. 244–52). They conclude: "Even in their most radical expressions, socialism and communism did not develop fundamentally different conceptions of representation and democracy, and as a result they repeated the founding nucleus of the bourgeois concept of sovereignty, trapped paradoxically in the need for the unity of the state" (p. 252).

Reiterating the limits of their inventive capacity, Hardt and Negri remind their readers: "We do not pretend to propose a concrete action program for the multitude but instead try to work out the conceptual bases on which a new project for democracy can stand" (p. 328). To this end, in imitation of the French revolutionaries of 1789, they compile a *"cahier de doléances"* – a "list of grievances" that the multitude charges against Empire. This list constitutes a negative map of the common and a precondition of the multitude's political organization. They survey a wide field, from Asia to Latin America, and they summarize the grievances under "three common points that return repeatedly as conditions for any project of a new, democratic world: the critique of existing forms of representation, the protest against poverty, and the opposition to war" (pp. 269–70). They examine several proposals for a new global representative body, a "people's assembly" or "global parliament," all of which collapse under the weight of the alienating representational logic they assume (pp. 293–5). The grievance of poverty, too, gives rise to unsatisfactory responses that do not escape from the logic of Empire itself:

> In general most existing propositions of reform of the basic functioning of the global economic system divide between two broad lines of action, which stand opposed to one another: a strategy that gives nation-states more regulatory power and one that strives to undercut control over the economy by either states or economic powers. (P. 300)

The former seeks to return to a pre-imperial logic that Empire is already able to defeat, while the latter seems to embrace and extend Empire's function. The opposition to war can only succeed, they suggest, if it recognizes the centrality of war to contemporary biopower and struggles against the overall system – and not just its military face. The reform proposals that are circulating now, while broadly positive, are insufficient. "What is necessary is an audacious act of political imagination to break with the past, like the one accomplished in the eighteenth century" (p. 308).

In the eighteenth and nineteenth centuries the main challenge to democratic politics was the conflict between the individual and the totality (generally the state); but the challenge now is to work out "the complementarity between the multiple singularities and our common social life," that is, the common (p. 310). The answer that both the capitalist and the socialist traditions gave to the earlier conflict was dialectical: the individual was incorporated into – and subordinated to – the unified totality, the party, the state or both, which expressed the individual's interests in mediated – and therefore alienated – form. The logic of sovereignty transformed the plurality of individual wills or powers into a single general will or Power, which could decide and act in the last instance. This logic was not limited to the political realm:

> The theory of modern sovereignty in politics dovetails with capitalist theories and practices of economic management. There must be a single, unitary figure that can take responsibility and decide in the field of production not only for there to be economic order but also for there to be innovation. (P. 331)

But the era in which this was true is passing, if not already past. The general socialization of labor, its "postmodernization," means that workers organize themselves in networks of production, and, in parallel fashion, "instead of an external authority imposing order on society from above, the various elements present in society are able collaboratively to organize society themselves" (p. 337). What does this mean? Most importantly, it means that unitary sovereignty in its modern form is no longer essential to contemporary social order. Decisions and innovations can be – and are – made collectively, in the processes of production and communication themselves. "The economic production of the multitude, in other words, is not only a *model* for political decision-making but also tends itself to *become* political decision-making" (p. 339). Politics no longer needs to be a professional specialty, limited to representatives acting in the name of a distant people, but can now merge with sociality itself. In other words, the autonomy of the political that Negri had been attacking for 40 years has finally run aground and lost any vestige of credibility. "Biopolitical production presents the possibility that we do the political work of creating and maintaining social relationships collaboratively in the same communicative, cooperative networks of social production, not at interminable evening meetings" (p. 350).

The final question of the book returns its readers to the beginning: the relationship of the democratic multitude to war and violence. As we have come to expect from Negri's work, *Multitude* does not espouse a pacifist position but instead acknowledges the necessity of force and violence. However, "[a] *democratic* use of force and violence is neither the same as nor the opposite of the war of sovereignty; it is different" (p. 342). In what way? The authors provide three criteria for distinguishing democratic violence from imperial violence: democratic violence is always subordinated to the common and does not command or expropriate it; democratic violence is always defensive (in contrast to the workers' violence that Negri theorized in the seventies, which could sometimes be offensive or pre-emptive; see chapter 3, pp. 100–2); and democratic violence is, as the phrase implies, organized democratically and not hierarchically (Hardt and Negri 2004: 342–5). Taken together, these criteria imply a further conclusion regarding democratic violence, insofar as the latter is revolutionary violence aimed at eliminating imperial sovereignty. "The force that the revolutionary organizes and imposes does not appear at the beginning but only at the end of the process: revolutionary realism produces and reproduces the becoming and proliferation of desire" (p. 356).[26] *Multitude* is committed to this becoming and proliferation, just as *Empire* was committed to the "irrepressible lightness and joy of being communist" (Hardt and Negri 2000: 413).

The critical response to *Multitude*, though significant, was much less voluminous and contentious than the response to *Empire* had been, and it has generally repeated the main themes of the earlier critiques. A few reviewers, such as Samir Amin, continued to express their conviction that classical imperialism is not over, and hence the model of Empire is nothing but a capitulation to capitalist euphoria over globalization (Amin 2005: 3–4). Amin's persistence in this matter is somewhat curious, since he is also the advocate of a theory of "collective imperialism" that in some ways resembles Empire:

> The growing centralization of oligopolistic capital has now given rise to the emergence of a "collective" imperialism of the triad (the United States, Europe, and Japan). In this respect, the dominant segments of capital share common interests in the management of their profit from this new imperialist system. But the unified political management of this system comes up against the plurality of states. (Amin 2005: 4).

Amin's assignment of Hardt and Negri to the role of unwitting capitalist ideologues seems to be based on his misreading of the multitude as a simple variation on bourgeois individualism, when in fact it is a critique of individualism (p. 9). This critique of individualism will become clearer when we discuss *Commonwealth*.

Other critics remain unconvinced of the Spinozian notion of constituent power, upon which the multitude's autonomy and efficacy are predicated. Hardt and Negri's most implacable opponent in this regard, Malcolm Bull, concludes his own survey of Spinoza's political legacy by insisting that, "[i]nsofar as Spinoza differs from Hobbes, his thought leads to Mandeville, Smith, Stewart and Hayek," the founding fathers of classical liberalism and capitalist libertarianism (Bull 2005: 38). Despite their strenuous efforts,

> [c]ontemporary champions of the multitude remain trapped within this history, committed to a position that is ultimately either Hobbesian or Hayekian. Seeking a route out of the impasse posed by the global market and its reactive populisms, they have retraced the path that led to it...Rather than being an agent of limitless potential, the multitude contracts political possibility to the primitivisms of the security state and the free market. (P. 39)

Bull's account parallels the standard liberal interpretation of Spinoza as an individualist thinker of the market, although Bull rejects rather than embraces Spinoza as a result. Jonathan Havercroft arrives at a different conclusion about Spinoza, but one that is equally incompatible with Hardt and Negri's reading. Focusing on the role of the state in maximizing positive encounters between subjects that will result in the growth of reason, he argues that "Spinoza's multitude – when it is properly guided by reason – will erase the differences among its constituent members, thereby undercutting one of the primary reasons that Hardt and Negri turned to the multitude in the first place: to provide a model of collective agency that preserves difference" (Havercroft 2010: 126). In his view, Spinoza remains an arch-rationalist even in his democratic theory. Even worse, the importance of this growth of reason and consensus implies that, "[u]nlike Hardt and Negri, Spinoza would suggest strengthening Empire and creating an absolute global (democratic) state" in order to accelerate the process of consensus formation (p. 129).

The absence of any account of articulation or of any tactical role granted to representation, noted in *Empire* by Laclau, Passavant and Dean among others, disturbs many readers of *Multitude* as well. Crystal Bartolovich expresses this dissatisfaction clearly when she reminds us that the multitude, as Hardt and Negri describe it, is not already separated from Empire but still embedded in it. Indeed, according to their own Foucauldian biopolitical assumptions,

> Empire *inhabits* the multitude to a greater or lesser extent and...this "internalization" must be confronted at the same time as Empire is

"refused" – or, rather, in order for it to be refused, as an alien force. Radical democratization, from this perspective, is a counterforce to consumerist, fundamentalist and liberal competition. (Bartolovich 2007: 85)

If this is true, then democratization cannot do without a theory of hegemony that will enable genuinely revolutionary desire to win the "*struggle* [that] is currently underway *for* the multitude by a variety of 'codes'" that seek to bind it ever more tightly to Empire (p. 89).

Related to this critique of the multitude's articulation as a political project are the doubts some readers express regarding Hardt and Negri's claim that the multitude decides and acts not through any form of delegated sovereignty, but in the very processes of its economic and social production. In other words, the technical composition of the class is implicitly presented *as* its political composition, in an odd and unexpected departure from workerist principles regarding class composition. Antoine Artous has noted this reversal: "All this is somewhat disquieting because under the apparently neutral surface lies a technical approach to decision-making that has nothing to do with a democratic approach to political debate. For democratic debate is precisely that which is not reducible to a decision-making technique" (Artous 2010: 125; my translation). This reversal has serious consequences for Hardt and Negri's conception of the democracy of the multitude: "In wishing to escape from democracy understood as the democratic self-institution of the social, Hardt and Negri fall into the phantasms of a technico-scientific approach to democracy," which resembles the procedural formalisms (of Rawls and Habermas, for example) that they denounce (p. 104; my translation).

The most widespread and compelling new critique of Hardt and Negri's thinking emerged from the analyses of feminist critics, who found the characterization of the multitude as "living flesh" that evades the organic order of the body to be deeply problematic and implicitly anti-feminist. The concept of affective labor in *Empire* had been attacked by feminists for obscuring the ferocious gendering of labor activities that persists throughout most of the world (see Quinby 2004: 240–2); but the new feminist critique went considerably further in denouncing *Multitude*'s implicit sexism. Negri's longtime friend, the critic and journalist Ida Dominijanni (one of the founders of the leftist newspaper *Il Manifesto*), summed up this perspective most cogently.

The authors write...that the multitude is "living flesh," and yet – in the best tradition of Western political thought that from ancient Greece onwards has transformed the body into a metaphor in order to rid itself of real bodies – it does not have a body. It is not a "political body" and it does not wish to be so...Consequently the multitude is not sexed. The difference between the sexes appears in the old form of the social condition of gender, not in the form of a sexed singularity[,] and the project is to neutralize its relevance rather than to give it significance in social, symbolic and political exchange...Lastly and most importantly, the multitude moves, like capital, in a linear and progressive temporality, ignoring the obstacles of regression...In short, it is neither traversed by the negative nor by negative feelings such as fear, anxiety and dependence. Thus, in one gesture it eliminates all the work done by feminist practices to reintroduce into the constitution of subjectivity the mass of material that has been disavowed by political rationality...(Dominijanni 2005: 32)

Dominijanni's critique of the absence of negativity from the concept of the multitude confirms Holloway's Adornian riposte to *Empire* and anticipates Bartolovich's emphasis on the struggle over the despotic "coding" of the multitude. Other feminist critics echoed these concerns and extended them to Hardt and Negri's account of differences in sexuality and ethnicity (see for example Hawkesworth 2006 and Mutman 2007: 154). Ingrid Hoofd speaks for many of these critics when she concludes: "The reader of *Empire* and *Multitude* cannot help but feel that the 'multitude' and 'the migrant' are rhetorical ploys to force the various differential feminist and anti-racist struggles under the umbrella of anti-capitalism, while effectively silencing them" (Hoofd 2005: 140).

Perhaps the gentlest, but at the same time most thought-provoking, rebuke of Hardt and Negri's work to date has come from friends and comrades who share the authors' workerist background. Recall that the workerist hypothesis states that the insubordination of labor precedes and drives capitalist innovation; Hardt and Negri explicitly pay homage to this notion (as well as to Foucault) in *Multitude*, when they state: "Even though common use of the term might suggest the opposite – that resistance is a response or reaction – *resistance is primary with respect to power*" (Hardt and Negri 2004: 64). Antonella Corsani, an Italian economist who collaborated with Hardt and Negri on the Parisian journal *Multitudes*, speaks for many workerists and post-workerists[27] when she writes: "Wishing to remain faithful to this revolutionary move at the very heart of Marxism, we could ask if the authors of *Empire* and *Multitude: War and Democracy in the Age of Empire* should not have begun with the Multitude, rather than as they did, with Empire" (Corsani 2007: 116). In this she echoes Holloway's rebuke: "Although [in *Empire*] they insist that refusal is the driving force of domination, refusal is in fact relegated to a subordinate place" in their writings in comparison to the logic of domination (Holloway 2005: 170). In one sense, this is a trivial objection; after all, don't Hardt and Negri in fact glorify – even if they don't adequately define – the multitude throughout *Empire*, despite giving the enemy pride of place on the book jacket? But in another sense the objection touches on perhaps the greatest challenge that the collaborators have set for themselves, and so far have failed fully to meet: how can their project of liberation find a foothold in collective militant practice, if it constantly defers an adequate definition of its ultimate agent? In order to define Empire in the first place, Hardt and Negri had to posit, in good workerist fashion, a subversive subject designed both to produce it and to destroy it: hence the multitude, maker of counter-Empire. But the concept of the multitude remains ambiguous and ambivalent, so they must write another book to clarify it, and in so doing they are compelled to introduce yet another concept, the common, which in turn requires re-definition in yet another book, *Commonwealth*.[28]

Published in the fall of 2009, shortly after Negri's 76th birthday, Hardt and Negri's fourth collaboration goes beyond the supplemental and somewhat defensive labor of *Multitude*, to offer a more robust and detailed – but not always less ambiguous – account of the multitude and its political organization that, directly or indirectly, responds to many of the critiques that the duo's earlier work inspired. They begin where *Multitude* left off, with the democracy of the multitude, which is "imaginable and possible only because we all share and participate in the common" (Hardt and Negri 2009: viii). The common to which they refer throughout this book is defined more broadly than it was in the previous book; whereas earlier it designated primarily the social feedback loop of the production of subjectivity through communication, now it expands to include the "common wealth of the natural world – the air, the water, the fruits of the soil, and all nature's bounty." Hardt and Negri call the latter the "natural common" and the former the "artificial common" (p. 250); and, while they assert the similarity of these forms of common, they also acknowledge their differences, the most important of which is the scarcity of the natural common in contrast to the abundance of the artificial common (p. 139).[29] The logic of this dual conception of the common stands opposed to the logic of capital and its legal structure, which the authors label "the republic of property" (p. 8) – by this they mean private property – and also to the homologous logic of classical socialism and its emphasis on public ownership. Hardt and Negri's quip that "what the private is to capitalism and what the public is to socialism, the common is to communism" (p. 273) could serve as a motto for the book. Their systematic investigation of the common as a concept beyond the false dialectics of the private and the public sets out from an interrogation and critique of the republic of property that parallels the histories of Empire's formal and material constitutions, outlined in *Empire*. Taking their cue from Marx and Engels' historical reconstruction of the stages of property that preceded capitalist forms of property, Hardt and Negri analyze the conjunction of property and subjectivity in slavery (where the laborer is property), in material wage slavery (where the laborer has only his or her labor-power as "property") and in immaterial labor (where the laborer "owns" not only abstract labor-power, but also the social skills that make autonomous cooperation possible). Property, as Proudhon recognized long ago, is theft, so the persistence and expansion of an anachronistic and unproductive regime of property constitutes one of the main challenges to militancy today.

"Property is the key that defines not only the republic but also the people, both of which are posed as universal concepts but in reality exclude the multitude of the poor" (p. 51). The individual subject of the nationalist "people" is defined, legally and metaphysically, as a property-owning subject, a "possessive individual" who has always been a minority in comparison with the full scale of the multitude. Thus, better to grasp the multitude, we must grasp how its production of the common exceeds the structures of property. In conventional economics, both the natural and the artificial common are modeled under the category of "externality," that is, as elements of production for which the capitalist doesn't directly pay: the oxygen in the air that allows combustion to take place in furnaces, the bees and butterflies that pollinate crops, but also the educational system that socializes workers, the public highways on which goods are transported or the domestic labor that restores the worker's energy every day. The process of real subsumption and the increasing demands of workers have brought many such externalities into the mechanisms of market pricing, but in the process the market itself has mutated and fractured. One of the most obvious sites of this incorporation of externalities (or of the common) is the recent urban real estate "bubble," the inflation of urban housing prices beyond any possible "internal" measure of value. What this bubble represents, according to Hardt and Negri, is an indirect attempt by market logic to measure the common and to snare it within conventional property valuation. Urban residence provides not only geographical convenience to employment sites, but also a huge array of additional social benefits in the form of access to cultural diversity, formal and informal education, entertainment, and other "goods" that cannot be directly measured (as well as negatives such as noise, smog and so on). "The theories of real estate economics, along with the practices of real estate agents, demonstrate how the metropolis itself is an enormous reservoir of the common, of not only material but also and moreover immaterial factors, both good and bad" (p. 156). Real estate prices measure the common externally, not in terms of its own socialized and communicational mode of production but in terms of the older capitalist model of private property that strives to capture the common.

At an even greater external distance and at a higher order of abstraction and scale, finance capital too constitutes an effort to measure the common and to incorporate it into market mechanisms. By means of its increasingly self-reflexive hierarchy of commodity futures, investment derivatives and credit default swaps,

> [f]inance capital is in essence an elaborate machine for *representing* the common, that is, the common relationships and networks that are necessary for the production of a specific commodity, a field of commodities, or some other type of asset or phenomenon...Insofar as biopolitical labor is autonomous, finance is the adequate capitalist instrument to expropriate the common wealth produced, external to it and abstract from the production process. (Pp. 157–8)

The "externality" of finance capital in this context means not "outside the capitalist market," as it does in conventional economics, but rather "parasitic upon cooperative production organized by the multitude itself," and thus both finance capital and urban real estate value constitute expropriations of the common. However, the same aspects of abstraction and externality that allow finance capital to represent and expropriate the common also leave it, like urban real estate prices, vulnerable to wild instability and to unpredictable breakdowns, such as the collapse of 2007–8. Indeed many analysts argue that the bursting of the real estate bubble, which underpinned many hedge funds, ignited the broader finance-sector collapse.

In Hardt and Negri's view, this failure of market mechanisms adequately to measure and manage the common within capitalist logic is only one symptom of the increasing desperation of the emerging global order. The other major symptom is the failure of the unilateralist *coup d'état* launched against Empire by the Bush administration in Afghanistan and Iraq. "The coup d'état was an effort to transform the emerging form of Empire back into an old imperialism, but this time with only one imperialist power" (p. 206). As was already becoming clear when *Multitude* was published in 2004, the military arm of this operation was unable to impose peace and order on the battlefield because of the network insurgency that arose to impede the extraction of petroleum wealth that was supposed to have paid for the conflict. But this is not the only problem the Iraq War brought to the surface. "In addition to failing militarily in Iraq, then, the U.S. unilateral project failed economically – failed, that is, to create a new economic regime that could generate and guarantee profits" (p. 215). This constitutes a broader, indeed global failure of neo-liberal Empire "to present a schema for stimulating and organizing production" (p. 266). On the contrary, the new security regime imposed globally after 9/11 has hamstrung capital's ability to produce surplus value by further impeding worker and commodity mobility and by redirecting productive resources into defense spending and surveillance. Only finance capital has managed to emerge from the crisis in an expansive mode, by further abstracting and cannibalizing all other forms of capitalist production.

The failure of US unilateralism has resulted in a paradoxical situation, in which the dominant forms of expropriation of the common are falling back into forms akin to earlier logics of property such as primitive accumulation (in the extraction of natural resources from the most subordinated sectors of the globe, under the cover of warfare – the "blood diamond" phenomenon) and rent (in the expansion of the regime of intellectual property to cover life forms and genetic codes, which we discussed briefly earlier),[30] which were thought to have been surpassed long ago (pp. 137–41). This means that, perversely, "[w]e need...to recognize a reciprocal movement also under way in the process of globalization, from the real subsumption to the formal, creating not new 'outsides' to capital but severe divisions and hierarchies within the capitalist globe" (p. 230; see also p. 245). This proposal may seem confusing in light of the tremendous emphasis Negri has put on the irreversible transition from formal to real subsumption in all his political writings since the seventies, but it is intended to grasp the emergence of genuine productive autonomy on the part of immaterial labor rather than any survival of pre-capitalist labor processes within capital (as the original formulation of formal subsumption did). Real subsumption *after* formal subsumption means that biopolitical production is increasingly autonomous from the internal organizational control of capital, as were pre-capitalist forms of labor; this is why capital is reviving pre-capitalist forms like primitive accumulation and rent. Biopolitical production itself, however, is not a regression to earlier labor forms. This aspect is the affirmative, militant flipside of the revival of older property forms.

Where do this autonomy and this militancy come from? As we learned from *Empire* and *Multitude*, it is always already there, in the ontologically prior resistance of the multitude itself, in its innate constituent power. In their earlier collaborative works, Hardt and Negri reformulated Negri's conception of the two modernities in order to historicize this resistance, and in *Commonwealth* they acknowledge that their prior formulations have spawned numerous dualist and dialectical misunderstandings and critiques. They recognize that the notion of counter-Empire, which they originally deployed to describe the multitude's project, is misleading, because "that term implies a second power that is homologous to the one it opposes" (p. 56). Similarly, the term "anti-modernity," which Negri had used in his work on Spinoza, implies a negation of modernity, often understood to entail a regression from, or refusal of, modernity that is actually contrary to the multitude's project as Hardt and Negri explain it. Modernity cannot simply be refused any more than Empire can; it has no outside, so it can only be resisted from within. Even postcolonial resistance is an aspect of modernity that cannot claim another territory for its activity than that of modernity.

> To understand modernity, we have to stop assuming that domination and resistance are external to each other, casting anti-modernity to the outside, and recognize that resistances mark differences that are within. The resulting geographies are more complex than simply the city versus the country or Europe versus its outside or the global North versus the global South. (P. 70)

To the extent that it implies a relation of exteriority or externality, "anti-modernity" is a misleading term for the multitude's project in the same way in which "anti-globalization" is a misleading term for the protest movements that have erupted in Seattle, Genoa and other global cities over the past decade. The protestors (or at least many of them) do not oppose their own global communications networks, mobility and cultural encounters, but rather they oppose the hierarchical command that constrains the freer flow of those very encounters. In France, militants have adopted the term *alter-mondialisation* ("alterglobalization") to denote this phenomenon, and Hardt and Negri appropriate the prefix for their own lexicon: "Altermodernity has a diagonal relationship with modernity. It marks conflict with modernity's hierarchies as much as does anti-modernity but orients the forces of resistance more clearly toward an autonomous terrain" within and against the repressive strain of modernity (p. 102), and thus it offers a better framework for understanding the multitude's actions.

Among the most common objections that critics have raised to the notion of the multitude is its undecidability, the difficulty of determining how to assess the liberatory potential of its protean activities. Skeptics find it impossible to use Hardt and Negri's concept to distinguish between progressive and reactionary collective behavior, and they themselves further confuse matters by establishing parallels between postmodern cultural theory and religious fundamentalism (in "Symptoms of Passage," discussed in the first section of this chapter, pp. 189–92). Their reluctance to acknowledge the negative subjective consequences of the multitude's enclosure within the form of the people, as well as the negative labor that escape from this enclosure demands, has alienated feminists like Dominijanni and Marxists like Holloway and Bartolovich. In *Commonwealth* the two of them finally address these critiques directly, and this makes the book a more significant advance than *Multitude* was. With regard to fundamentalism, they propose a simple criterion for determining its political valence: its attitude toward the body. Following Foucault once again (as well as Althusser on ideology), they propose the "double relation to the body – at once focusing on it and making it disappear – [as] a useful definition for fundamentalism, allowing us to bring together the various disparate fundamentalisms on this common point and, through contrast, cast into sharper relief the characteristics and value of the biopolitical perspective" (p. 32). Fundamentalisms

focus obsessively upon the body – its purity, its rituals, its relationships – as signs of conformity to the spiritual norm; but that focus
is really an effort to look beyond the body to the soul, or to take
the body as a symptom of the soul's condition. Thus the body is
central, but ultimately disposable. If this criterion is accurate, then
"[b]iopolitics...is the ultimate antidote to fundamentalism because
it refuses the imposition of a transcendent, spiritual value or structure, refuses to let the bodies be eclipsed, and insists instead on
their power" (p. 38).

Hardt and Negri's analysis of the city as a crucial site of the
biopolitical production of the common offers further criteria for
distinguishing progressive or democratic practices from reactionary or imperial ones. As they note, "elements of the common contained in the city are not only the prerequisite for biopolitical
production but also its result; the city is the source of the common
and the receptacle into which it flows" (p. 154); but the contemporary city is still a functional link in the drivetrain of Empire, so not
every metropolitan activity advances the liberation of the common.
Since *the metropolis is to the multitude what the factory was to the
industrial working class*" (p. 250), it demands a specific form of political activity and organization, just as the factory did. In Spinozian
terms, "[t]he politics of the metropolis is the organization of encounters. Its task is to promote joyful encounters, make them repeat,
and minimize infelicitous encounters" (p. 255). Joyful encounters
with persons, cultures, ideas and objects increase the individual
and collective body's powers of acting, and a radical politics of the
metropolis must encourage such encounters by breaking down the
new divisions and hierarchies that capital is building in and around
cities while simultaneously eliminating the disempowering effects
of sad or fearful encounters with violence, coercion and command.

Even if we accept the validity of these criteria of judgment for
fundamentalism and urban life, the question remains: what about
the rest of the multitude, the singularities that occupy neither of
those categories? Hardt and Negri also offer a more general critique
of the "corruption" the multitude undergoes in the present social
order. "The three most significant social institutions of capitalist
society in which the common appears in corrupt form are the
family, the corporation, and the nation" (p. 160). All three present
themselves as forms of community in and through which the multitude can express its singularities, but in their standard forms each
of these structures constrains singularity into the mold of identity
and divides the multitude from itself. Therefore "[t]he multitude

must flee the family, the corporation, and the nation but at the same time build on the promises of the common they mobilize" (p. 164). All these forms are organized around claims to love – exclusive romantic and familial love; office camaraderie and brand loyalty; patriotism and jingoism – that are really corruptions of the multitude's love of singularities and of the common, corruptions that Hardt and Negri polemically label "evil": "Evil is the corruption of love that creates an obstacle to love, or to say the same thing with a different focus, evil is the corruption of the common that blocks its production and productivity" (p. 192). The upshot of this perspective is that evil – the corrupt forms of the common that are consistent with capitalist command – has no power of its own beyond the distortion of the love or common that it expropriates. A politics of love must critique these corrupt forms, re-socialize and re-orient the distorted love that drives them. In this way the politics of love is parallel to the politics of the metropolis and to anti-fundamentalism: all are practices of self-critique and self-construction that update the Renaissance humanist project for the context of the struggle against Empire.

Beyond these differentiations and negations that help us decide what actions of the multitude to affirm and what corruptions of the multitude to combat, *Commonwealth* also offers a grander political vision, if not quite a concrete organizational project, for an absolute democracy based on the common. Perhaps the clearest way to approach this vision is through Hardt and Negri's engagement with identity politics, which underpins many contemporary postcolonial, ethnic and gender struggles. In contrast to their dismissal of this logic in *Empire*, in *Commonwealth* they propose a tactical use for identity politics as the initial stage of a more revolutionary "singularity politics" of the multitude. The danger of identity politics is the trap its conception of identity often conceals: if the affirmation of a repressed or marginalized identity is the only telos of struggle, then one likely result of this struggle is merely the promotion, fossilization and reproduction of that identity once it achieves a degree of recognition. In a global order based on "universal" or "imperial" racism/sexism and not on exclusionary racism/sexism, such recognition will not destroy the hierarchies, and it will function by demanding the constant re-performance of the asserted identity as a condition of economic and political participation. Identity politics abets imperial racism by yoking subjective agency to possessive individualism, transforming identity into a form of property. For Hardt and Negri, this trap highlights the difference between the emancipation of a stable identity and the liberation of singularities defined by becoming: "whereas emancipation strives for the freedom of identity, the freedom to be *who you really are*, liberation aims at the freedom of self-determination and self-transformation, the freedom to determine *what you can become*" (p. 331). The latter is the freedom not *of* but *from* fixed identity; and, for Hardt and Negri, only the latter constitutes a revolutionary politics – although they hasten to say: "The point is not to pose a division between identity politics and revolutionary politics but, on the contrary, to follow the parallel revolutionary streams of thought and practice within identity politics, which all, perhaps paradoxically, aim toward an abolition of identity" (p. 326).[31]

Inspired by Spinoza's immanent conception of the relationship between the distinct attributes of mind and body (see chapter 4, p. 123), Hardt and Negri propose parallelism as a method to preserve the singularities of the multitude from conformity to a unitary or hierarchical principle of struggle, while linking them together in a common project – one based on the correspondences among their antagonisms and innovations.

> A translation process is required to reveal and understand these potential correspondences, a process that both acknowledges the autonomy of the language of each domain and facilitates communication among them. And a political process of articulation is required to address their conflicts and link them together. (Pp. 341–2)

Laclau, Passavant and Dean would welcome this admission of the need for political articulation in the making of what we called earlier "the multitude for itself," but they might be puzzled by the practical work this notion of articulation implies. Hardt and Negri distinguish it from the traditional "Popular Front" policy of alliance or coalition building, which "simply couple[s] identities like links in a chain," because it "can never get beyond the fixed identities striving for emancipation that form them." Parallel articulation, on the other hand, "transforms singularities in a process of liberation that establishes the common among them" (p. 350). It does not consolidate a given identity but opens up new transformations and becomings, which define the field of variation for both the common and the multitude. Although the common is the precondition of biopolitical production as well as its result, it is not simply given but must continually be produced or made. The same is true of the multitude as a political project. "Focusing on the

making of the multitude, then, allows us to recognize how its productive activity is also a political act of self-making" (p. 175). Moreover, "[m]ultitude is…a concept of applied parallelism, able to
grasp the specificity of altermodern struggles, which are characterized by relations of autonomy, equality, and interdependence
among vast multiplicities of singularities" (p. 111).

In parallel articulation, Hardt and Negri offer a theoretical
method for conceiving political organization anew, but no concrete
tools for applying it. As we know from *Multitude*, the authors posit
that the multitude can perform the sovereign function of decision-
making by means of – indeed, as a consequence of – its biopolitical,
network productive processes. They repeat the point in *Commonwealth*: the "three characteristics of biopolitical labor – cooperation,
autonomy, and network organization – provide solid building
blocks for democratic political organization" (p. 353). In order to
meet Empire head on, this potential for democratic political organization must find institutional forms, but not in the conventional
sense explicated by Foucault, Althusser and the Weberian tradition
in sociology. According to those models, institutions are staging
areas or construction sites for individual subjects – the subject
accedes to agency, whether intellectual, political, economic or spiritual, by passing through one or more institutions. This is the dis-
cursive (for Foucault) or ideological (for Althusser) function of
institutions: to reproduce the fabric of social existence by means of
subjective individuation, interpellation and discipline. The institutional process that Hardt and Negri conceive for the multitude is
different because it is predicated on the ontological priority of singularities and of their becoming. Institutions in this model are the
means of articulation that produce parallelism by providing staging
grounds for joyful encounters among singularities; like biopolitical
cities, they increase the speed and frequency of the swerves that
bring parallel lines of struggle and innovation into contact.

> This institutional process allows singularities to achieve some con-
> sistency in their interactions and behaviors, creating in this way a
> form of life, but never are such patterns fixed in identity. The central
> difference, perhaps, has to do with the locus of agency: whereas
> according to the conventional sociological notion institutions form
> individuals and identities, in our conception singularities form insti-
> tutions, which are thus perpetually in flux. (P. 358)

Such institutions, like the singularities they channel, must be
protean, perhaps even aleatory; in any case they will bear little

resemblance to contemporary political institutions of constituted power. The multitude's "institutions form a constituent rather than a constituted power" (p. 359) and, as such, they may look more like dance companies, free-jazz bands or hacker collectives than like legislatures or churches (and this analogy is not intended as a criticism of the idea).

At the conclusion of *Commonwealth*, Hardt and Negri renew the demands they first expressed in *Empire* and repeated in *Multitude*: basic income, global citizenship and re-appropriation of the common (pp. 380–1). But their most startling and provocative suggestion comes a few pages earlier, when they pose the question of how the multitude might actually govern while it sloughs off the shell of Empire and afterward. What mechanisms would be adequate for it beyond the level of constituent institutions for the coalescence of singularities? Their answer: the same de-centered mechanisms of "governance without government" that allow Empire to function now.

> The governance mechanisms of Empire do have the merit, in fact, of interpreting the biopolitical context and registering the increasing autonomy of the networks of singularities, the overflowing and unmeasurable forms of value produced by the multitude, and the ever greater power of the common. Our inclination is to appropriate this concept of governance, subvert its imperial vocation, and reformulate it as a concept of democracy and revolution. (Pp. 372–3)

In light of Hardt and Negri's penchant for illuminating reversals of perspective, this proposition is less shocking than it initially appears. However, while it may be simple enough to appropriate and subvert the *concept* of imperial governance, it's not as simple to reformulate it in practical terms. Nevertheless, the suggestion is audacious enough to take seriously, as a challenge to hidebound habits of militant thinking. if nothing else.

How might imperial governance be subverted, then? In order to become democratic and incorporate the demands of the multitude,

> [g]overnance gives up any vain attempt to bring unity to global legal systems (based on international law or consensus among nation states) and tries instead to establish a network logic that can manage conflicts and achieve a normative compatibility among the fragments of global society. Since the society they regulate and manage is full of exceptions, the structures of governance always remain

contingent and aleatory – floating structures, we could say, on the clashing waves of global society. (P. 373)

Like the institutions that will stage the encounters among singularities that will make the parallel articulation of struggles work without hierarchy or center, a democratic global governance cannot be a static, constituted form of power, but rather a fluid, constituent one.

> A constituent governance that inverts the imperial form would have to present not simply a normative figure of rule, and not only a functional structure of social consensus and cooperation, but also an open and socially generalized schema for social experimentation and democratic innovation. (P. 374)

It is not immediately clear how to derive a normative figure of rule from the common, although it does offer an innovative model of consensus formation – consensus as the swerve into parallelism of singular dissent. Perhaps the best gloss on this organizational proposition is still Negri's salute to Spinoza's absolute conception of democracy, which constantly transcends every fixed constitution, moving toward an asymptotic perfection that will never be achieved (see chapter 4, pp. 129–31). This is the result of his half-century search for an organizational form that would be adequate for a fully socialized and autonomous collective subject; and it is perhaps no less paradoxical than the party of mass vanguards that he proposed in the midst of the tumultuous seventies (see chapter 3, pp. 83–4). In *Commonwealth* Hardt and Negri reject the mosaic metaphor of static multicultural identity politics in favor of the metaphor of a kaleidoscope – singularities in constant becoming – and such an image is perhaps the best figure available for the institutions of global democratic governance as well.

***

Hardt and Negri's three collaborations since 2000, *Empire*, *Multitude*, and *Commonwealth*, do not constitute a trilogy, despite Fredric Jameson's, Giuseppina Mecchia's and other critics' use of that term to describe them. "Trilogy" is a narrative category that describes tripartite fictional works governed by a single overarching plot or theme (like Negri's *Trilogy of Resistance*, which is focused on the role of violence in revolutionary action). In the history of philosophy, only Kant's trio of critiques approximates this model; and it does so not in terms of a coherent plot or theme, but in terms of a logical architecture of faculties and concepts that is awe-inspiring in its rigidity as well as in its profundity. What Kant's work shares with narrative trilogies is unity and closure, and those qualities are precisely what Hardt and Negri's three works eschew. In drawing together, updating and expanding many ideas that first emerged in Negri's single-author writings of the preceding 50 years and more, these works organize, extend and modify themselves in unexpected and sometimes exasperating ways. Like Spinoza's *Ethics* and Marx's *Grundrisse*, they are essentially open works, in Umberto Eco's sense of artefacts that demand the participation of their audience in the constitution of their meaning. There is no other way to interpret Hardt and Negri's resolute refusal to dictate the forms that the multitude's political organization should take. This openness no doubt accounts for at least some of the perplexity their work has caused; not every reader is prepared to join a de-centered collective subject on repeated journeys among the fractured and antagonistic histories of modernity. Mecchia expresses the challenge of the pair's work very well: "The desire for the gay science contained in these books has to be already at work in their readers, lest the necessary translations and interpretations become impossible" (Mecchia 2010: 140). That desire, and others parallel to it, must be encouraged however and wherever they arise.

6

Envoi: Time to Come

As he approaches his 80th birthday, Negri remains remarkably acute and active. In 2010 he published a new study of Spinoza, *Spinoza et nous* (*Spinoza and Us*) (Negri 2010b), which extends his earlier work, and he embarked on the composition of another set of thematically linked plays – a "trilogy of critique" to complement the *Trilogy of Resistance*. His readership, for works both singly authored and collaborative, continues to expand in unexpected directions. For example the Italian graphic novelist Claudio Calia recently produced a comic-book interview-cum-biography of Negri entitled *È primavera* (*It's Springtime*) (Calia and Negri 2011), and Negri has also been the subject of documentary films in German, French, English, Spanish and Italian designed to introduce his work to new audiences. Patrick Cuninghame argues that worker-ism or autonomism, the mode of communist critique and militancy of which Negri is the most prominent contemporary exponent, is perhaps the most vital force in the network of altermodern and alterglobal movements today:

> Today autonomism can be seen as a global network of alliances between occupied social centers and media activists in Europe, Zap-atistas and Piqueteros in Latin America, Black Blockers in North America, cyber hacktivists in Japan, and autonomous workers, unemployed youth, students, dispossessed peasants, and urban squatter movements in South Korea, South Africa, and India ... united in their disparity and diversity by the overriding principle and prac-tice of autonomy from all forms of capitalist institution, authority, or power, but also along the lines of the autonomy of one section of

the multitude from the rest in order to prevent their absorption by traditional socialist "workers' centrality" ...(Cuninghame 2010: 451)

The key to this ever expanding engagement lies in Negri's ceaseless effort not only to speak *of* and *to* the singularities of the multitude – including those who, though gone, still have much to say, like Machiavelli, Spinoza, Leopardi and Marx, and those who, though they are here now, have been given little or no chance to speak, like the poor and the migrants – but also *with* them, to bring their voices, ideas and affects into his writings and actions without subordinating them to his own subjective singularity. Like Nietzsche, Deleuze and Guattari, Negri is a thinker of the multiple, the singular and the potential – which means that he is also a thinker of the future or, as he prefers to call it, of a time to come. We can say of him what he often says of Marx: when we pass beyond him, we find him waiting for us up ahead.

Notes

Notes to Chapter 1 Who Is Toni Negri, and Why Are They Saying such Terrible Things about Him?

1 Biographical information in the next sections is derived from Negri's remarks in *Negri on Negri* (Negri and Dufourmentelle 2004) and in *In Praise of the Common* (Casarino and Negri 2008), as well as from Yann Moulier's chronology in *Italie: Rouge et noire* (Negri 1985) and from my own personal correspondence with Negri.

2 Complete runs of three of these journals have recently been reissued in digital format: *Quaderni rossi* 2008; Trotta and Milana 2008; and De Lorenzis, Guizzardi and Mita 2008.

3 The best English-language sources on the Italian radical movements of the sixties and seventies are Lumley 1990 and above all Wright 2002; in Italian, see Balestrini and Moroni 1997, Borio, Pozzi and Roggero 2005, and Bianchi and Caminiti 2007–8.

4 In addition to the Amnesty International Reports, see also Ginsborg 1990: 386–7, as well as Portelli 1985. For a sampling of the international reaction to the case, see also *Working Class Autonomy and the Crisis* 1979; *Italy 1980–81: After Marx, Jail!* 1981; Leonetti and Rambaldi 1983; and the special issue of *Semiotext(e)* on *Autonomia: Post-Political Politics* (Lotringer and Marazzi 2007).

5 For a legal analysis of the failure to extradite Negri and other exiles, see Ruggiero 1993. For a detailed analysis of Negri's arrest and trial, see my "Editor's Introduction" to Negri's *Books for Burning* (Negri 2005).

6 Gilles Deleuze too participates in the general critique of humanism that characterizes postwar continental philosophy; but, like Foucault, he also furnishes Negri with elements for a revival of non-essentialist humanism, as we will see in chapters 4 and 5.

7   See "The Specter's Smile," Negri's essay on Derrida's *Specters of Marx*, and the full text of Derrida's reply – both in Sprinker 1999. Nealon 2006 provides a sophisticated and even-handed analysis of the Negri–Derrida debate.

8   This is not to deny that Negri often polemicized against universal or essentialist humanism, especially during the seventies; but even then he did so with the proviso that not every critical engagement with human subjectivity constituted a return to such humanism. In *Marx beyond Marx*, for example, he noted: "In avoiding humanism, some would also seek to avoid the theoretical areas of subjectivity. They are wrong. The path of materialism passes precisely through subjectivity. The path of subjectivity is the one that gives materiality to communism" (Negri 1984: 154).

Notes to Chapter 2 A Critical Genealogy of the Modern State – In Reverse

1   Negri's studies of Dilthey and Meinecke were published in 1959 as *Saggi sullo storicismo tedesco: Dilthey e Meinecke* (Negri 1959), and his study of Weber appeared in *Annuario bibliografico di filosofia del diritto* 1 as "Studi su Max Weber (1956–1965)" (Negri 1967b). His work on Troeltsch has never been published.

2   Negri's work on German historicism, while not totally sidelined by the shift in his interests that followed his encounter with Marx, became less central to the later development of his thinking. The exception to this is his work on Meinecke's analysis of *raison d'état*, which would continue to figure prominently in many of Negri's studies of the changing form of the modern capitalist state.

3   Negri makes no explicit use of the virtue/fortune dichotomy in *Political Descartes*, but he introduced it for the first time in the related methodological essay published a few years earlier: "Problemi di storia dello stato moderno – Francia: 1610–1650" (Negri 1967a). There he summarizes the Renaissance conception of freedom as follows: "The new Renaissance naturalism, in art and philosophy alike, wherever one looks, constitutes the framework within which the new vision of the world is defined. The world: an immense but certain projection of the microcosm, itself animated by this tension that emanates from the individual. The state: also a microcosm parallel to the individual. All the hierarchical gradations, the static links that configure the state – and nature – in the medieval vision collapse; the relation between the individual and the totality is direct, immediate; there is continuity between man and heaven. Freedom, to do or to struggle, is entirely positive. Like nature, the individual is essentially productive. 'Virtue' corresponds to 'fortune,' virtue produces or conquers fortune. Yes, it is a world that does not know

impossibility, that has no sense of limits – but when has a revolution ever known impossibility?" (pp. 190–1, my translation).

4   A more judicious approach to the problem of Descartes' politics can be found in Cavaillé, whose work broadly parallels Negri's in analyzing Descartes' consistent denial and disavowal of the political: "although it has been possible to speak of a 'political Descartes', it is completely against his stated intentions" (Cavaillé 1987: 119).

5   Negri's dispute with Cacciari would continue through the seventies, as each one marshaled abstruse metaphysical arguments to support concrete political programs; see Mandarini 2009 for a perceptive explication of this conflict.

6   To grasp the full significance of Negri's works on Kant and Hegel, we must first grasp an important terminological point: both works use the German term *Recht*, which, as the distinguished Hegel translator T. M. Knox notes, "is the German equivalent of *jus, droit* and *diritto*, as distinct from *lex, loi* and *legge*. There is no corresponding distinction in English" (Knox 1952: vi). This distinction of terms permits a distinction of conceptual levels between individual positive laws (the level of *legge* in Italian) and their abstract source or foundation (*diritto* in Italian). *Recht* refers to the foundational level that makes positive law possible; in English that level is sometimes called "law," as in "constitutional law," and other times it is called "right." English translations of Hegel tend to use the term "right" to translate the German *Recht*, though this introduces a certain subjectivism, because "right" in English is associated with individual properties and privileges, which is not the case with equivalents in other languages.

7   Negri's immersion in eighteenth-century juridical formalism did influence his earliest Marxist work on the role of labor in the Italian Constitution; see the introduction to chapter 3. His youthful studies also sensitized him to the pitfalls of twentieth-century formalisms like that of John Rawls' *Theory of Justice* (Rawls 1971), which he and Michael Hardt critique in *Labor of Dionysus*; indeed, Hardt and Negri interpret Rawls and his communitarian critics, like Michael Sandel, as repeating the development of juridical formalism from Kant to Hegel (see Hardt and Negri 1994: 247–52, 256–7).

8   See Macpherson 1962. Negri contributed an introduction to the Italian translation of this book; see Negri 1973.

9   In *Labor of Dionysus* Hardt and Negri interpret Richard Rorty's "postmodern" extension of John Rawls' theory of justice as a restaging of the subjective idealist version of juridical formalism; see Hardt and Negri 1994: 235–9.

10 In *Labor of Dionysus* Hardt and Negri see a similar operation, whereby the state is hypostasized as the source and guarantor of all intersubjective communities, their underlying subject as it were, at work in modern communitarian theories of justice as well; see Hardt and

Negri 1994: 252–7. The critique of the people as national subject in *Empire* is essentially a reiteration of this analysis of historicism from *Alle origini del formalismo giuridico*; see chapter 5, pp. 182–3.

11 Although Negri ultimately broke with Lukács' interpretation of Hegel, his later work on ontology (which we will discuss in chapter 4) shows interesting parallels with Lukács' own ontological speculations; on this parallelism, see Murphy 2003.

12 Hegel's analysis of the German Constitution was an early model for Negri's own important transitional essay "Labor in the Constitution," written in 1964 but unpublished until 1977. See the introduction to chapter 3.

13 The popular state is also the generic form of the nation state that Negri's later work, from "Labor in the Constitution" to *Empire*, will attack.

14 A revised but no less harsh and implicitly self-critical version of this essay was published in French under the title "Hegel: La fin de la modernité et la possibilité du communisme" ("Hegel: The End of Modernity and the Possibility of Communism") (Negri 1995). Negri's return to this essay after 25 years attests to its importance as the marker of a caesura in his intellectual development.

15 In the 1995 version of this essay Negri puts it even more bluntly: "In what follows I posit Hegel's philosophy of right and the State as the most perfect definition of modern 'politics,' that is, as the expression of the hegemonic project of domination and exploitation of living labor produced by the bourgeoisie" (Negri 1995: 157).

16 Negri first articulated the centrality of labor to the state in his 1964 essay "Labor in the Constitution," which we will examine briefly in the introduction to chapter 3.

Notes to Chapter 3 Workerism between State and Party

1 See Hardt and Negri 2000: 102–5, as well as chapter 5, pp. 182–3.

2 On Negri's analysis of the Italian Constitution, see also Mandarini 2005: 198–200.

3 The closest English-language analogs for class composition analysis can be found in the historical work of E. P. Thompson (Thompson 1963) and George Rawick (Rawick 1972).

4 For a more robust history of early workerism, see Wright 2002: Chs. 1–3. For a more thorough explication of Tronti's overall theoretical contribution, see Toscano 2009: 114–22.

5 This typology is spelled out fully in Bologna 1974.

6 In 1976 Negri published *La fabbrica della strategia: 33 lezioni su Lenin* (*The Strategy Factory: 33 Lessons on Lenin*), the result of a seminar he had taught on Lenin's work in which he found a precedent for the workerist conception of class composition in Lenin's concept of

the "determinate social formation." That book offers an explication of the basis and limits of Negri's Leninism that parallels the analysis we will present in the next section of this chapter; but we do not have space to analyze it here. For an overview of that book, see Hardt 2005: 14–21.

7   In 1977 Tronti published a book-length defense of this perspective, entitled *Sull'autonomia del politico* (Tronti 1977).

8   See Wright 2002: 161–75 for an overview of these critiques.

9   For detailed accounts of self-reduction, see Cherki and Wieviorka 1980 and Ramirez 1992, as well as Wright 2002: 158–161. For a historical reconstruction of the refusal of work in Marxist theory more generally, see Weeks 2005.

10 On the many competing organizational proposals that circulated throughout the Italian extra-parliamentary left during the seventies, see Wright 2005, who describes as follows Negri's regional organization, the Collettivi politici operai (CPO: Workers' Political Collectives): "Able to draw upon the prestige both of Negri as an intellectual, and of *Rosso* as a paper... the CPO was long the leading component of Autonomia organizzata within the Milan radical left. On the other hand, in the face of competition from Senza Tregua and a number of other 'organized autonomist' groupings, the CPO was never able to attain the sort of local hegemony secured by the CAO [Comitati Autonomi Operai or Workers' Autonomous Committees] in Rome or the CPV [Collettivi Politici Veneti or Venetian Political Collectives] in the Veneto" (p. 88).

11 What Negri calls the "crisis-state" has many of the features that later commentators will associate with the neo-liberal state. See for example Harvey 2005.

12 In addition to this political argument against the autonomy of the political, Negri also pursued a metaphysical version of the same argument in his ongoing debate with Massimo Cacciari (discussed briefly in chapter 2, pp. 37–8). As Matteo Mandarini shows in explicating the latter debate, Cacciari's conception of negative thought privileges technical rationality over Negri's conception of a constitutive ontology of historical subjective forms, and therefore the autonomy of the political can only be understood as "the decisionistic management of the multiplicity of fragmentary rationalities, as the working class – in the form of the PCI – taking control of the administration of the state," because "it is only once one has abandoned faith in a political subject as foundation of revolutionary political change that one can rediscover a professional political class that can take over the administration of the actual to bring change from above" (Mandarini 2009: 61–2). In an argument that prefigures Lyotard's *Postmodern Condition*, Cacciari adapts Wittgenstein's notion of language games to justify political opportunism: "On the one hand, the Political is a language game like the others, with its

own specific rules and immanent possibilities of transformation and, on the other hand, it has other language games for its content. The Political then situates itself in such a way as to keep the confrontation between the various language games continuously open" (p. 67). The metaphysical transcendence that negative thought eliminated by negating the ontological referents of all language games returns in the form of the political sphere itself, and the dialectical synthesis of capitalist development is reborn as socialist reformism, as Negri demonstrates.

13 In *Labor of Dionysus*, Michael Hardt and Negri endorse a version of Bologna's suggestion when they argue that the "withering of civil society" in the postmodern era produces a situation in which, "as every reality or even semblance of social dialectic disappears, the autonomy of the political from the social becomes total" (Hardt and Negri 1994: 270).

14 Historian Steve Wright expands this critique so as to encompass most of the factions comprising Autonomia. If the overall project of a party of Autonomia failed, this was primarily a result of "the inability of the great majority of Autonomia organizzata to rethink its role as a *ceto politico* [political elite] in the face of the rich and complex class composition thrown up in the late 1970s" (Wright 2005: 100–1).

15 "Toward a Critique of the Material Constitution" was first published in Negri's book *La forma-stato: Per la critica dell'economia politica della Costituzione* (Negri 1977), which also contained the first publication of "Labor in the Constitution."

16 This concept of "invention-power" was first proposed by Negri's Padua colleague Ferrucio Gambino in Gambino 1968.

17 At the time when "Workers' Party" was written, the recently formed Red Brigades had not yet adopted the strategy of vanguard terrorism that would later define them, and members of Negri's circle worked with Red Brigades members on the journal *Controinformazione*; see Tari 2007.

18 As his collaborative volume *Reading Capital* suggests, Althusser was certain that *Capital* is the work "by which Marx has to be *judged*. By it alone, and not by his still idealist 'Early Works' (1841–1844); not by still very ambiguous works like *The German Ideology*, or even the *Grundrisse...*" (Althusser 1971: 71). Callinicos (2007: 176–7) echoes the charges of idealism that Althusser levels at the *Grundrisse*.

19 Negri adopts a similar procedure a few years later, when he proposes to complete Spinoza's *Political Treatise* by finishing its unfinished chapter on democracy; see Negri 2004a: 28–58 and chapter 4, pp. 128–31.

20 Mahmut Mutman extends Ryan's deconstructive critique of Negri's essentialism to Hardt and Negri's concept of the multitude, arguing that "Negri's reversal of transcendental humanism with an *immanent*

one...remains, being a reversal, humanism, i.e. a philosophy of subject" (Mutman 2007: 149).

Notes to Chapter 4 From Solitude to Multitude

1   For an analysis of Negri's arrest, imprisonment and trial, see my "Editor's Introduction" to Negri 2005. For Negri's own account of the trial, see Negri 2010a: § 1.
2   See the subtitle to Nietzsche's *Ecce Homo*: *How One Becomes What One Is* (in Nietzsche 1968: 671).
3   On this terminology, see Hardt 2005: 29–30 and Read 2007: 30–6.
4   Negri is not the only theorist to take up the concept of multitude from Spinoza, but he is one of the most influential. For a different perspective on the multitude, which derives from some of the same sources, see the work of Negri's longtime comrade Paolo Virno (Virno 2004), to be discussed in chapter 5.
5   And not just by specialists: Manfred Walther reports that, "in the Netherlands...a review of the book by Wim Klever in a weekly newspaper provoked a long debate by the readers, many of the participants not being philosophers at all; all of them were passionately engaged in the debate" (Walther 1990: 286).
6   According to Deleuze, for Spinoza "The principle of consent (pact or contract) becomes the principle of political philosophy, and replaces the rule of authority" (Deleuze 1990a: 260; see also p. 390 n. 29 on the "second contract").
7   Spinoza often sums up this conception in the phrase *Tantum juris quantum potentiae*, "as much right as there is power." See Negri 2004a: 33, where he specifies that the contract is "an alienation that, although it constitutes sovereignty through the medium of transfer, restores to subjects a freedom and a series of rights that have been transformed (in the transfer and by sovereignty) from natural rights into juridical rights."
8   Resistance to the delegation of power has been central to many forms of anti-institutional left militancy over the past century; for example the workers' council tradition (see Pannekoek 1948 and Bologna 1976), and that of the Situationists and the May '68 militants (see Debord 1967 and Cohn-Bendit 1968).
9   For a sophisticated and fascinating attempt to synthesize all these intellectual currents, see Read 2003.
10 The linguistic turn also connects his work to that of Paolo Virno, Christian Marazzi, Maurizio Lazzarato and others working in the field of "cognitive capitalism."
11 The chapter "...And Nietzsche Went to Parliament" in *Domination and Sabotage* (Negri 2005: 253–8) is a sarcastic polemic against

Cacciari's Nietzschean/Heideggerian conception of *krisis* or "negative thought" and against its relevance for workers' struggles; it was written in response to Cacciari's election to the Italian Chamber of Deputies. See Mandarini 2009 for a fuller elaboration on this polemic.

12 In 1991 Negri published a manifesto outlining his approach to Spinoza; it was entitled "Spinoza's Anti-Modernity" (Negri 2004a: 79–93).

13 Negri also notes similarities between Leopardi and Spinoza that drew him to both thinkers during his time in prison, and, while these overlap with the similarities between Leopardi and Nietzsche, they are ultimately distinct. See "Between Infinity and Community: Notes on Materialism in Spinoza and Leopardi," in Negri 2004a.

14 For a quick outline, in English, of Leopardi's materialism, see Negri 2004a: 63–4.

15 This critique of Hegelian teleology is the aspect of Nietzsche's work that was most significant for Foucault; see Revel 2007: 96–100.

16 Throughout this section I cite J. G. Nichols' translation of "The Broom" from *The Canti* (Leopardi 1994), pp. 141–8. Further references to it by line numbers will be included parenthetically in my text.

17 See, among other things, the final aphorisms (1066 and 1067, pp. 548–50) in Nietzsche's *Will to Power* (Nietzsche 1967).

18 See passages in Leopardi's *Zibaldone* such as the following: "imagination is the source of reason, as it is of feeling, passions, poetry. This faculty that we suppose to be a principle, a distinct and determined quality of the human soul, either does not exist or it is merely the same thing, the same disposition along with a hundred others that we distinguish absolutely from it, and with the same thing we call reflection or the faculty to reflect, and with what we call intellect etc. Imagination and intellect are the same" (Leopardi 1992: 149).

19 Compare to Deleuze's reading of Nietzsche as a critic of Kantian morality in Ch. 3 of *Nietzsche and Philosophy* (Deleuze 1983), and Michael Hardt's identification of this "triangulation" with Deleuze's general project of anti-Hegelianism (Hardt 1993: 27–30).

20 This line of thinking later leads Negri to a similar rebuke of Adorno: "It's not straightforwardly true anymore that poetry has become impossible after Auschwitz, as Adorno claimed, just as it's no longer straightforwardly true that all hope has perished after Hiroshima, as Günther Anders asserted; poetry and hope have been revitalized by the postmodern multitudes, yet their measure is no longer homogeneous with that of the poetry and the hope of modernity" (Negri 2007: 51).

21 As Miguel Vatter summarizes: "Arendt analyzes constituent power in order to understand revolution as the origin of *the state*, so that revolution comes to mean the process of *constitutio libertatis*, the process of giving freedom a legal constitution such that the political

remains separate from the activities that constitute the social dimension of the world. Negri, for his part, analyzes constituent power in order to understand *revolution* as the origin of the state, so that revolution comes to mean the process of the permanent crisis of the state, of constituted power. For Negri, the political is also a power of separation, but one that breaks away from every constituted power, from institutionalized politics, in order to effect a return of constituent power back to the social, to the domain of living labor" (Vatter 2007: 54).

22 We will refer to the English translation, *Insurgencies*, throughout this chapter, but we will sometimes modify the citations because that edition departs from the convention we have followed so far of using "Power" for *potere* and "power" for *potenza*.

Notes to Chapter 5 Empire and Counter-Empire

1 Most of Negri's earlier discussions of multinationals were indebted to the work of his friend, Paduan colleague and later fellow prisoner Luciano Ferrari Bravo, who worked extensively on the topic throughout the seventies; see Ferrari Bravo 1975, as well as Negri's tribute to him in an anthology of Ferrari Bravo's works that he edited (Negri 2003b).

2 For a sampling of *Futur antérieur*'s concerns and proposals, see Virno and Hardt 1996.

3 For Hardt's background and a description of Hardt and Negri's method of collaborative writing, see Hardt 2004b.

4 For a more detailed explication of this convergence, see Murphy 2008.

5 For a critique of this "totalizing" proposal of a global cognitive map, see Villalobos-Ruminott 2001.

6 Hardt and Negri do not really discuss these institutions in *Empire*, an omission that their critics see as a serious weakness in their analysis; see Aronowitz 2003: 24, and Buchanan and Pahuja 2004: 79–81. They provide a more in-depth account of the World Trade Organization, International Monetary Fund and World Bank in *Multitude* (see Hardt and Negri 2004: 169–75, 290–1).

7 For Foucault's own formulation of the concept, see Foucault 1978, 2007 and 2008.

8 This account of the rise of the nation state out of feudalism has been disputed by Ernesto Laclau: "That the transference of control of many social spheres to the new social states is at the root of the new forms of biopower is incontestable, but the alternative to that process was not autonomous power of any hypothetical multitude but the continuation of feudal fragmentation. It is more: it was only when this process of centralization had advanced beyond a certain point

that something resembling a unitary multitude could emerge through the transference of sovereignty from the king to the people" (Laclau 2004: 25). Thus, for Laclau, the multitude could only be the product of the nation state, not its antagonist.

9   This interpretation of US constitutional history has been criticized by many scholars, most pertinently by Paul Passavant and Peter Fitzpatrick. Passavant uses an examination of the rhetorical and generic source texts of the Declaration of Independence to deconstruct the opposition between the constituent power that Hardt and Negri attribute to the Declaration and the constituted power of the constitution, and he thereby shows how both documents explicitly produce an exclusionary concept of the people (Passavant 2004: 108–14). Likewise, Fitzpatrick reminds readers of important Supreme Court cases from early and recent US history that explicitly repudiated the inclusive logic that Hardt and Negri attribute to US constitutional functionality (Fitzpatrick 2004: 50–1).

10 Susan Koshy objects that Hardt and Negri's analysis of the UN focuses on a single participant in its theoretical founding, the formalist Hans Kelsen (Hardt and Negri 2000: 4–9), and ignores the complexity of the rights regime instantiated in the organization: "the first generation of civil and political rights, associated with Western liberal democracies, developed out of the bourgeois revolutions in France and America in the late eighteenth century; the second generation of social and economic rights were the product of socialist revolutions in the early decades of the twentieth century; and the third generation of solidarity rights, like the right to development and the rights of peoples, emerged from the post-World War II anti-colonial revolutions. Thus to identify the project of universalism embedded in human rights norms as Western, whether as an act of genealogical valorization by globalization theorists or as an act of repudiation by radical scholars, is mistaken and short-sighted, because it surrenders a crucial arena of struggle in the current global conjuncture" (Koshy 2005: 115).

11 Hardt and Negri note that a similar transition brought about the collapse of the Soviet system of "real socialism": "The Soviet machine turned in on itself and ground to a halt, without the fuel that only new productive subjectivities can produce. The sectors of intellectual and immaterial labor withdrew their consensus from the regime, and their exodus condemned the system to death" (Hardt and Negri 2000: 279). In his model of the multitude, Paolo Virno similarly attributes the form of capitalist restructuring in the seventies and eighties – the transition to post-Fordism – to the forms of resistance pioneered by the counter-culture; see Virno 2004: 98–9.

12 Just as the original formulation of immaterial labor in *Labor of Dionysus* was castigated (by George Caffentzis 2003, for example) for its marginalization of the kinds of intensive manual labor – including

overt slavery – that predominate in the less developed regions of the global economy, so has its redeployment as symbolic and affective labor been attacked as ambiguous and reductive. Nick Dyer-Witheford argues that the "theory of immaterial labor seems very like a Marxian mirror image of the 'knowledge work' celebrated by managerial savants from Peter Drucker through Daniel Bell to Alvin Toffler and Robert Reich...Such a direct inversion of managerial orthodoxy, however, evidently risks entrapment in the arms of its bourgeois doppelgänger" (Dyer-Witheford 2005: 147). Paolo Virno's concept of the multitude's "virtuosity" embodies most of the characteristics of immaterial labor but avoids the negative connotations that these critics have registered in Hardt and Negri's version; see Virno 2004: 52–6.

13   This "epochal" revision – and division – of Foucault's concept of biopower, which presents it as achieving subjective hegemony under Empire, has been disputed by several of Hardt and Negri's critics. Alberto Toscano offers the sharpest version of this critique: they aim, he says, to "generate a new distinction between biopolitics and biopower at a remove from Foucault's own...This realignment of the terms means that biopower is on the side of subjection and control, while biopolitics is rethought in terms of subjectivity and freedom...This idea of biopolitics as an extension or even (following Negri's reading of real subsumption) an intensification and culmination of class struggle requires that Foucault's concept be presented as one that may be complemented (rather than displaced or abolished) by a Marxian analysis of class and its composition" (Toscano 2007: 118). See also Mutman 2001: 46–53 and Quinby 2004: 244–8.

14   Negri's onetime ally Michael Ryan found this dismissal of deconstruction and related critical approaches so troubling that he accused Hardt and Negri of bad faith: they dispense with deconstruction, he writes, "because they recognize that they cannot advance as the answer to the Marxist political quandary an ontological and uncritical materialist ideal such as the multitude and allow to go unchallenged (I should say undenounced) a powerful school of thought that suggests that all such ideals should be treated with suspicion" (Ryan 2001).

15   For a survey of some of the groups that made up these protests, see On Fire (2001), which includes a reprint of Hardt and Negri's New York Times op-ed piece "What the Protestors in Genoa Want" (pp. 101–3). For a more recent survey of Hardt and Negri's influence on global militancy, see Cuninghame 2010.

16   For a selection of Tute Bianchi materials in English, see http://www.nadir.org/nadir/initiativ/agp/free/tute/. Hardt and Negri salute the Tute Bianchi in Multitude; see Hardt and Negri 2004: 264–7.

17   Such suggestions were echoed on the left, in the quasi-psychoanalytic polemic attributed to the pseudonym "Ugo D. Rossi," which

accuses Hardt and Negri of a "proto-fascist" desire to replace Empire with its mirror image, a "great Rival for world hegemony," which would simply establish "a new domination" as well as "a desire to establish a total control of truth, which would at the same time be a control of thought by and within self-enclosed communities" ("Rossi" 2005: 191, 197, 200, 216). "Rossi" concludes that "the Counter-Empire remains a captive thought, subordinated to the Desire of a great Other, which is the contrary of liberation", p. 217), echoing Lacan's famous rebuke to the students occupying the University of Paris in 1969: "What you, as revolutionaries, aspire to is a Master. You will have one" (Lacan 1990: 126).

18 Most of the contents of Balakrishnan's volume were previously published in periodicals, as reviews of *Empire*, in the six months immediately following 9/11.

19 In addition to the *Rethinking Marxism*, Balakrishnan, and Passavant and Dean collections discussed below, the journal *Strategies* also published a special issue on *Antonio Negri: From Autonomia to Empire* (*Strategies* 16 (2), 2003); but it is more concerned with Negri's earlier work and its context than with *Empire*, so it is less central to the present discussion. See also Murphy and Mustapha 2005 and 2007.

20 Wood's essay was written for the Balakrishnan collection; Boron's was intended for that collection but grew too large to be accommodated, and was ultimately published as a separate book (Boron 2005). Néstor Kohan, a professor at the University of Buenos Aires like Boron, articulates a critique of *Empire* that is very similar to Boron's (Kohan 2005). For other, more restrained critiques of *Empire* that remain committed to classical imperialism, see Bull 2003, and Buchanan and Pahuja 2004. In an interesting essay focused on Marx and the history of British colonialism in India, John Hutnyk makes essentially the opposite claim that, from the viewpoint of the relative autonomy of corporations vis-à-vis nation states, classical imperialism was already Empire (see Hutnyk 2001: 121–7).

21 Malini Johan Schueller has taken this critique much further, accusing Hardt and Negri of a "universal theorizing" that amounts to intellectual colonialism (Johan Schueller 2009: 236). She argues that "global theories [such as that expressed in *Empire*] can operate as colonizing forces which it is our ethical task to resist, to decolonize" (Johan Schueller 2009: 237). Her critique of the language of inevitability in *Empire*'s opening pages is suggestive, but her overall argument concludes ambiguously with the assertion that we can never imagine that "the task of decolonization is ever complete," which would seem implicitly to claim a similar sort of transhistorical universality for postcolonial criticism.

22 For similar criticisms, see also Arrighi 2003: 36–7, Brennan 2003: 104–5, Dunn 2004: 158 and Shapiro 2004: 308.

23 Timothy Brennan's *ad hominem* attack was an exception; see Hardt and Negri 2003. In *Multitude* they offer a general response to several broad categories of critique without identifying any critics by name; see Hardt and Negri 2004: 222–7. Only in *Commonwealth* do they respond to a few of their critics individually; see Hardt and Negri 2009: 166–9.

24 This represents the maturation and confirmation of Negri's insight, from *Domination and Sabotage*, that "[o]nly a diffuse network of powers can organize revolutionary democracy" (Negri 2005: 279).

25 Virno's account of Marxian "general intellect" as the expansion of "common places" offers a similar theory of what is common to the multitude – one that is also based on the linguistic powers of subjects; see Virno 2004: 35–40, 106–8. Negri has occasionally embraced the concept of general intellect, both in his single-author and in his collaborative works, but he usually seeks to get past its implicit disembodiment and to emphasize its necessary relation to the "flesh" of the multitude and to the subversive potential of biopolitics; see Negri 2008a: 112–13, 152–4, Negri 2008b: 196–9, and Hardt and Negri 2000: 28–30, 364–7.

26 Negri investigates the different modalities of revolutionary or democratic violence in his first set of plays, *Trilogy of Resistance* (Negri 2011); on the self-critique of his own prior conceptions of violence that he carries out in the plays, see my introduction to Negri 2011.

27 For a selection of post-workerist writings, see Virno and Hardt 1996 and Henninger, Mecchia and Murphy 2007. *Multitudes* is the successor of *Futur antérieur*, which ceased publication shortly after Negri returned to prison in 1997.

28 Many of the criticisms of *Multitude* that we have examined, as well as the previously discussed criticisms of *Empire*, are brought together in Dardot, Laval and Mouhoud 2007, which nevertheless expresses considerable sympathy for Hardt and Negri's project.

29 This expansive ontological conception of the common is perhaps Hardt and Negri's most significant contribution to the recent revival of interest in the history and prospects of the commons among critics like Dyer-Witheford, Peter Linebaugh and Naomi Klein.

30 Hardt and Negri specify that "[r]ent operates through a *desocialization of the common*, privatizing in the hands of the rich the common wealth produced" (Hardt and Negri 2009: 258).

31 This emphasis on the liberation of singularities, which do not correspond to political or economic citizen-subjects, refutes the accusation of bourgeois individualism that Amin made against Hardt and Negri's concept of the multitude.

Works Cited

Agamben, G. 1998. *Homo Sacer: Sovereign Power and Bare Life* [1995], trans. D. Heller-Roazen (Stanford: Stanford University Press).

Alquati, R. 1975. *Sulla FIAT e altri scritti* (Milan: Feltrinelli).

Althusser, L. 1969. "Marxism and Humanism." In L. Althusser, *For Marx*, trans. B. Brewster (New York: Verso), pp. 219–47.

Althusser, L. 1970. "The Object of Capital." In Althusser and Balibar 1970, pp. 73–198.

Althusser, L. 1971. *Lenin and Philosophy and Other Essays*, trans. B. Brewster (New York: Monthly Review).

Althusser, L. 1999. "Machiavelli's Solitude." In L. Althusser, *Machiavelli and Us*, trans. G. Elliott (New York: Verso), pp. 115–30.

Althusser, L., and E. Balibar. 1970. *Reading Capital*, trans. B. Brewster (New York: Verso).

Amin, S. 2005. Review of *Empire* and *Multitude*, trans. J. H. Membrez. *Monthly Review* 57 (6) (November), pp. 1–12.

Anderson, B. 1983. *Imagined Communities: Reflections on the Origin and Spread of Nationalism* (New York: Verso).

Anderson, B. C. 2009. "Brothers in Marx." *The Wall Street Journal*, October 7. Available online at: http://online.wsj.com/article/SB10001424052748703298004574457113221769116.html.

Antonio Negri: From Autonomia to Empire. 2003. Special Issue of *Strategies: Journal of Theory, Culture and Politics* 16 (2) (November).

Arendt, H. 1963. *On Revolution* (New York: Penguin).

Aronowitz, S. 2003. "The New World Order." In Balakrishnan, ed., 2003, pp. 19–25.

Arrighi, G. 1994. *The Long Twentieth Century: Money, Power, and the Origins of Our Times* (New York: Verso).

Arrighi, G. 2003. "Lineages of Empire." In Balakrishnan, ed., 2003, pp. 29–42.

Artous, A. 2010. *Démocratie, citoyenneté, émancipation* (Paris: Syllepse).

Balakrishnan, G., ed. 2003. *Debating Empire* (New York: Verso).

Balestrini, N., and P. Moroni. 1997. *L'orda d'oro: 1968–1977: La grande ondata rivoluzionaria e creativa, politica e esistentiale*, new edition by S. Bianchi (Milan: Feltrinelli).

Balibar, E. 1994. *Masses, Classes, Ideas: Studies on Politics and Philosophy Before and After Marx*, trans. J. Swenson (New York: Routledge).

Balibar, E., and I. Wallerstein. 1991. *Race, Nation, Class: Ambiguous Identities* (New York: Verso).

Bamyeh, M. 2001. "Life and Vision Under Globalization." *Dossier on* Empire 2001, pp. 199–208.

Bartolovich, C. 2007. "Organizing the (Un)Common." *Angelaki* 12 (3), pp. 81–104.

Bianchi, S., and L. Caminiti, eds. 2007–8. *Gli Autonomi: Le storie, le lotte, le teorie*, vols. 1–3 (Rome: DeriveApprodi).

Bobbio, N. 1995. *Ideological Profile of Twentieth-Century Italy*, trans. L. G. Cochrane (Princeton: Princeton University Press).

Bologna, S. 1974. "Moneta e crisi: Marx corrispondente della 'New York Daily Tribune', 1856–57." In S. Bologna, P. Carpignano, and A. Negri, *Crisi e organizzazione operaia* (Milan: Feltrinelli, 1974), pp. 9–72.

Bologna, S. 1976. "Class Composition and Theory of the Party at the Origin of the Workers Councils Movement," trans. B. Ramirez. In *The Labour Process and Class Strategies* (London: CSE Pamphlet 1), pp. 68–91.

Bologna, S. 2003. Review of Wright, *Storming Heaven*. In *Antonio Negri: From Autonomia to Empire* 2003, pp. 97–105.

Bologna, S. 2005. "Negri's *Proletarians and the State*: A Critique" [1976], trans. Ed Emery. In Murphy and Mustapha, eds., 2005, pp. 38–47.

Borio, G., F. Pozzi and G. Roggero. 2002. *Futuro anteriore: Dai "Quaderni rossi" ai movimenti globali – Ricchezze e limiti dell'operaismo italiano* (Rome: DeriveApprodi).

Borio, G., F. Pozzi and G. Roggero, eds. 2005. *Gli operaisti* (Rome: DeriveApprodi).

Boron, A. 2005. *Empire and Imperialism: A Critical Reading of Michael Hardt and Antonio Negri*, trans. J. Casiro (London: Zed Books).

Brecht, B. 1994. *Life of Galileo*, trans. J. Willett (New York: Arcade).

Brennan, T. 2003. "The Italian Ideology." In Balakrishnan, ed., 2003, pp. 97–120.

Buchanan, R., and S. Pahuja. 2004. "Legal Imperialism: *Empire*'s Invisible Hand?" In Passavant and Dean, eds., 2004a, pp. 73–93.

Bull, M. 2003. "You Can't Build a New Society with a Stanley Knife." In Balakrishnan, ed., 2003, pp. 83–96.

Bull, M. 2005. "The Limits of Multitude." *New Left Review* 35 (September/October), pp. 19–39.

Cacciari, M. 1970. "*Vita Cartesii est simplicissima.*" *Contropiano* 2 (May/August 1970), pp. 375–99.

Caffentzis, C. G. 2003. "The End of Work or the Renaissance of Slavery? A Critique of Rifkin and Negri." In W. Bonefeld, ed., *Revolutionary Writing* (Brooklyn: Autonomedia), pp. 115–33.

Calia, C., and Negri, A. 2011. *Antonio Negri Illustrated: Interview in Venice*, trans. J. F. McGimsey (Ottawa: Red Quill Books). [Originally published as *È primavera: Intervista a Antonio Negri* (Padua: BeccoGiallo, 2008).]

Callinicos, A. 2003. "Toni Negri in Perspective." In Balakrishnan, ed., pp. 121–43.

Callinicos, A. 2007. "Antonio Negri and the Temptation of Ontology." In Murphy and Mustapha, eds., 2007, pp. 169–97.

Casarini, L. 2001. "Capitalism and War: Theories of Conflict" [interview of Casarini by A. Callinicos]. *Socialist Review* 258 (December). Available online at: http://pubs.socialistreviewindex.org.uk/sr258/callinicos.htm.

Casarino, C., and A. Negri. 2008. *In Praise of the Common: A Conversation on Philosophy and Politics* (Minneapolis: University of Minnesota Press).

Cavaillé, J.-P. 1987. "Politics Disavowed: Remarks on the Status of Politics in the Philosophy of Descartes," trans. R. Scott Walker. *Diogenes* 35 (138), pp. 118–38.

Cherki, E., and M. Wieviorka. 1980. "Autoreduction Movements in Turin." *Autonomia: Post-Political Politics* (New York: Semiotext[e]), pp. 72–8.

Chiesa, L., and A. Toscano, eds. 2009. *The Italian Difference: Between Nihilism and Biopolitics* (Melbourne: re.press).

Cohn-Bendit, D., and G. 1968. *Obsolete Communism: The Left-Wing Alternative*, trans. A. Pomerans (New York: McGraw-Hill).

Comitato 7 aprile. 1979. *Processo all'Autonomia* (Cosenza: Lerici).

Corsani, A. 2007. "Beyond the Myth of Woman: The Becoming-Transfeminist of (Post-)Marxism," trans. T. S. Murphy. In Henninger, Mecchia and Murphy, eds., 2007, pp. 106–38.

Cox, L. 2001. "Barbarian Resistance and Rebel Alliances: Social Movements and *Empire*." *Dossier on* Empire 2001, pp. 155–67.

Cuninghame, P. 2010. "Autonomism as a Global Social Movement." *Working USA: The Journal of Labor and Society* 13 (December), pp. 451–64.

Dardot, P., C. Laval and E. M. Mouhoud. 2007. *Sauver Marx? Empire, multitude, travail immatériel* (Paris: La Découverte).

Dean, J. 2004. "The Networked Empire: Communicative Capitalism and the Hope for Politics." In Passavant and Dean, eds., 2004a, pp. 26–88.

Debord, G. 1967. *Society of the Spectacle*, trans. D. Nicholson-Smith (New York: Zone Books, 1994).

Deleuze, G. 1954. "Review of Hyppolite's *Logique et existence*." In J. Hyppolite, *Logic and Existence*, trans. L. Lawlor and A. Sen (Albany, NY: SUNY Press, 1997), pp. 191–5.

Deleuze, G. 1982. Preface to Negri, *L'Anomalie sauvage: Puissance et pouvoir chez Spinoza*, trans. F. Matheron (Paris: Presses universitaires de France), pp. 9–12.

Deleuze, G. 1983. *Nietzsche and Philosophy*, trans. H. Tomlinson (New York: Columbia University Press).

Deleuze, G. 1988. *Spinoza: Practical Philosophy*, trans. R. Hurley (San Francisco: City Lights).

Deleuze, G. 1990a. *Expressionism in Philosophy: Spinoza*, trans. M. Joughin (New York: Zone Books).

Deleuze, G. 1990b. *The Logic of Sense*, trans. C. Stivale, M. Lester, C. Stivale and C. Boundas (New York: Columbia University Press).

Deleuze, G. 1995a. *Negotiations 1972–1990*, trans. M. Joughin (New York: Columbia University Press).

Deleuze, G. 1995b. "Postscript on Control Societies." In Deleuze 1995a, pp. 177–82.

De Lorenzis, T., V. Guizzardi and M. Mita, eds. 2008. *Avete pagato caro non avete pagato tutto: La rivista "Rosso" (1973–1979)* (Rome: DeriveApprodi).

Derrida, J. 1982. "The Ends of Man." In J. Derrida, *Margins of Philosophy*, trans. A. Bass (Chicago: University of Chicago Press), pp. 109–36.

Derrida, Jacques. 1999. "Marx and Sons." In Sprinker, ed., pp. 213–69.

Dominijanni, I. 2005. "Rethinking Change: Italian Feminism between Crisis and Critique of Politics." In *Italian Effects* (Special Issue of *Cultural Studies Review* 11 (1), September), pp. 25–35.

Dossier on Empire. 2001. Special Issue of *Rethinking Marxism* 13 (3/4) (fall/winter).

Dunn, K. C. 2004. "Africa's Ambiguous Relation to Empire and *Empire*." In Passavant and Dean, eds., 2004a, pp. 143–62.

Dyer-Witheford, N. 2001. "Empire, Immaterial Labor, the New Combinations, and the Global Worker." In *Dossier on* Empire 2001, pp. 70–80.

Dyer-Witheford, N. 2005. "Cyber-Negri: General Intellect and Immaterial Labor." In Murphy and Mustapha, eds., 2005, pp. 136–62.

Eakin, E. 2001. "What is the Next Big Idea? Buzz is Growing for *Empire*." *The New York Times*, July 7, B7.

Elliott, M. 2001a. "The Wrong Side of the Barricades." *Time Magazine*, July 23, p. 39.

Elliott, M. 2001b. "Innovators – *Time* 100: The Next Wave." *Time Magazine*, December 17, pp. 68–9.

Ferrari Bravo, L. 1975. *Imperialismo e classe operaio multinazionale* (Milan: Feltrinelli).

Fitzpatrick, P. 2004. "The Immanence of *Empire*." In Passavant and Dean, eds., 2004a, pp. 31–55.

Foucault, M. 1970. *The Order of Things: An Archaeology of the Human Sciences* (New York: Vintage).

Foucault, M. 1972. "The Discourse on Language." In M. Foucault, *The Archaeology of Knowledge*, trans. A. M. Sheridan Smith (New York: Pantheon), pp. 215–37.

Foucault, M. 1977. "Revolutionary Action: 'Until Now'" [1971]. In M. Foucault, *Language, Counter-Memory, Practice: Selected Essays and Interviews*, ed. and trans. D. F. Bouchard (Ithaca, NY: Cornell University Press), pp. 218–33.

Foucault, M. 1978. *The History of Sexuality*, vol. 1: *An Introduction*, trans. R. Hurley (New York: Vintage).

Foucault, M. 2007. *Security, Territory, Population: Lectures at the Collège de France, 1977–1978*, ed. M. Senellart, trans. G. Burchell (New York: Palgrave).

Foucault, M. 2008. *The Birth of Biopolitics: Lectures at the Collège de France, 1978–1979*, ed. M. Senellart, trans. G. Burchell (New York: Palgrave).

Fukuyama, F. 1992. *The End of History and the Last Man* (New York: Free Press).

Gambino, F. 1968. "Forza-invenzione e forza-lavoro: Ipotesi." *Altreragioni* 8 (1999), pp. 147–50.

Ginsborg, P. 1990. *A History of Contemporary Italy: Society and Politics 1943–1988* (New York: Penguin).

Guaraldi, A. 1965. Review of *Alle origini del formalismo giuridico*. *Journal of the History of Philosophy* 3 (1) (April), pp. 135–6.

Guattari, F., and E. Alliez. 1984. "Capitalist Systems, Structures and Processes," trans. B. Darling. In G. Genosko, ed., *The Guattari Reader* (Oxford: Blackwell, 1996), pp. 233–47.

Guattari, F., and A. Negri. 1985. *New Lines of Alliance, New Spaces of Liberty*, trans. M. Ryan, J. Becker, A. Bove and N. Le Blanc (Brooklyn: Autonomedia, 2010). [Original publication: *Les nouveaux espaces de liberté* (Paris: Dominique Bedou, 1985).]

Hardt, M. 1993. *Gilles Deleuze: An Apprenticeship in Philosophy* (Minneapolis: University of Minnesota Press).

Hardt, M. 1997. "Prison Time." In *Genet: In the Language of the Enemy* (Special Issue of *Yale French Studies* 91), pp. 64–79.

Hardt, M. 2004a. "Sovereignty, Multitudes, Absolute Democracy: A Discussion between Michael Hardt and Thomas L. Dumm about Hardt's and Negri's *Empire*." In Passavant and Dean, eds., 2004a, pp. 163–73.

Hardt, M. 2004b. "The Collaborator and the Multitude," interview by C. Smith and E. Minardi. *Minnesota Review* 61/2. Available online at: http://www.theminnesotareview.org/journal/ns61/index.shtml.

Hardt, Michael. 2005. "Into the Factory: Negri's Lenin and the Subjective Caesura (1968–73)." In Murphy and Mustapha, eds., 2005, pp. 7–37.

Hardt, M., and A. Negri. 1994. *Labor of Dionysus: A Critique of the State-Form* (Minneapolis: University of Minnesota Press).

Hardt, M., and A. Negri. 2000. *Empire* (Cambridge, MA: Harvard University Press).

Hardt, M., and A. Negri. 2001. "Adventures of the Multitude: Response of the Authors." In *Dossier on* Empire 2001, pp. 236–43.

Hardt, M., and A. Negri. 2003. "The Rod and the Forest Warden: A Response to Timothy Brennan." *Critical Inquiry* 29 (2) (winter), pp. 368–73.

Hardt, M., and A. Negri. 2004. *Multitude: War and Democracy in the Age of Empire* (New York: Penguin Press).

Hardt, M., and A. Negri. 2009. *Commonwealth* (Cambridge, MA: Harvard University Press).

Harvey, D. 2005. *A Brief History of Neoliberalism* (Oxford: Oxford University Press).

Havercroft, J. 2010. "The Fickle Multitude: Spinoza and the Problem of Global Democracy." *Constellations* 17 (1), pp. 120–36.

Hawkesworth, M. 2006. "The Gendered Ontology of *Multitude*." *Political Theory* 34 (2) (June), pp. 357–64.

Hegel, G. W. F. 1962. *Scritti di filosofia del diritto (1802–1803)*, trans. A. Negri (Bari: Laterza).

Hegel, G. W. F. 1993. *Introductory Lectures on Aesthetics*, trans. B. Bosanquet (New York: Penguin).

Heidegger, M. 1947. "Letter on Humanism," trans. F. Capuzzi, J. G. Gray and D. F. Krell. In L. Cahoone, ed., *From Modernism to Postmodernism: An Anthology* (Oxford: Basil Blackwell, 1996), pp. 274–308.

Henninger, M., G. Mecchia and T. S. Murphy, eds. 2007. *Italian Post-Workerist Thought* (Special Issue of *SubStance* 36.1 (112)).

Holloway, J. 2005. *Change the World Without Taking Power: The Meaning of Revolution Today*, new edition (London: Pluto Press).

Hoofd, I. M. 2005. "The Migrant Metaphor within Radical Italian Thought." In *Italian Effects* (Special Issue of *Cultural Studies Review* 11 (1), September), pp. 129–46.

Hutnyk, J. 2001. "Tales from the Raj." In *Dossier on* Empire 2001, pp. 119–36.

Italy 1980–81: After Marx, Jail! 1981. London: Red Notes.

Jameson, F. 1991. *Postmodernism, or, The Cultural Logic of Late Capitalism* (Durham, NC: Duke University Press).

Johar Schueller, M. 2009. "Decolonizing Global Theories Today: Hardt and Negri, Agamben, Butler." *interventions* 11 (2), pp. 235–54.

Kimball, R. 2001. "The New Anti-Americanism." *The New Criterion* 20 (2) (October). Available online at: http://www.newcriterion. com/articles.cfm/antiamericanism-kimball-2111.

Knox, T. M. 1952. "Translator's Foreword" to *Hegel's Philosophy of Right*, trans. T. M. Knox (New York: Cambridge University Press), pp. v–xii.

Kohan, N. 2005. *Toni Negri e gli equivoci di Impero*, trans. L. Cordidonne (Bolsena: Massari).

Koshy, S. 2005. "The Postmodern Subaltern: Globalization Theory and the Subject of Ethnic, Area, and Postcolonial Studies." In F. Lionnet and Shu-mei Shih, eds., *Minor Transnationalism* (Durham, NC: Duke University Press), pp. 109–31.

Lacan, J. 1977. "The Agency of the Letter in the Unconscious." In J. Lacan, *Écrits: A Selection* (New York: Norton), pp. 146–59.

Lacan, J. 1988. *The Seminar of Jacques Lacan*, Book 2: *The Ego in Freud's Theory and in the Technique of Psychoanalysis 1954–55*, ed. J.-A. Miller, trans. S. Tomaselli (New York: Norton).

Lacan, J. 1990. *Television: A Challenge to the Psychoanalytic Establishment*, ed. J. Copjec, trans. D. Hollier, R. Krauss and A. Michelson (New York: W. W. Norton).

Laclau, E. 2004. "Can Immanence Explain Social Struggles?" In Passavant and Dean, eds., 2004a, pp. 21–30.

Lawlor, L. 1997. "Translator's Preface" to Hyppolite, *Logic and Existence*, trans. L. Lawlor and A. Sen (Albany, NY: SUNY Press), pp. vii–xviii.

Leonetti, F., and E. Rambaldi, eds. 1983. *Il dibattito sul processo dell'Autonomia* (Milan: Multhipla).

Leopardi, G. 1992. *Zibaldone: A Selection*, trans. M. King and D. Bini (New York: Peter Lang).

Leopardi, G. 1994. *The Canti*, trans. J. G. Nichols (London: Carcanet).

Levinson, B. 2001. "*Empire*, or, The Limit of Our Political Choices." In *Dossier on* Empire 2001, pp. 209–15.

Lotringer, S., and C. Marazzi, eds. 2007. *Semiotext(e): Italy/Autonomia – Post-Political Politics* [1980], 2nd edition (New York: Semiotext(e)).

Lukács, G. 1971. *History and Class Consciousness: Studies in Marxist Dialectics*, trans. R. Livingstone (Cambridge, MA: MIT Press).

Lukács, G. 1975. *The Young Hegel: Studies in the Relations between Dialectics and Economics*, trans. R. Livingstone (Cambridge, MA: MIT Press).

Lumley, R. 1990. *States of Emergency: Cultures of Revolt in Italy from 1968 to 1978* (New York: Verso).

Lunn, E. 1982. *Marxism and Modernism: An Historical Study of Lukács, Brecht, Benjamin and Adorno* (Berkeley: University of California Press).

Lyotard, J.-F. 1984. *The Postmodern Condition: A Report on Knowledge* [1979], trans. G. Bennington and B. Massumi (Minneapolis: University of Minnesota Press).

Lyotard, J.-F. 1992. *The Postmodern Explained*, trans. J. Pefanis, D. Barry, B. Maher, V. Spate and M. Thomas (Minneapolis: University of Minnesota Press).

Macciocchi, M. A. 1973. *Letters from inside the Italian Communist Party to Louis Althusser*, trans. S. M. Hellman (London: New Left Books). [Original Italian 1969, *Lettere dall'interno del P.C.I. a Louis Althusser* (Milan: Feltrinelli).]

Macherey, P. 2007. "Negri's Spinoza: From Mediation to Constitution," trans. T. Stolze. In Murphy and Mustapha, eds., 2007, pp. 7–27.

Macpherson, C. B. 1962. *The Political Theory of Possessive Individualism* (Oxford: Clarendon Press).

Mandarini, M. 2005. "Antagonism, Contradiction, Time: Conflict and Organization in Antonio Negri." In C. Jones and R. Munro, eds., *Contemporary Organization Theory* (Oxford: Blackwell), pp. 192–214.

Mandarini, M. 2009. "Beyond Nihilism: Notes toward a Critique of Left-Heideggerianism in Italian Philosophy of the 1970s." In Chiesa and Toscano, eds., pp. 55–79.

Mandarini, M., and A. Toscano. 2007. "Antonio Negri and the Antinomies of Bourgeois Thought." In Negri 1970b, pp. 1–25.

Marx, K. 1973a. *Grundrisse: Foundations of the Critique of Political Economy (Rough Draft)*, trans. M. Nicolaus (New York: Penguin).

Marx, K. 1973b. *The Revolutions of 1848: Political Writings*, vol. 1, ed. D. Fernbach (New York: Penguin).

Marx, K., and F. Engels. 1998. *The German Ideology*, no trans. listed (Amherst, NY: Prometheus Books).

Matheron, F. 1982. Preface to Negri, *L'Anomalie sauvage: Puissance et pouvoir chez Spinoza*, trans. F. Matheron (Paris: Presses universitaires de France), 19–25.

Mecchia, G. 2010. "Foreign Theories: On the Completion of the *Empire* Trilogy." In *Minnesota Review* 75, "Franco-Italian Political Thought," pp. 133–42.

Mishra, P. K. 2001. "The Fall of the Empire or the Rise of the Global South?" In *Dossier on* Empire 2001, pp. 95–9.

Mitchell, S. 1972. "Extended Note to Ian Burchall's Paper." In Paul Walton and Stuart Hall, eds., *Situating Marx: Evaluations and Departures* (London: Human Context Books, 1972).

Montag, W. 1998. Preface to E. Balibar, *Spinoza and Politics* (New York: Verso), pp. vii–xix.

Moreiras, A. 2001. "A Line of Shadow: Metaphysics in Counter-Empire." In *Dossier on* Empire 2001, pp. 216–26.

Murphy, T. S. 2003. "The Ontological Turn in the Marxism of Georg Lukács and Antonio Negri." In *Antonio Negri: From Autonomia to Empire* 2003, pp. 163–85.

Murphy, T. S. 2008. "To Have Done with Postmodernism: A Plea (or Provocation) for Globalization Studies." In R. M. Berry and J. Di Leo, eds., *Fiction's Present: Situating Contemporary Narrative Innovation* (Albany, NY: SUNY Press, 2008), pp. 29–45.

Murphy, T. S., and A.-K. Mustapha, eds. 2005. *The Philosophy of Antonio Negri: Resistance in Practice* (London: Pluto Press).

Murphy, T. S., and A.-K. Mustapha, eds. 2007. *The Philosophy of Antonio Negri*, vol. 2: *Revolution in Theory* (London: Pluto Press).

Mutman, M. 2001. "On *Empire*." In *Dossier on* Empire 2001, pp. 43–60.

Mutman, M. 2007. "Difference, Event, Subject: Antonio Negri's Political Theory as Postmodern Metaphysics." In Murphy and Mustapha, eds., 2007, pp. 143–68.

Nealon, J. T. 2006. "Post-Deconstructive? Negri, Derrida and the Present State of Theory." *symploke* 14 (1/2), pp. 68–80.

Negri, A. 1958. *Stato e diritto nel giovane Hegel: Studio sulla genesi illuministica della filosofia giuridica e politica di Hegel* (Padua: Cedam).

Negri, A. 1959. *Saggi sullo storicismo tedesco: Dilthey e Meinecke* (Milan: Feltrinelli).

Negri, A. 1962. *Alle origini del formalismo giuridico: Studio sul problema della forma. Kant e nei giuristi kantiani tra il 1789 e il 1802* (Padua: Cedam).

Negri, A. 1967a. "Problemi di storia dello Stato moderno – Francia: 1610–1650." *Rivista critica di storia della filosofia* 22 (2) (April/June) 1967, pp. 182–220. Florence: La Nuova Italia Editrice.

Negri, A. 1967b. "Studi su Max Weber (1956–1965)." *Annuario bibliografico di filosofia del diritto* 1 (Milan: Dott. A. Giuffré Editore), pp. 427–59.

Negri, A. 1970a. "Rileggendo Hegel, filosofo del diritto." In F. Tessitore, ed., *Incidenza di Hegel: Studi raccolti in occasione del secondo centenario della nascita del filosofo* (Naples: Morano, 1970), pp. 251–70.

Negri, A. 1970b. *Descartes politico o della ragionevole ideologia* (Milan: Feltrinelli). [Trans. M. Mandarini and A. Toscano, *Political Descartes: Reason, Ideology and the Bourgeois Project* (New York: Verso, 2007). All parenthetical references in the main text are to this English edition.]

Negri, A. 1973. "Prefazione" to C. B. Macpherson, *Libertà e proprietà alle origini del pensiero borghese: La teoria dell'individualismo possessivo da Hobbes a Locke* (Milan: Istituto editoriale internazionale [ISEDI]), pp. 13–22.

Negri, A. 1977. *La forma-stato: Per la critica dell'economia politica della Costituzione* (Milan: Feltrinelli).

Negri, A. 1979. Appendices to *Crisi e organizzazione operaia*. In *Working-Class Autonomy and the Crisis*, trans. E. Emery (London: Red Notes), pp. 32–65.

Negri, A. 1980. "Il memoriale difensivo di Toni Negri." *Lotta continua*, 19–21 January.

Negri, A. 1981. "Note sulla storia del politico in Tronti." In A. Negri, *L'anomalia selvaggia: Saggi sul potere e potenza in Baruch Spinoza* (Milan: Feltrinelli), pp. 288–92.

Negri, A. 1982. *Macchina tempo: Rompicapi liberazione costituzione* (Milan: Feltrinelli).

Negri, A. 1984. *Marx beyond Marx: Lessons on the Grundrisse*, trans. H. Cleaver, M. Ryan and M. Viano (South Hadley, MA: Bergin and Garvey). [Original Italian 1979, *Marx oltre Marx: Quaderni di lavoro sui Grundrisse* (Milano: Feltrinelli).]

Negri, A. 1985. *Italie: Rouge et noire*, trans. Y. Moulier (Paris: Hachette).

Negri, A. 1988. *Revolution Retrieved: Writings on Marx, Keynes, Capitalist Crisis and New Social Subjects 1967–1983*, trans. E. Emery (London: Red Notes).

Negri, A. 1991. *The Savage Anomaly: The Power of Spinoza's Metaphysics and Politics*, trans. M. Hardt (Minneapolis: University of Minnesota Press). [Original Italian 1981, *L'anomalia selvaggia: Saggi sul potere e potenza in Baruch Spinoza* (Milan: Feltrinelli).]

Negri, A. 1995. "Hegel: La fin de la modernité et la possibilité du communisme." In Henri Maler, ed., *Hegel passé, Hegel à venir* (*Futur antérieur* supplement) (Paris: L'Harmattan), pp. 157–78.

Negri, A. 1999. *Insurgencies: Constituent Power and the Modern State*, trans. M. Boscagli (Minneapolis: University of Minnesota Press). [Original Italian 1992, *Il Potere costituente: Saggio sulle alternative del moderno* (Milan: SugarCo).]

Negri, A. 2001. *Lenta ginestra: Saggio sull'ontologia di Giacomo Leopardi* [1987] (Milan: Mimesis).

Negri, A. 2002. "The Imperialist Backlash on Empire," interview with I. Dominijanni. *Il Manifesto*, September 14. [English translation available online at: http://www.generation-online.org/t/backlash.htm.]

Negri, A. 2003a. *Time for Revolution*, trans. M. Mandarini (New York: Continuum).

Negri, A. 2003b. *Luciano Ferrari Bravo: Ritratto di un cattivo maestro* (Rome: ManifestoLibri).

Negri, A. 2004a. *Subversive Spinoza: (Un)Contemporary Variations*, trans. T. S. Murphy, Michael Hardt, Ted Stolze and Charles T. Wolfe (Manchester: Manchester University Press). [Original Italian 1992, *Spinoza sovversivo: Variazioni (in)attuali* (Roma: Pellicani.]

Negri, A. 2004b. "Wittgenstein and Pain: Sociological Consequences," trans. T. S. Murphy. In *Genre: Forms of Discourse and Culture*, 37 (3–4), pp. 353–67.

Negri, A. 2005. *Books for Burning: Between Civil War and Democracy in 1970s Italy* [1971–7], trans. T. S. Murphy, Arianna Bove, Ed Emery and Francesca Novello (New York: Verso).

Negri, A. 2007. "Art and Culture in the Age of Empire and the Time of the Multitudes," trans. M. Henninger. *SubStance* 36.1 (112), pp. 48–55.

Negri, A. 2008a. *Reflections on Empire*, trans. E. Emery (Cambridge: Polity Press). [Original Italian 1003, *Guide: Cinque lezioni su Impero e dintorni* (Milan: Raffaello Cortina).]

Negri, A. 2008b. *Empire and Beyond*, trans. E. Emery (Cambridge: Polity Press). [Original Italian 2006, *Movimenti nell'Impero: Passaggi e paesaggi* (Milan: Raffaello Cortina).]

Negri, A. 2009a. *Il lavoro nella Costituzione, e una conversazione con Adelino Zanini* (Verona: Ombre Corte).

Negri, A. 2009b. *The Labor of Job: The Biblical Text as a Parable of Human Labor*, trans. M. Mandarini (Durham, NC: Duke University Press). [Original Italian 1990, *Il Lavoro di Giobbe: Il famoso testo biblico come parabola del lavoro umano* (Milan: SugarCo).]

Negri, A. 2010a. *Diary of an Escape*, trans. E. Emery (Cambridge: Polity Press). [Original Italian 1986, *Diario di un'evasione* (Milan: MBP).]

Negri, A. 2010b. *Spinoza et nous*, trans. J. Revel (Paris: Galilée).

Negri, A. 2011. *Trilogy of Resistance*, trans. with an introduction by T. S. Murphy (Minneapolis: University of Minnesota Press). [Original French 2009, *Trilogie de la différence* (Paris: Stock).]

Negri, A., and A. Dufourmantelle. 2004. *Negri on Negri*, trans. M. B. Debevoise (New York: Routledge). [Original French 2002, *Du retour: Abécédaire biopolitique* (Paris: Calmann-Levy).]

Nietzsche, F. 1911. "We Philologists." In *The Complete Works of Nietzsche*, vol. 8, ed. O. Levy and trans. J. M. Kennedy (Edinburgh: T. N. Foulis). Available online at: http://www.gutenberg.org/cache/epub/18267/pg18267.txt.

Nietzsche, F. 1967. *The Will to Power*, trans. W. Kaufmann (New York: Vintage).

Nietzsche, F. 1968. *Basic Writings*, trans. W. Kaufmann (New York: Random House).

Nietzsche, F. 1974. *The Gay Science*, trans. W. Kaufmann (New York: Vintage).

Nietzsche, F. 1979. "On Truth and Lies in a Nonmoral Sense." In *Philosophy and Truth: Selections from Nietzsche's Notebooks of the Early 1870s*, ed. and trans. D. Brazeale (Atlantic Highlands, NJ: Humanities Press, 1979), pp. 79–91.

Nietzsche, F. 1983. *Untimely Meditations*, trans. R. J. Hollingdale (Cambridge: Cambridge University Press).

On Fire: The Battle of Genoa and the Anti-Capitalist Movement. 2001. London: One Off Press.

Pannekoek, A. 1948. *Workers' Councils* (Oakland, CA: AK Press, 2003).

Passavant, P. A. 2004. "From Empire's Law to the Multitude's Rights: Law, Representation, Revolution." In Passavant and Dean, eds., 2004a, pp. 95–120.

Passavant, P. A., and J. Dean, eds. 2004a. *Empire's New Clothes: Reading Hardt and Negri* (New York: Routledge).

Passavant, P. A., and J. Dean. 2004b. "Representation and the Event." In Passavant and Dean 2004a, pp. 315–28.

Portelli, A.. 1985. "Oral Testimony, the Law and the Making of History: The 'April 7' Murder Trial." *History Workshop: A journal of socialist and feminist historians* 20 (autumn), pp. 5–35.

Quaderni rossi. 2008. Rome: Sapere. DVD-ROM.

Quinby, L. 2004. "Taking the Millennialist Pulse of *Empire*'s Multitude: A Genealogical Feminist Diagnosis." In Passavant and Dean, eds., 2004a, pp. 231–51.

Ramirez, B. 1992. "Self-Reduction of Prices in Italy." In Midnight Notes Collective, *Midnight Oil: Work, Energy, War 1973–1992* (Brooklyn: Autonomedia), pp. 185–92.

Rawick, G. 1972. *From Sundown to Sunup: The Making of the Black Community* (Westport, CT: Greenwood Press).

Rawls, J. 1971. *A Theory of Justice* (Cambridge, MA: Belknap Press).

Read, J. 2003. *The Micro-Politics of Capital: Marx and the Pre-History of the Present* (Albany, NY: SUNY Press).

Read, J. 2007. "The *Potentia* of Living Labor: Negri and the Practice of Philosophy." In Murphy and Mustapha, eds., 2007, pp. 28–51.

Resnick, S., and R. Wolff. 2001. "*Empire* and Class Analysis." In *Dossier on* Empire 2001, pp. 61–9.

Revel, J. 2004. *Fare moltitudine* (Soveria Manelli: Rubbettino).

Revel, J. 2007. "Antonio Negri, French Nietzschean? From the Will to Power to the Ontology of Power," trans. T. S. Murphy. In Murphy and Mustapha, eds., 2007, pp. 87–108.

"Rossi, Ugo D." 2005. "The Counter-Empire to Come or the Discourse of the Great Rival: An Attempted Decoding of Michael Hardt's and Toni Negri's Empire." *Science and Society* 69 (2) (April), pp. 191–217.

Ruggiero, V. 1993. "Sentenced to normality: The Italian political refugees in Paris." *Crime, Law and Social Change* 19, pp. 33–50.

Ryan, M. 1989. *Politics and Culture: Working Hypotheses for a Post-Revolutionary Society* (Baltimore: Johns Hopkins University Press).

Ryan, M. 2001. "The Empire of Wealth." *Politics and Culture* 1. Available online at: http://www.politicsandculture.org/2010/08/10/the-empire-of-wealth-by-michael-ryan-2/.

Sartre, J.-P. 2007. *Existentialism Is a Humanism*, trans. C. Macomber (New Haven: Yale University Press).

Shapiro, K. 2004. "The Myth of the Multitude." In Passavant and Dean, eds., 2004a, pp. 289–314.

Spinoza, B. 1985. *Collected Works*, vol. 1, ed. and trans. E. Curley (Princeton: Princeton University Press).

Spinoza, B. 2000. *Political Treatise*, trans. S. Shirley (Indianapolis: Hackett).

Sprinker, M., ed. 1999. *Ghostly Demarcations: A Symposium on Jacques Derrida's Specters of Marx* (New York: Verso).

Steiner, G. 1984. *Antigones* (Oxford: Clarendon Press).

Tari, M. 2007. "Fuochi di Autonomia a nordest: I Collettivi politici veneti per il potere operaio." In Bianchi and Caminiti, eds., vol. 1, pp. 242–54.

Taylor, Q. 2001. "Descartes's Paradoxical Politics." *Humanitas* 14 (2), pp. 76–103.

Thompson, E. P. 1963. *The Making of the English Working Class* (New York: Vintage).

Togliatti, P. 1979. "The Communist Policy of National Unity (1944)" [1944]. In P. Togliatti, *On Gramsci and Other Writings* (London: Lawrence and Wishart), pp. 29–65.

Torealta, M. 1980. "Painted Politics." In S. Lotringer and C. Marazzi, eds., *Semiotext(e): Italy/Autonomia – Post-Political Politics* (New York: Semiotext[e]), pp. 102–6.

Toscano, A. 2007. "Always already only now: Negri and the Biopolitical." In Murphy and Mustapha, eds., 2007, pp. 109–28.

Toscano, A. 2009. "Chronicles of Insurrection: Tronti, Negri and the Subject of Antagonism." In Chiesa and Toscano, eds., pp. 109–28.

Tronti, M. 1964. "Lenin in England." In M. Tronti, *Working-Class Autonomy and the Crisis*, trans. E. Emery (London: Red Notes, 1979).

Tronti, M. 1971. *Operai e capitale*, enlarged edition (Turin: Einaudi).

Tronti, M. 1977. *Sull'autonomia del politico* (Milan: Feltrinelli).

Trotta, G., and F. Milana. 2008. *L'operaismo degli anni Sessanta: Da "Quaderni rossi" a "classe operaia"* (Rome: DeriveApprodi).

Vatter, M. 2007. "Legality and Resistance: Arendt and Negri on Constituent Power." In Murphy and Mustapha, eds., 2007, pp. 52–83.

Vattimo, G. 1988. "The Crisis of Humanism." In G. Vattimo, *The End of Modernity: Nihilism and Hermeneutics in Postmodern Culture*, trans. J. R. Snyder (Baltimore: Johns Hopkins University Press), pp. 31–47.

Villalobos-Ruminott, S. 2001. "*Empire*, A Picture of the World." In *Dossier on Empire* 2001, pp. 31–42.

Virno, P. 2004. *Grammar of the Multitude*, trans. I. Bertoletti, J. Cascaito and A. Casson (Los Angeles: Semiotext[e]).

Virno, P., and M. Hardt, eds. 1996. *Radical Thought in Italy: A Potential Politics* (Minneapolis: University of Minnesota Press).

Walther, M. 1990. "Negri on Spinoza's Political and Legal Philosophy." In E. Curley and P.-F. Moreau, eds., *Spinoza: Issues and Directions* (Leiden: Brill), pp. 286–97.

Weeks, K. 2005. "The Refusal of Work as Demand and Perspective." In Murphy and Mustapha, eds., 2005, pp. 109–35.

Wolfe, A. 2001. "The Snake." *The New Republic*, October 1. Available online at: http://www.handl.net/pol45/trends/on_empire_by_hardt_negri.htm.

Wolfe, C. T. 2007. "Materialism and Temporality: On Antonio Negri's 'Constitutive Ontology'". In Murphy and Mustapha, eds., 2007, pp. 198–220.

Wood, E. M. 2003. "A Manifesto for Global Capitalism?" In Balakrishnan, ed., 2003, pp. 61–82.

Working Class Autonomy and the Crisis. 1979. London: Red Notes.

Wright, S. 2002. *Storming Heaven: Class Composition and Struggle in Italian Autonomist Marxism* (London: Pluto Press).

Wright, S. 2005. "A Party of Autonomy?" In Murphy and Mustapha, eds., 2005, pp. 73–106.

Wu Ming 1 (R. Bui). 2001. "Myth-Making and Catastrophes." *Giap Digest* 11. Available online at: http://www.wumingfoundation. com/english/giap/giapdigest11.html.

Žižek, S. 2001. "Have Michael Hardt and Antonio Negri Rewritten the *Communist Manifesto* for the Twenty-First Century?" In *Dossier on* Empire, 2001, pp. 190–8.

Žižek, S. 2004. "The Ideology of the Empire and Its Traps." In Passavant and Dean, eds., 2004a, pp. 253–64.

Index

(A lower-case "n" in an entry indicates a numbered endnote on the listed page.)